PENGUIN BOOKS

THE FALL OF YUGOSLAVIA

'Standing back from the catastrophe, one begins to see, with the help of Misha Glenny's fine book, that Western failures of policy were caused by something deeper than inattention, misinformation, or misguided good intentions' – Michael Ignatieff in *The New York Review of Books*

'Anyone baffled by Yugoslavia's civil war should read this short book . . . a speaker of Serbo-Croat, Misha Glenny has talked to the leaders, fighters and victims of this vile war . . . vivid reporting and analytical verve' – *Economist*

'This book has all his usual gusto and readability . . . probably no other English-language reporter has met more of the key personalities, or covered the ground more assiduously' – Mark Thompson in the *New Statesman & Society*

'An essential guide for anyone who wants to understand the conflicts' – Nicholas Lezard in the *Guardian*

'In this fine cocktail of reportage and analysis the BBC's distinguished Central European correspondent tells us why it happened and what it felt like to be there' – *Observer*

D0345630

ABOUT THE AUTHOR

Misha Glenny is a writer and broadcaster living in Thessaloniki in northern Greece. During most of the Yugoslav crisis, he was the Central European correspondent of the BBC World Service based in Vienna, working throughout central and south-eastern Europe. In 1993 he won the Sony Radio Award for Special Contribution to broadcasting for his coverage of Yugoslavia. Before joining the BBC, he reported from the same area for the *Guardian*. A speaker of German, Czech, Serbo-Croat and Greek, he has developed an inside knowledge of Eastern Europe and the Balkans that few other journalists possess. In articles and broadcasts he frequently predicted the outbreak of war in both Croatia and Bosnia-Hercegovina. He was stationed permanently in Yugoslavia from the beginning of June 1991, during which time he travelled throughout the country, including assignments on most of the major fronts of the war. Before taking up journalism, he worked in publishing, having studied in Bristol, at the Freie Universität in Berlin and Charles University in Prague. His book, *The Rebirth of History*, analyses the collapse of communism in Eastern Europe and its implications for European stability. It is also published by Penguin.

MISHA GLENNY

———

THE FALL OF YUGOSLAVIA

THE THIRD BALKAN WAR

PENGUIN BOOKS

In memory of Lenka Raos

PENGUIN BOOKS

Published by the Penguin Group
Penguin Books Ltd, 80 Strand, London WC2R 0RL, England
Penguin Putnam Inc., 375 Hudson Street, New York, New York 10014, USA
Penguin Books Australia Ltd, 250 Camberwell Road, Camberwell, Victoria 3124, Australia
Penguin Books Canada Ltd, 10 Alcorn Avenue, Toronto, Ontario, Canada M4V 3B2
Penguin Books India (P) Ltd, 11 Community Centre, Panchsheel Park, New Delhi – 110 017, India
Penguin Books (NZ) Ltd, Cnr Rosedale and Airborne Roads, Albany, Auckland, New Zealand
Penguin Books (South Africa) (Pty) Ltd, 24 Sturdee Avenue, Rosebank 2196, South Africa

Penguin Books Ltd, Registered Offices: 80 Strand, London WC2R 0RL, England

www.penguin.com

First published 1992
Second edition 1993
Third edition 1996

022

Map of Bosnian Land Transfers under the Dayton Agreement.
Source Map © British Crown copyright. Reproduced with the permission
of the Controller of Her Britannic Majesty's Stationery Office.

The moral right of the author has been asserted

Typeset by Datix International Limited, Bungay, Suffolk
Set in 10/12 pt Monophoto Bembo
Printed in England by Clays Ltd, St Ives plc

Acknowledgements

I would like to thank all those who helped me in writing this book in such a short
space of time. In particular, I wish to acknowledge the assistance of those who
offered me invaluable comments on the text – my editor Jon Riley, Laura Silber,
Alison Smale and Juliet Sydenham. I would also like to thank Snežana, Miljan and
Alexandra for the patience and support I received from them while writing this.

M.G., June 1992

ISBN-13: 978–0–140–26101–1

www.greenpenguin.co.uk

Contents

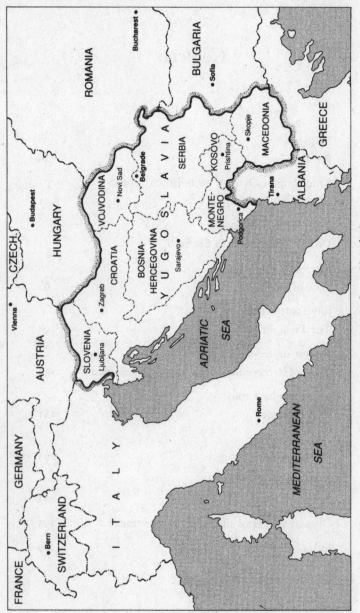

The Republics of the former Yugoslavia

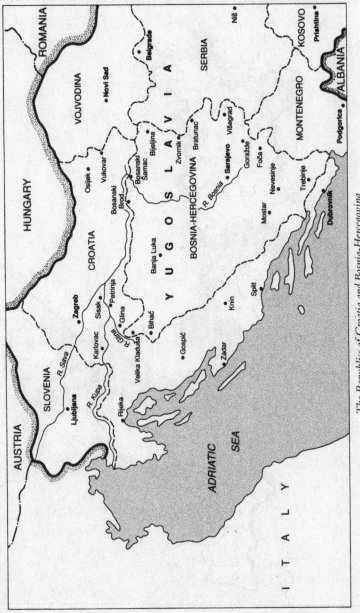

The Republics of Croatia and Bosnia-Hercegovina

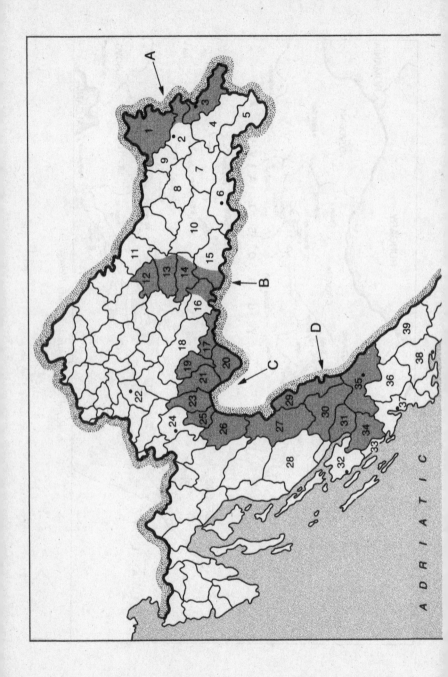

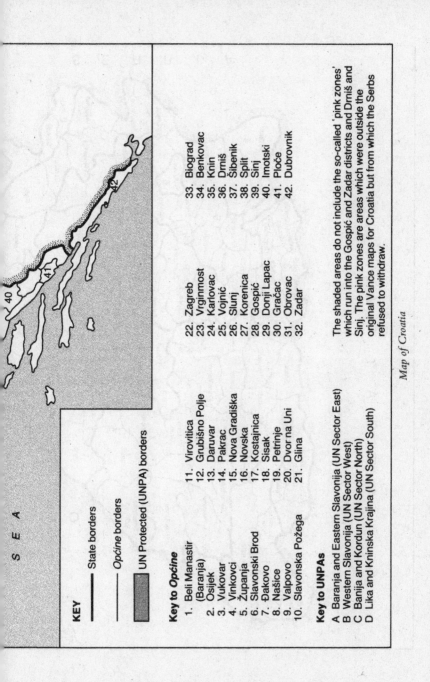

S E A

KEY

—— State borders

—— Općine borders

▓ UN Protected (UNPA) borders

Key to Općine

1. Beli Manastir (Baranja)
2. Osijek
3. Vukovar
4. Vinkovci
5. Županja
6. Slavonski Brod
7. Đakovo
8. Našice
9. Valpovo
10. Slavonska Požega
11. Virovitica
12. Grubišno Polje
13. Daruvar
14. Pakrac
15. Nova Gradiška
16. Novska
17. Kostajnica
18. Sisak
19. Petrinje
20. Dvor na Uni
21. Glina
22. Zagreb
23. Vrginmost
24. Karlovac
25. Vojnić
26. Slunj
27. Korenica
28. Gospić
29. Donji Lapac
30. Gračac
31. Obrovac
32. Zadar
33. Biograd
34. Benkovac
35. Knin
36. Drniš
37. Šibenik
38. Split
39. Sinj
40. Imotski
41. Ploče
42. Dubrovnik

Key to UNPAs

A Baranja and Eastern Slavonija (UN Sector East)
B Western Slavonija (UN Sector West)
C Banija and Kordun (UN Sector North)
D Lika and Kninska Krajina (UN Sector South)

The shaded areas do not include the so-called 'pink zones' which run into the Gospić and Zadar districts and Drniš and Sinj. The pink zones are areas which were outside the original Vance maps for Croatia but from which the Serbs refused to withdraw.

Map of Croatia

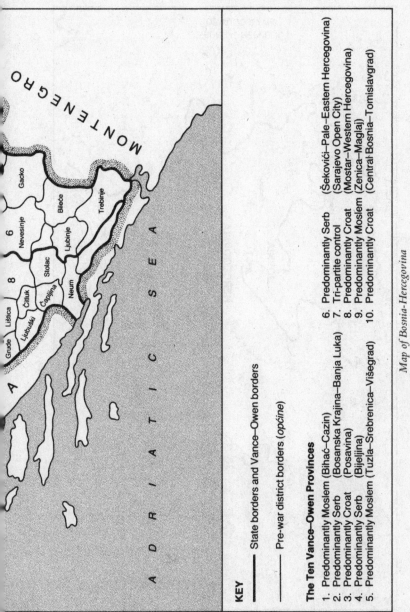

KEY

— State borders and Vance–Owen borders

— Pre-war district borders (općine)

The Ten Vance–Owen Provinces

1. Predominantly Moslem (Bihać–Cazin)
2. Predominantly Serb   (Bosanska Krajina–Banja Luka)
3. Predominantly Croat   (Posavina)
4. Predominantly Serb   (Bijeljina)
5. Predominantly Moslem (Tuzla–Srebrenica–Višegrad)
6. Predominantly Serb   (Šekovići–Pale–Eastern Hercegovina)
7. Tri-partite control   (Sarajevo Open City)
8. Predominantly Croat   (Mostar–Western Hercegovina)
9. Predominantly Moslem (Zenica–Maglaj)
10. Predominantly Croat   (Central Bosnia–Tomislavgrad)

Map of Bosnia–Hercegovina

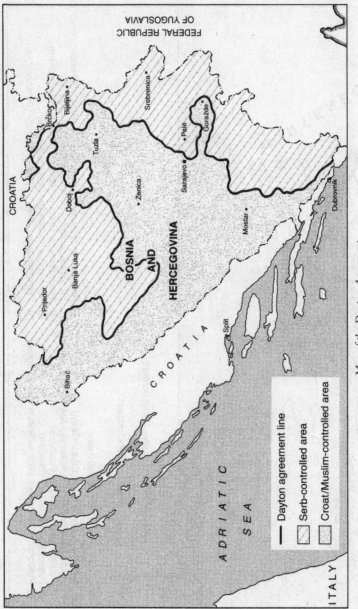

Map of the Dayton Agreement

FEDERAL REPUBLIC
OF YUGOSLAVIA

CROATIA

Brčko
Bijeljina
Srebrenica
Tuzla
Goražde
Pale
Doboj
Zenica
Sarajevo
Banja Luka
BOSNIA AND HERCEGOVINA
Mostar
Prijedor
Dubrovnik
Bihać
CROATIA
Split

ADRIATIC
SEA

ITALY

— Dayton agreement line
  Serb-controlled area
  Croat/Muslim-controlled area

Preface

1992

'All of us have had, now and then, a terrible, horrifying dream, a nightmare, from which we wake up in the middle of the night or at dawn bathed in sweat from the terror we have experienced. We're overcome by joy to find that it was only a dream and not reality. Sadly, what is happening around us today, this horror, this chaos on our soil, in the heart of Europe, at the beginning of the twenty-first century, this destruction, this killing, this hatred – this, alas, is no dream but a living nightmare.

'It is all so unreal, so inconceivable, that it is hard to grasp, at least for me. It leaves me quite unable to judge what is going on or to adopt a rational attitude towards it. It really is like that dream, that ugly nightmare. And if that is how I feel living in Belgrade, where I am threatened by no physical danger, only the psychological torture inflicted by the media, I can imagine what it must now be like for the people in Dubrovnik, Zadar, Cavtat, Knin, Glina, Sisak and especially Vukovar. I can imagine how people must feel who have lost everything they had, everything they worked for all their lives, their homes in ruins, burned to the ground – the feelings of families, mothers and fathers who have lost their precious son, sister, brother, grandmother or whoever it may be. Terrible.

'To what end, and in whose name, I ask myself (you probably do the same), this senseless nationalist imperative, which enforces membership of a nation to which you are driven and in which you are instructed by those who until yesterday were champions of the League of Communists, fighters for brotherhood and unity, secretaries of various committees from the commune to the Central Committee?

'Well, if that is the case, comrade secretaries, don't count on me: I won't go along with you. You won't teach me to hate anyone. And, to tell you the truth, the more you call on me and remind me of my nationality, the less I feel I belong to it. The more you appeal to my patriotism, the less patriotic I feel because of you. There you have it. That is my stand.'

Statement made by the Belgrade actor Boro Todorović to the independent television station YUTEL on 2 November 1991

1996

I have twice revised my original text, once in 1993 and once in 1996. In an important respect, 1993 marked a break in international policy towards the former Yugoslavia. After the collapse of the Vance–Owen Peace Plan, international mediators offered diplomatic solutions, all of which implied the partition of Bosnia–Hercegovina. After the Dayton Agreement was signed at the end of 1995, enshrining effective partition in international law, I felt it appropriate to add a final epilogue to this book. I suspect that the wars of Yugoslav succession are now over. I am not yet convinced that the stability of the Balkans has been secured.

I   KNIN,
AUGUST/OCTOBER 1990–JANUARY 1992:

The Heart of the Matter

Driving eastwards up steep spiralling roads, I am always struck how the paradise of Dalmatia's coast is so swiftly consumed by the forbidding mountains and stony plateaux of its hinterland. In some parts, it is only a matter of a few miles before the deep blue of the Adriatic yields to the destitute flatland surrounded by inhospitable, if spectacular Dinaric peaks. As the roads rise, the palm trees of the seafront give way to clumps of scrub. Sickly but tenacious, they inexplicably resist the winds which lash the barren rock formations. These winds, which mostly originate not from the balmy sea to the west but from the harsh continent to the east, seem to have played the dominant role in sculpting this landscape. Yet they always convey a curt but vital message of hope which persists in defiance of the grim surroundings – this is the soothing smell of pine, present even when dreadful winter cold suffocates all other signs of life. Alas, the aroma is never anything more than symbolic. By the time a small town called Knin approaches, forty miles into the interior, Šibenik, one of Dalmatia's majestic ports where in winter the temperature can tickle the low seventies, has been almost completely erased from memory by the dust which dries my throat and settles as a thick, grey mantle on my car. In ordinary times this region, Kninska Krajina, would be just another of those bleak Balkan vistas, destined to drift out of my mind as swiftly as I drive through them. But in these times, Knin is a bridge stretching from paradise to hell.

The road plunges suddenly, dipping into the town which is well protected by mountains on all sides. To outsiders, Knin is an insignificant regional blob with as much to offer as Reading or Walsall. It is a vapid town which is gloomy when it rains and oppressive when the sun blazes. When it snows, it is the coldest and most isolated place in the Balkans. Despite its intrinsic emptiness, when the dark ghosts of Knin began to wail, almost all Croats and Serbs responded to this call to arms. The lure of Knin proved fatal for both nations.

From the south, Knin is shielded by a grand hill which seen from the town looks like the nose to another string of mountains. In fact, if one slips round the back, the hill reveals itself to be nothing but an enormous mound, strangely adrift in this dense cluster of jagged peaks. The hill is crowned by a fortress, a tenth-century monument which thanks to repeated renovations looks youthful and sturdy. From atop the fortress, Knin looks as innocent and uninteresting as a small industrial settlement can. From here it is hard to spot the town's fascinating historical landmarks that inadvertently bear an unspoken responsibility for the revival of the conflict between Serbs and Croats. Instead, the chimney-stacks of the Tvik screw factory stand out, pumping out the foul exhaust of a forlorn and long-failing enterprise which is still the largest employer in Knin even though it no longer has any market where it can sell its shoddy nuts, bolts, nails and screws. But the outstanding features of this panorama are the railway station and the track running in and out of Knin. Thus the eye is drawn immediately to one of the keys to the entire Yugoslav conflict. Knin, with a population of just 10,000 in peacetime, is known to all as an economic backwater, under-developed and with little to offer. It has, however, one undisputed asset – its obstinate location as the central communications' junction between the Croatian capital, Zagreb, and the tourist magnets of Dalmatia, the geese which bless Croatia's economy with gold. With Knin outside its control, Croatia faces insurmountable difficulties in developing its tourist industry. Without Knin, Croatia is an economic cripple.

Once the place of enthronement of medieval Croatian kings, Knin is now home to a militant tradition of Serb nationalism. With the exception of a much smaller area in the region of Lika, this was the only stronghold of the extreme Serb-nationalist Chetnik movement in Croatia during the war. Everywhere else in the republic, the Serb communities and later many Croat communities identified themselves with Tito's Partizans. But it is here in Knin, where the Croats least need it, that the toughest Serbs in Croatia happen to live.

Just as Zagreb needs the Krajina, Knin without Croatia is equally damned. Yet the primitive, hardy peasants of the region are reared on a diet of poverty which has apparently inured them to the temptations of Croatia's economic potential. This was the fatal error that President Tuđman and his learned advisers made in the months after the victory of the Croatian Democratic Union (HDZ) in Croatia's democratic elections of April 1990. The majority of the 600,000 Serbs in Croatia are urbanized. Before the war, they were generally well integrated into Croatian society and relations between these Serbs and the Croats could hardly have provoked the ferocious conflict which ripped through Croatia in 1991. The mellow Croat academics who helped fashion Tuđman's policy in the first months after his election were acquainted with the sophisticated Serbs from Zagreb, but their knowledge of their cousins in the country was vague and even dismissive. Yet it is these rural Serbs who control the broad swathes of countryside in Krajina, and in the other, now ravaged regions: Kordun, Banija and Slavonija. These Serbs, who did much of the fighting in 1991, are very different from their compatriots in the cities who are known rather frivolously as *Hrbi*, a conflation of *Hrvati* (Croats) and *Srbi* (Serbs). The economic horizons of the rural Serbs are limited, but the early post-feudal concepts of land and home are central to their thinking and sense of security. Passive for decades, when they believed their homes were under threat, their harmless ignorance transformed itself into something extremely dangerous. (Equally unpredictable, it must be said, are their Croat *alter egos* from the Dinaric region and from western Hercegovina, where the least compromising Croat peasants live.) Cosseted by the moderation of the urban Serbs, the Tuđman team after the elections assumed arrogantly and stupidly that the passivity and adaptability of the urban communities was the way of the Serbian world in Croatia. In Croatia's extremities of eastern Slavonija, Krajina and the region around Split and Zadar, Tuđman's government was represented by a very different type of Croat whose antipathy towards Serbs would soon lead to conflict. Tuđman's inability to recognize the complexity of Serbian society within Croatia was probably the most costly mistake he has ever made in his life. The conflict between Zagreb and Knin was not only the dispute which provoked the war, it remains the most powerful engine of fratricidal strife.

★

Up on the hilltop, the fortress testifies to Knin's depressing history as disputed territory. In a report on their Dalmatian territories delivered in 1394, the Venetian senate was told that 'As a town in the regions which surround Dalmatia, Fortress Knin is more important and useful to us than anywhere else because it is the main key to the routes into Dalmatia and the main bastion preventing those who would penetrate the province, from doing so.' The various empires and states which have dominated the area have all afforded Knin's strategic position similar respect.

Throughout the seventeenth century, successive Habsburg emperors strengthened and expanded the Military Frontier (in Serbo-Croat, Vojna Krajina). This enormous defensive strip eventually stretched across the border lands of the Habsburg southern possessions from Dalmatia eastwards to the western edge of Transylvania in what is now Romania. It was developed both to block Ottoman expansion into Europe and in order to launch offensives against the Turks. Serb fighters in pursuit of their own political struggle with the Sublime Porte in Constantinople had frequently collaborated with the invading Habsburg forces against the Ottoman army. In the wake of one such failed Habsburg assault in the late seventeenth century, Arsenije III, the Serb patriarch of Peć in Kosovo, led 30,000 families into the Habsburg empire to escape the wrath of the janizaries, the peculiar social class which doubled as the sultan's elite fighting corps. From Vienna, the Emperor, Leopold I, agreed to allow these Serbs religious freedom and a measure of self-government. They were thus granted a charter to establish a metropolitanate in Sremski Karlovci, an enchanting little town in Vojvodina, whose many Orthodox spires still poke through lush forests.

Suspicion of Rome was a mighty force within the Serbian Orthodox Church, but the political struggle of the day was directed against the temporal lords of Islam. The fratricidal antipathy which now stains the relationship between so many Serbs and Croats can perhaps trace its roots back a long way, but its flowering has been a relatively recent development. Soon after Sremski Karlovci was founded, the Porte closed down the Peć patriarchy, the old spiritual home of the Serbian Church. Sremski Karlovci thus became a powerful symbol of the religious and political freedom which the Habsburgs granted Serbs. In return for these privileges, the Serbs swore allegiance to Vienna and agreed to populate many parts of the Vojna Krajina as military colonists. There had been Serbs in the Knin area before this and claims that the region was purely Croat until the settlement are disingenuous and unsubstantiated. But the migration led by Arsenije III effectively established the territorial problems between Serbs and Croats which remain, all too evidently, unsolved to this day.

The Krajina was wild country. If the Serb or Croat soldiers there were not fighting on behalf of Vienna, they were providing for their families or villages. Many became involved in banditry and the practice of merciless looting and plundering was widespread. In 1991, Montenegrin and Serb soldiers, who returned home clutching videos, malt whisky and cartons of Marlboro cigarettes from many areas of Croatia which they had defiled, were following a tradition with deep roots in the region. One reservist who was mobilized from Bosnia and stationed on the front line near the Dalmatian coast described to me how his commander from the eastern Vojvodina town of Kikinda screamed at his troops before entering a Croat holiday resort: 'If I catch anyone looting the place before I've finished, I'll shoot them!'

Partly to curb the flourishing tradition of banditry, the Habsburgs during the eighteenth century and especially during the reformist reign of Maria-Theresa embarked on a concerted effort to discipline the territories of the Vojna Krajina. They curtailed the rather generous provisions for self-rule they had afforded the Serbs. The Vojna Krajina was subdivided into military districts, each with its own headquarters. The Krajina was controlled from Karlovac, a town thirty miles south of Zagreb, which was constructed exclusively for military purposes. The Krajina soldiers were drafted into regiments, and dependency on their masters in Vienna was increased. The efficacy of the Military Frontier improved quite dramatically.

The Vojna Krajina was always ruled directly from Vienna with orders going over the heads of the Croat and Hungarian nobility. The Croats were forced to observe as large parts of what they considered the historic Triune Kingdom of Slavonija, Croatia and Dalmatia were administered by Vienna and peopled by Serbs. The Habsburgs made a certain effort to soothe the Croat wrath by placing one region under the direct jurisdiction of the Croatian Ban (the chief administrator). Thus the area became known as Banija. To the west of Banija and just south of Karlovac lay Kordun, a bastardization of the French, *cordonne*. Aside from Banija, the regions were ruled by *vojvode* (or dukes), who gave their name to another area of the Vojna Krajina, Vojvodina. These were the parts of Yugoslavia which ran red with innocent blood in 1991. The areas over which the Croats demanded to assume control from Vienna in the eighteenth and nineteenth centuries were the same over which they fought with Belgrade in the late twentieth century.

The Vojna Krajina can claim to be one of the most active and disruptive historical fault lines in Europe. Apart from forming the border between the empires of Islam and Christendom for three centuries, it is also the line of fissure between Rome and Constantinople, the Roman Catholic and Orthodox Christian faiths. Without question, the economic traditions of Slovenia and Croatia to the west of this line have developed in closer harmony with Western ideas in the twentieth century, whereas to the east of the divide, the corrupt barter mentality of the Ottomans still dominates the rural economies of Serbia, Bulgaria, Macedonia, Bosnia, Montenegro and Albania. It is no coincidence that the war between Tito's Partizans and the Croat fascists, the Ustashas, one of the most bestial struggles within the myriad conflicts of the Second World War, erupted largely along this strip of south-eastern Europe.

Settled in the Krajina as fighters and moulded by the Dinaric surroundings, the Serbs developed an extraordinary affinity with weaponry. Of all the region's traditions, this is probably the most enduring to this day. Children are schooled in weaponry at an early age, learning to handle and control first shotguns and later handguns before they reach their teens. Thus guns are not just a central part of the people's character. A person's standing will be enhanced and confirmed by his or her (there are many female fighters in the Krajina) ability to wield a gun. One piece of local folklore tells how every house in Krajina has three defenders. The first is a snake which lives in the roof of the house (Krajina is home to many snakes and other species attracted to semi-arid and mountainous environments), the second is houseleek, a plant which grows on and around the house and is known colloquially throughout Serbia as the guardian of the home (*čuvarkuća*) and the third is the gun of the house. The *Krajišnici*, as people from Krajina are called, say that the gun was born with this land and will never disappear.

In December 1991, the leader of the Krajina, Milan Babić, rejected the plan brokered by Cyrus Vance on behalf of the UN which envisaged the deployment of some 10,000 UN troops in the Krajina and other troubled districts. One of Babić's main arguments was that nobody must be permitted to disarm the Krajišnici. Although the Krajina's president was using this to further his own murky political aims, he knew instinctively that this logic would find almost unanimous support among the people he represents. He was correct. When I travelled to Knin in January 1992, all the people I spoke with made a point of stressing that the idea of disarming them was a dishonour in itself. During the period of civil peace which reigned for forty years after the Second World War, the guns were important aids in the economy of this rural area, but as soon as relations between Knin and Zagreb began to deteriorate, the weapons assumed a new, more sinister role.

In late September 1990, I was confronted with the Serbs' warrior consciousness for the first time. Until then, this had been parcelled in cosy tales of the Partizan struggle during the Second World War or in the myths surrounding the great nineteenth-century Serbian uprisings against the Turks and before that, the heroes of the medieval Serbian empire, in particular those who fell during the Serbian Golgotha, the Battle of Kosovo in 1389. This sugary illusion was easily shattered by the swagger and aggression which I observed in Knin.

The road from Gračac to Knin is long and lonely. There are few settlements on the way as the mountains begin to close around you. I was travelling to Knin at a time when tension in the area was still palpable following the first armed confrontation between the Krajina Serbs and the government of Franjo Tuđman which flared on the weekend of 17 August. As I approached the town, a white estate car with a Zagreb registration shot past me in the other direction at a speed which raised eyebrows even by Yugoslav standards. Perhaps this was the first sign of the looming *straža*, as the Serb guard posts on the outskirts of Knin were known. Three miles further on, where the road begins to rise slowly, my path was blocked by a colossal tree. I slowed down, encouraged to do so by the two barrels of an old shotgun which a burly young man in jeans and a tatty lumberjack shirt had levelled at my forehead. I jumped out of my car, making it clear that I was completely harmless and addressed the man while firmly clasping his hand, '*Zdravo, druže!*' During the Titoist state, the word *drug* in Serbo-Croat was used to mean comrade in the sense of the Russian word *tovarishch*. However, *drug* also means friend. But it is a word which is associated in particular with the Serbs who still use it frequently whether talking to comrades or not. The Croats, who to a large extent had the greeting forced on them, find the word distasteful – it reminds them explicitly of what they say was Tito's Serbian-dominated brand of socialism. It also reflects what most Croats believe to be the Serbs' peasant-like culture. During my conversations in Knin, the use of the word *drug* and my heavy dependence on the eastern, that is the Serbian, variant of Serbo-Croat was an important way of establishing my credibility, even though ironically in Knin, the Serbs all speak the Croatian variant. When I shook his hand vigorously, the young man on the *straža* could afford to look quizzical and relaxed as only then did I notice two, more senior members of his group twenty yards up on the hillside with their automatic weapons trained on me.

The faces confronting me were those of the peasantry. They were round, wide-eyed, with large amounts of roughly trimmed hair – demons with the trigger, but no Einsteins. Over the next year, I would become very used to these ill-defined, rural features. In my best Serbian, I explained that I had come on the invitation of Lazar Macura, the Deputy President of Knin's Town Council who was elevated in 1991 to the position of Information Minister in the Republic of the Serbian Krajina, as the local Serbs were to call their enclave state. The name of Macura relaxed the members of the *straža* and the man in charge slipped down from the hillside to examine my passport. The tree on the main road, he detailed, was immovable and I was told instead to travel along the back route into town. He gave me directions but before I left, I asked him who was in the car with the Zagreb plates. 'That was a team from HTV (Croatian Television),' he told me, 'they made great target practice.' At this point, he burst out laughing. The others quickly took up the chorus and with their squeals of mischievous delight ringing in my ears, I turned the car in the direction of the back route. The theatrical smile on my face disguised the frightening realization that I was entering a very hostile and volatile environment.

The back route comprised exhausting, steady climbs and descents on a stony track which kicked up so much dust as to obscure my visibility. For just under an hour, I travelled on this track before finally arriving on some asphalt again, two hundred metres away from a small run-down café. Outside this little dive stood another *straža*. I was waved down by a boy who could not have been more than fourteen, holding a handgun. Some six men, all pointing their weapons at me, told me to get out of the car. I again explained that I was going to see Mr Macura, saying that I had arranged the visit with him and he was expecting me at the studio of Serbian Radio Knin (in areas under *de facto* Serb control, the word 'Serbian' often prefaced the names of the local media, in response to the renaming of Yugoslav Television, Studio Zagreb, as Croatian Television). This was not, however, accurate – I had been unable to get through to Macura to warn him of my arrival and although he would be pleased to welcome me, he would have naturally denied that he was expecting me. In contrast to the previous *straža*, however, Macura's name was not an impressive enough passport to see me through the barricade. 'I'll go and phone him,' said the boss of the *straža*, looking me up and down through black eyes which were hooded by inhumanly dense brows. He disappeared to the telephone. Time passed. While still swaggering in suitably confident Serbian, inside I was panicking that if they rumbled my Macura ruse, then their natural suspicion might turn yet more cancerous. (Despite the dangers to which I exposed myself throughout the conflicts in Yugoslavia and Croatia, I never succeeded in discarding my unswerving cowardice. Although I gradually learned what was a stupid course of action to take and what was less stupid – they were all stupid – every time I pointed the car in the direction of a crisis region, I was always aware that I was doing so against my essential will.) After half an hour of waiting by the café, during which time I had conjured up all conceivable tortures awaiting me, this strange troll of a *straža* commander shuffled back out and announced: 'I can't get though – the line's down.' I bit my tongue to stop a shriek of delight. 'Thank

God for good old, lousy socialist infrastructures,' I muttered to myself. 'They can't even manage a phone line across a couple of miles.' None the less, the men still wanted to give the car a thorough search. This led to the next revelation, a regrettable burden which I have borne throughout the Yugoslav conflict: seen through certain eyes, the equipment of a radio journalist (batteries, Blu-Tack, cassette recorders, wires, insulating tape, screwdrivers and pliers) is difficult to distinguish from the tools of an itinerant bomb-maker. I finally persuaded the troll that I had not the remotest idea how a bomb is constructed. 'We have to see if you have weapons,' he growled. And then I said it: 'I can assure you, even if I did have weapons, I wouldn't know how to use them.' This ignited a deafening explosion of laughter. A man who uses no gun is no man. Thus they allowed me to pass into Knin as if I were a member of some harmless sub-human species.

It was later on that lazy day of Yugoslavia's Indian summer of 1990 that I became convinced how the country had now been programmed along a trajectory which needs must lead to armed conflict between Croats and Serbs. Once I arrived in Knin, I succeeded in tracking down Macura, who promised he would take me to meet Milan Babić, the President of Knin's Town Council and the *enfant terrible* of Krajina politics. Lazar Macura was my guide through the land of Knin. As an English teacher from the local secondary school, he is more at ease communicating with foreigners than many of Knin's inhabitants. He has a striking face with a firm square-shaped jaw and rather intimidating black eyes which have the unnerving habit of staring deep into your own with an apocalyptic glare. Within the narrow boundaries of life in the Krajina, he commands considerable respect and his company is entertaining. Without question, he is a Babić loyalist who defends the local strongman against all criticism, and yet despite this deadening political and intellectual loyalty and indeed frequently bellicose rhetoric, Macura's behaviour betrays an unhappiness about the Krajina's gun culture. He is the only man I have met in Knin whom I never see bearing arms.

After what seemed to me to be a number of unnecessarily conspiratorial phone calls, Macura told me that he would be guiding me to Babić's military headquarters. We set off along the northern road out of Knin in the direction of Bosnia which is about twelve miles away. The sun descended out of sight towards the Adriatic, generating a breath-taking shade of orange, left to glow behind the desolate silhouettes of Dinaric granite. As the orange yielded to deep blue and then black, I felt as if I was moving still deeper inside the beast's belly. We had to negotiate two barricades (although Macura's presence ensured this was the swiftest of formalities) before entering the village of Strmica. We drove up a hillside into a farmhouse where we were shown into a darkened living-room with few decorations or ornaments. We were, however, surrounded by several people bearing ostentatious weapons. For the first time in the conflict, I saw a massive machine-gun with a circular magazine which was toted by Babić's personal bodyguard. This man, with huge laser-like blue eyes, his jaw and forehead wrought from stainless steel, his frame that of a Spanish fighting bull, would startle the cast of an Arnold Schwarzenegger film. He glowered in the shadows of the room collecting nervous respect from all around him, as brute force always will.

The discussion around the table was inarticulate, but it none the less revealed how these simple Serb peasants have been traumatized by unscrupulous politicians wishing to realize their politics of nationalist fantasy. A confused tale of real and perceived discrimination emerged. It was largely but not exclusively based on hearsay from friends and relations elsewhere in Krajina, as Knin was safe country for Serbs from the beginning. The rural Serbs in Krajina, but also some Serbs in other parts of Croatia, were absolutely convinced that following the victory of Franjo Tuđman and his Croatian Democratic Union (HDZ) in April 1990, Croats began to install the infrastructure of a fascist state in Croatia. The Krajina Serbs understood fascism above all to be a state system promoting virulent Croatian nationalism, and the revival of Croat national sentiment in any form was *ipso facto* interpreted by them as the return of fascism. The port of Split, just forty miles from Knin, was a new centre of militant Croat nationalism and it was in such regions, far from Zagreb's cosy Central European consciousness, that the more radical Croats started political experiments which simply confirmed the Serbs' erroneous conviction that fascism was awakening from its slumber and therefore they must answer the call to arms.

*

Tuđman's political inclinations were authoritarian but not expressly undemocratic. His greatest obsession was with the creation of a state which would be identified with the Croatian people. The elections in Croatia were characterized by an excess of symbols and bunting, as they were everywhere else in Eastern Europe as it shook off the burden of neo-Stalinist repression. In many parts of Yugoslavia, the stress on nationalist iconography was particularly intense as a central feature of the Titoist state; indeed, the very mechanism which brought such a swift end to enmity between Serbs and Croats in 1945 had been the suppression of all national political rights: Serb, Croat, Macedonian, Albanian, Hungarian, Italian, Moslem and Slovene alike. Individual national identity was consumed by the all-purpose Yugoslav ideal which enjoyed a strong appeal among many for sustained periods of the Titoist state. But having discarded their Titoist garb during 1990 in the unimpeachable name of democracy, Croats now wanted a state in their Yugoslav borders which they could call their own in every respect. In Tuđman's eyes that meant hanging the red and white chequered shield, the *šahovnica*, the core of Croatian heraldry, from every building; it meant demoting the Serbs from their status within Croatia as a majority Yugoslav nation to that of a minority nation within Croatia; it entailed pronouncing literary Croat as the only language of administration in Croatia and dismissing the Serbs' Cyrillic script as well. The move was as senseless as it was provocative. According to moderate Knin Serbs I met in 1990, only about 5 per cent of the local Serbs used the Cyrillic script, the rest not only spoke the Croatian variant, they used the Latin script. Eighteen months later, on my return, I witnessed the extraordinary spectacle of a Knin Serb attempting to write the address of his relations in Belgrade in Cyrillic – he could not do it. Half-way through the address, he gave up and wrote it in Latin. The Croatian language was already dominant in Knin and Tuđman did not need to force it on people. As soon as he did, this helped to drive them away from Croatian culture.

There was another, yet more sensitive problem which Tuđman foolishly decided to solve in his typically insensitive fashion. Under the Titoist state, the Serbs in Croatia, especially in the cities, occupied a disproportionately high number of posts in the state administration. The reasons for this were complex, but part of the explanation lies in the high percentage of Serbs in the Communist Party (especially in Croatia). It also reflects Tito's delicate system of balance between the national groups which was in certain respects a highly sophisticated game of divide and rule. Over the years (but especially after the violent reform period in Croatia in 1971 known as the 'Croat Spring'), Tito realized that Yugoslavia could only exist if Serbia's bureaucracy was kept on a relatively short leash, while the regional centres of power, say in Zagreb, Prishtina or Ljubljana, enjoyed a significant degree of autonomy from Belgrade. In the complicated dialectics of Yugoslav administration, this policy had an antithesis which was the relative dominance of Serbs within the Croat state and party bureaucracy. This was Tito's unconscious and unsatisfactory solution to the infernal conundrum posed by this region of the Balkan peninsula – the central problem of a Yugoslav state is the dominance of Serbs over Croats; the central problem of an independent Croatia is the dominance of Croats over Serbs.

After the collapse of communism, the latent and quite understandable resentment among Croats of the undue influence enjoyed by Serbs in the republic was quickly revived. Many Croats believed this influence was the bastard ideology spawned by the unholy union of two demons, Greater Serbian arrogance and Bolshevism. President Tudman decided to amend matters by examining nationality as a criterion for the employment of many workers in the state administration. This policy led to large numbers of Serbs being made redundant. The purge was not restricted to the police forces, although this became the focus of considerable attention. The police was merely the most sensitive profession because it involved depriving Serbs of their most important possession, the gun. Yet Tudman failed to take into account how these Serbs, who were suddenly and inexplicably deprived of their livelihood, were unaware that they might have been appointed to their position because of their nationality. When the militant dogs of the HDZ were unleashed and allowed to organize purges of the state administration, Serbs throughout Croatia were shaken by the spectre of persecution. Their misery was compounded when it became clear that they would be replaced by Croats. For many urban Serbs who fell victim to the policy, this was distressing to say the least. When the

HDZ government attempted to start redressing the imbalance in the police forces where rural Serbs dominated, the spectre of persecution was able to invoke their worst nightmare: the return of the Ustashas, the Croat fascists.

This perceived fear engendered a sparkling variety of myths inside the Krajina. It was claimed, for example, that Serbian newspapers and magazines were banned throughout Croatia, a charge which was palpably untrue. None the less, wherever he could, Tudman inadvertently sprinkled oil on the burning fire with gay abandon. For instance, the Croatian President decreed that biscriptual signs in Latin and Cyrillic should be replaced with Latin ones alone. His various advisers and colleagues have described how Tudman was obsessed with control of the Krajina. 'Knin is sacred, Knin is sacred,' he allegedly repeated over and over to Stipe Mesić, the then Croat Prime Minister, who under the influence of some perceptive Croat intellectuals tried to persuade Tudman to reassess his policy towards Krajina in the summer of 1990. With every provocative decision taken by Zagreb, the people of Knin were driven ever faster towards the heart of darkness, the leadership of the Socialist Party of Serbia (SPS) and Prince Milošević.

As I sat in the darkened room waiting for Milan Babić to turn up, I heard how Knin would never again be part of Croatia. I also heard predictions of how their fellow Serbs and in particular the Yugoslav People's Army (JNA) would not allow the imposition of Tudman's policies on the Serb minority. I could almost feel the grubby fighters in that room bracing themselves for the fight and the clammy hands of Milošević four hundred miles away rubbing together in delighted but mistaken anticipation.

Despite this educational discussion with the Knin peasants, I had still not succeeded in securing an audience with Babić. After an hour, the telephone rings in the farmhouse. The master of the house mutters down the mouthpiece before whispering his message to Macura. The Deputy President of Knin Town Council informs me solemnly that his President will not be coming to the military headquarters in which we are sitting and we are all obliged to head back towards Knin. As we get into the car, Macura mumbles almost to himself how there are some disreputable elements in the movement, adding an indistinct reference to some of the 'gorillas' we had left behind in the farmhouse. Again he reveals something of the unhappiness beneath his warrior skin.

I am now becoming irritated as I suspect the meeting with Babić, my main purpose in coming to Knin, may just end up as a wild-goose chase. But true to the spirit of his future job, Macura tracks his boss down, ironically only five minutes' walk from where we departed on our trek to the farmhouse in Strmica.

Rather unexpectedly and certainly unawares, Macura also predicts the discord which much later would spread through the various Serbian communities in what remained of Yugoslavia. We talk about Kosovo, the province of southern Serbia where a small Serb and Montenegrin minority is thoroughly outnumbered by a large Albanian majority. Kosovo is one of the great Serbian myths, regarded by Serbs as the cradle of their civilization. Peć, the seat of the patriarchate abolished by the Turks after the migration of Arsenije III, is in Kosovo. In the autumn of 1987, Slobodan Milošević exploited the powerful anti-Albanian sentiment among Serbs by placing Kosovo at the top of his political agenda as a way of toppling his mentor, Ivan Stambolić, as head of the Serbian League of Communists. Milošević's tactic of forcing a nationalist question into the political limelight of Yugoslavia signalled the beginning of the struggle which ended in the war of 1991. Kosovo was crucial and to most Serbs sacred, even though demographic trends shall ensure that within the next few decades, it will become almost exclusively an Albanian area (unless the Serbian government embarks upon a massive recolonization of the area). Instead of losing himself in a dewy-eyed saga about the inviolability of Serbia's historic province, Macura sighs in a matter-of-fact way, 'Kosovo's lost,' he says. 'Why don't they recognize what we all know and pull out of Kosovo now? It's a mystery to me.' The great motor behind Serbian nationalist politics is the search for unity. The most powerful example of Serbian iconography is the symmetrical cross adorned with four Cs (the Cyrillic letter S), the two left-hand ones being printed as mirror images. This is an acronym for the phrase '*Samo Sloga Srbina Spašava*' (Only Unity Can Save the Serb). Most nationalisms are based on the assumption that a state which encompasses all members of one nation can overcome all major social and economic evils. This is a deeply irrational assumption and one which Serbs, more than many nations, unwittingly expose – Serbian society is so deeply riven by provincial rivalry and indeed suspicion, that if the Serbs ever were to succeed in creating a state which encompassed them all, they would be tearing one another to shreds within minutes. For Macura, Kosovo was an irritation which deflected the attention of Serbs from the problem which he considered the central issue, which was, of course, the fate of the Krajina Serbs. This prediction of disunity came true over a year later when Milošević, having created the leviathan, Babić, attempted to overrule the Krajina leader on the issue of United Nations' peace deployment. The accusations which flew backward and forward between Knin and Belgrade were as acidic as anything hurled between Croats and Serbs in the preceding eighteen months. As the collapse of Yugoslavia intensified and the war become more intense and more bloody, the myth of Serbian unity was rent asunder with shocking force.

Babić is sitting in a front room, perhaps it is his own, but nobody tells me. He is watching television. We are in a flat which would not look out of place in any moderately prosperous suburban estate in Western Europe. He looks like a man in his thirties who is, none the less, still recovering from adolescence. His boyish face is plump and unappealing behind some square spectacles. To the delight of the assembled acolytes, mainly women, he is swinging a Luger around and cracking jokes which are either vaguely obscene or vaguely grotesque but consistently unfunny.

Babić is a dentist, a first-generation professional, who joined the Croatian Communist Party (which after the crackdown following the so-called 'Croatian Spring' of 1971 was renowned as one of the most Stalinist parties inside Yugoslavia's federal Communist League, the LCY). Indeed he was a delegate of the Croat League of Communists at the final fiasco of the LCY, its Fourteenth Congress held at the beginning of 1991. After the collapse of communist power, he joined the Serbian Democratic Party (SDS) which was formed during the early months of 1990 in Donji Lapac, a small town north of Knin in a wholly Serb region of Croatia. The leader of the SDS was Dr Jovan Rašković, a respected psychiatrist who was a consultant in Šibenik's General Hospital. Rašković is a mild man with small eyes and an enormous bushy beard. His main political strategy as leader of the SDS was to avoid armed conflict between Serbs and Croats. But although a moderate himself, as a politician he was cursed with a fatal blind spot: he believed in the essential goodness of most other Serb politicians, including two of the palpably least good – Slobodan Milošević and Milan Babić.

According to his own testimony, it was Rašković who nurtured Babić's early career in the SDS after the Croat elections in April 1990. In a move guaranteed to provoke Tuđman's HDZ, Rašković organized a referendum on political autonomy for the Krajina Serbs which was held in August and September of 1990. This was the event which led to the armed confrontation on the weekend of 17 August. It was during the preparation of the Krajina referendum that Rašković was impressed by the organizational skills of the young President of Knin's Town Council. With Rašković's help, Babić was soon elevated to become the second most influential politician in the Krajina. Babić persistently requested Rašković to put him in touch with the leadership of the SPS, Milošević's party, in Belgrade. Rašković obliged. It was then that Rašković, rather naively, decided to travel to the United States for two months.

During this period, Babić travelled regularly to Belgrade where he built up a substantial network of political and military contacts. Rašković insists he does not know whether Babić was in direct contact with Milošević. If anybody does know, they have not revealed this particular secret, but to judge by Milošević's overall political behaviour, it is extremely likely that the two men were personally acquainted and that Babić's programme received the express approval of Milošević. The result was the transformation of Krajina's ragbag shotgun resistance movement into an extremely well-armed and highly motivated militia quite capable of bloodying the nose of Tuđman's nascent army, at the time comprised policemen and special reservists alone. The Krajina Militia was conceived and nurtured by a man who was initially regarded as Babić's most trusted bosun, Milan Martić. Slightly rounded and plump, with a clipped moustache, a cartoonist would not have been able to draw such a comic rural Slav policeman (or inspector, as Martić sternly pointed out to me). Although Martić was thrown into the job as Babić's Interior Minister and military organizer, as he himself insists, he was no slouch in creating one of the most terrifying organizations which participated in the fighting between Serbs and Croats – the Martićevci. When he exchanged his blue police outfit for camouflage fatigues, the war between Serbs and Croats moved one large step nearer.

Later on, Martić was to fall out badly with Babić when the latter was beginning to challenge the political monopoly enjoyed by Milošević. But he always displayed a certain loyalty to Babić which ensured a degree of cooperation. After Babić had successfully side-lined Rašković, Knin became in the eyes of many Serbs the centre of a new Serb renaissance. Perhaps the dentist from Knin would lead his people to one of the Balkans' most elusive sacred grails – Serbian unity.

The tales of Babić's authority were already legion. Similarly renowned was his importance as an actor on the Yugoslav stage in a performance which already resembled the plot of an Elizabethan revenge tragedy. It was thus a shock to meet a man whose personal-ity was so lifeless and behaviour so child-like. Only when I talked to him did I realize why he should not be underestimated. He was articulate and calm about his resistance to Croatia (and later on to anybody who crossed his path, like Milošević). Babić had clearly realized that Knin, the SDS and the fears of the rural Serbs in Croatia could be mixed together, and spiked with a potent spirit of violence to make up a recipe for his political success. As he sat there explaining his demands of Zagreb, swinging his Luger with a supercilious smile on his face, I appreciated that I was listening to what was within the context of the political culture of the Balkans a very serious figure. His initial success was dependent on Milošević, the supreme manipulator of Serb politics. But Babić's dogged, even insolent resistance of Milošević in December 1991 and January 1992 over the issue of the UN peace-keeping force deployment inside Krajina proved that he was one of Milošević's only equals in the politics of deceit and manipulation. Perhaps he was his only equal.

After assuming power in the SDS, Babić added more demands of Tuđman than those Rašković had been pressing for. Initially, Rašković had hoped to strike a deal with Tuđman which would have granted Serbs cultural autonomy, including such privileges as control over the local school system in Serb majority areas. Tuđman and Rašković failed to find a compromise, which resulted in the Serbs also demanding political autonomy which they would legitimize through a referendum. After being denounced as illegal by Zagreb, the decision to hold a referendum was followed by the formation of a Serbian National Council in Krajina. At no point did Rašković express an interest in taking Serb areas out of Croatia. The autonomy he demanded would be realized within a Croatian state, whether part of Yugoslavia or not. Babić introduced the idea of territorial autonomy which later developed into a policy of secession from Croatia. While both Milošević and Tuđman stoked the fires, Babić stirred the pot vigorously.

Although nationalist politicians throughout Yugoslavia were constantly raising the stakes in their dangerous political game, they had not yet thrown their greatest asset into the pot. This was the people, or *narod* as the Slavs call them. Before May 1991, Croats and Serbs lived together in relative contentment throughout the regions which have now been so dreadfully ravaged. They were perfectly aware that the rotten ship of the Yugoslav state was entering troubled seas. Yet nobody in their wildest fantasy would have predicted that within a little more than twelve months, the peaceful town of Vukovar would be levelled to the ground in one of the most merciless bombardments of modern history. Nor would they have dreamed it possible that Croat soldiers would massacre innocent Serbs, while Serb fighters would mutilate innocent Croats. When I first arrived in Knin, although the *narod* was being prepared for the forthcoming events, this had not yet affected the everyday friendships of Serbs and Croats. Later on during the war, I witnessed how the tightest and oldest personal bonds were slashed into ribbons by the blades of hate and prejudice. But it was a gun-carrying, Ustasha-hating Serb who put me in touch with his old Croat friends in Knin when I first travelled there. 'Most of the Croats in Knin are fine people,' he explained. 'They're not like those dreadful Ustashas in Split.' I developed a friendship with the Croat family whose fate is now a mystery to me. Even by 1990, it had become clear to me that in Croatia one's nationality was not important. The only fact of significance for individuals in Croatia was whether they were members of the local minority or not. In Knin, the Croats were definitely a minority. Although the fabric of their life was still intact, my Croat family did explain how their thirty-year-old son had been warned to stay away from public places and, indeed, to consider leaving Knin lest the Martićevci, as the Krajina Militia was labelled, should try and mobilize him.

It was through these Croats that I uncovered a network of Serbs in Knin who believed that Babić was driving them towards a senseless war. These were relatively sophisticated Serbs from Knin who protested in particular against Babić's methods in organizing the referendum and the *straža*. They described how the followers of Babić and Martić would knock on the door of recalcitrant Serb males at all hours to demand why they had failed to volunteer for duty on the *straža*. They painted a convincing picture of the general fear which Babić had created to guarantee his order. They also explained how Babić's most faithful people came not from Knin itself but from the surrounding villages. Although I was convinced by these men's story, I am similarly convinced that Babić could have survived in Knin without resorting to such crude totalitarian methods, as support for him in the town was substantial.

I visited Knin once after the war had begun. The house of my Croat friends had been taken over by Serb refugees from somewhere on the Dalmatian coast who had prominently replaced the Croat names with their own written in Cyrillic, and although I succeeded in briefly meeting one of the Serb dissidents of eighteen months earlier, his commitment was now one of unquestioning and genuine loyalty to Babić. It was as though the whole town had suffered the fate of the American mid-west town featured in Don Segal's film, *Invasion of the Body Snatchers*: some alien virus had consumed their minds and individual consciences. Mercifully, this virus had not been so effective in the Krajina areas to the north of Knin where opposition to Babić began to grow. But in Knin nobody had a bad word to say about Babić anymore and they were all being sincere. I hope I will be able to meet my Croat friends from Knin again some day. More than this, I hope they are still alive.

Without doubt one of the most important actors on the Knin stage which transformed the consciousness of this dozy town was Srpski Radio Knin (Serbian Radio Knin). On the main street in Knin, right opposite the railway station, Srpski Radio Knin shares its offices with various ministers and politicians from the Republic of Serbian Krajina. The first time you enter this building, you are subjected to a thorough, menacing search by the two armed irregulars on the door. But it's not long before they welcome you with an almost imperceptible raising of the eyebrow, which among the Chetniks and irregulars is the equivalent of a broad, beaming smile. From a professional point of view, Srpski Radio Knin is an impressive affair. The radio has little if any money, one tiny studio, while the studio manager is squeezed into a little box surrounded by the thousands of discs which any self-respecting radio station, local or national, has to own. In the front office sits the indefatigable Petar Popović, the journalistic mastermind behind Radio Knin. Popović buzzes around like a bumble-bee caught in a glass jar – although his work presents him with one insurmountable problem after the next, he will not rest until he has done what he set out to do. He gathers information, writes the stories and broadcasts them, while all the time being remarkably polite (inasmuch as a radio journalist can be) to the flotsam forever drifting in and out of his small front office. The people of Knin are extremely dependent on this radio station and although much of the news broadcast about the political situation in the local region is tendentious nonsense put out by the army or Babić, when Popović himself is on a story, he works with scrupulous attention to detail and accuracy. And yet like all other media in Yugoslavia, with a few dazzling exceptions, Srpski Radio Knin is a vital accomplice in the dissemination of falsehoods and the perpetuation of divisive myth which has turned one hapless *narod* against another equally innocent one. The only truth in the Yugoslav war is the lie.

Returning to Knin in January 1992 was a strange experience. The intervening period had exacted massive destruction on Croats and Serbs alike in the republic of Croatia. Knin had been one of the great pistons in the engine of war, tirelessly pumping out armed conflict fuelled by prejudice, persecution, aggression and an incomprehensible love of destruction. The town itself had not been a theatre of war but one of the main bases of the Yugoslav army inside Croatia. Knin was now heaving with people, as its population had almost doubled, soaking up large numbers of Chetniks, irregulars and reservists as well as over 5,000 Serb refugees from the Dalmatian coast, the region of Lika and towns like Zadar, where Croatia's innocent Serbs were subject to some of the most irrational and unpleasant retribution which traumatized Croats began handing out after the war began in June 1991.

This time I am travelling to Knin from Sarajevo where it is bright and very cold, with frozen snow lining the way to Zenica and deepening as I head westwards. I pass through Travnik, the birthplace of Ivo Andrić, who is known to a very small percentage of the outside world as the only Yugoslav winner of the Nobel Literature Prize. Since the war began, Andrić has once again become a symbol not of majestic writing but of Serbia's greatness, particularly among Serbs in Bosnia. It is Andrić who articulated with great fluency the history, suffering and historical mission of the Serbs in Bosnia. With all the irony that this opaque conflict can muster, it is usually forgotten that Andrić was a Croat.

Some fifty miles after Travnik, the road plunges into a valley and my car is smothered by a visibly toxic yellow fog. I know I have entered a town but I can no longer see even a metre in front of me. The fumes which have swallowed the town penetrate my vehicle and I feel a sharp knife at the back of my throat, while a nauseating odour invades my nose. This is how Jajce looked the day after the European Community announced it would recognize Slovenia and Croatia as independent states. The town where Tito's state, AVNOJ Yugoslavia, was proclaimed in 1943 was mourning not only the death of its child but its own fate as well. Surrounded by a beautiful lake and celebrated for its gorgeous, steep waterfalls in the middle of town, Jajce became a repository for some of the most devilish industrial cocktails mixed in Bosnia, when Yugoslavia's communists decided to turn the Switzerland of the Balkan peninsula into its Black Country.

The last town I drive through in Bosnia before reaching Krajina is Titov Drvar. Eight towns were blessed with the epithet 'Tito's', one in each republic and one in each Socialist Autonomous Province. Titov Drvar, like all others so honoured that I have visited, has nothing to recommend it except the surrounding countryside. Drvar is an industrial complex and nothing more. Like Jajce and many other towns in the area, Drvar is in a valley guarded by high mountains, making it an ideal victim of the phenomenon known as temperature inversion, when cold air in the town, made even heavier by atmospheric waste from the unregulated industry, is trapped by hot air above. The damage this does to the health of the local population is well documented by scientists in northern Bohemia where one of the worst manifestations of temperature inversion occurs regularly. Whether scientists will ever make the tiring trip to Drvar or not is another matter. I suspect not. But having been awarded the prized prefix 'Titov', Drvar must live up to its mythical reputation which was won during the Second World War. Tito was cornered in Drvar with a German parachute unit hot in pursuit. Despite overwhelming odds, brave Tito and his faithful dog outwitted with cunning the ruthless German killers. So it is told in the comic-book legend which the wartime struggle became at the hands of Titoist historians. Svetozar Vukmanović Tempo, one of the most colourful and interesting figures in Serbian and Yugoslav history, has a slightly different version of the heroism at Drvar. According to Tempo, Tito was so terrified by the approaching Germans, that he was not only unable to move, but he defecated in his trousers. At the last moment, Aleksandar Ranković, later the head of Tito's secret police, succeeded in organizing Tito's escape with a local Partizan unit. Paralysed with fear, Tito was literally carried out of the cave where he was hiding, which for many years was one of the most sacred goals of the Titoist pilgrim.

The eerie orange glow throbbed behind the mountains, as the military guard waved me down on the border of the self-proclaimed Republic of Serbian Krajina. The soldier's border hut was almost obscured under an enormous Serbian flag which was clearly raised as a warning and provocation to all Croats, even though few Croats are ever likely to clap their eyes on it. The soldier glanced at the slip of paper issued by the headquarters of the Yugoslav People's Army (JNA) in Belgrade and then gave a cursory search of the car boot for weapons which he knew he would not find. As he returned my passport, he said: 'So why did you British cowards capitulate to the Germans?' He was referring to the British government's decision of the previous day to recognize an independent Croatia along with the eleven other members of the European Community. I merely replied that Croatia had been recognized by the British government and not by me. I had by now become weary of entering into disputes with people who had large, angry guns pointing somewhere in my vicinity, but no sense of logic. He let me drive back into the heart of darkness.

Although the shabby streets were as I had remembered them, they were now bristling with uniforms of all sorts: Chetniks, the Krajina Militia, Partizans, JNA regulars, Arkanovci and Šešeljovci (which followed two of the most notorious supporters of Milošević, Arkan and Vojislav Šešelj), JNA reservists and a dazzling spectrum of volunteers. I even met a group of Moslems from Bosnia who had come to Knin to fight for Yugoslavia. Bosnia's Moslems are Serbo-Croat speaking Slavs who were converted during five centuries of Ottoman rule, and the overwhelming majority has displayed an implacable hostility to the neurotic and unstable intentions of Serbs. Following the collapse of communism, the Bosnian Moslems formed a political alliance with the Bosnian Croats. Everybody knew that this was a marriage of convenience, aware that a divorce could be easily applied for and granted. But despite this tactical arrangement, there were a large number of Moslems, particularly intellectuals in Sarajevo, who refused to give up the Yugoslav idea. They believed genuinely and reasonably that the chaotic mix of Slavs and non-Slavs on the territory of what was Yugoslavia forced everybody to live together. For them, Sarajevo was the most obvious and indeed successful example where Croats, Moslems and Serbs had no choice but to live together. Despite this Yugoslav consciousness among a minority of Moslems, to find a band of armed Moslems in Knin, the nerve centre of psychopathic Serb nationalism, was one of the many surreal experiences of the Serb–Croat conflict.

Probably the most bizarre fighter of all milling about Knin was a sixty-year-old volunteer from Vojvodina who despite his decidedly unintellectual origins spoke fluent French. He had come to Knin from his home region of Vojvodina as a hired hand. Although a Serb, he had absolutely no commitment to the nationalist cause. He had run out of money in Vojvodina and indicated that he had run up large debts in Serbia. He described without sensation how he had been working as a driver on the front line and from his understated style of story-telling, he appeared to be somebody who had lived a fairly risky life. After some discussion, it emerged that he had worked as a driver within the French underworld for many years, ending up eventually as a bodyguard for the French film star, Alain Delon. He described the criminal scandal by which the Delon entourage was finally exposed. His attention to detail and his disarming style convinced me that this, one of the truly ridiculous stories of a war built on lies, exaggerations and distortions, was probably the most reliable I had heard in eighteen months.

Not all these walking 'Armoured Personnel Carriers' were quite so genial as this lovable rogue. Most were highly motivated by nationalism, and the English (there was no talk of the British, while the Scots are considered by many Serbs to be the enemy because of the prominent support given by some Scottish mercenaries to the Croat National Guard) were newly reviled because of the decision by the Court of St James to capitulate to Germany's insistence on the recognition of Croatia. I spent some time in the main café in Knin either trying to evaluate youth culture, talking to the warriors or, frankly, anaesthetizing myself from what was happening around me by drinking double Scotches. One afternoon I erred by sitting next to a reservist in his mid-thirties who, with the few brain cells still available to him, was staring threateningly at a glass of *rakija* (one of the local spirits). Even in this advanced state of cerebral decay, he was able to recognize that I was not of his world and he grabbed my hand. *'Zdravo, druže! Odakle si?'* ('Hello, comrade! Where have you sprung from?') I told him I was English, and that sparked it off. 'Why did you fucking English capitulate to the fucking Nazis? You fucking bastard, go fuck your mother, you spineless motherfucker!' It was at this point that he started waving his gun and I started to weigh up my options. Next to this being who had just parachuted in from the set of *Night of the Living Dead* sat a uniformed man with elegantly clipped grey hair. He calmly soothed the reservist. My saviour looked different from many others roaming Knin. He was a Serb from Zagreb, Yugoslavia's most sophisticated metropolis, and he was clearly on a different intellectual plane from all his comrades. Regrettably, he did not wish to talk but his dignified demeanour and his helpless expression told me that he was a man mixed up in hell with no chance of even buying a ticket back to purgatory.

The day after I return to Knin, I am granted the privilege of a private audience with General Ratko Mladić, the commander of the Knin corps. General Mladić is a single-minded, resolute career officer for whom the Serb–Croat conflict has finally confirmed his crusty analysis of the human condition. In Zagreb, but particularly in Gospić, Zadar and other areas where Mladić's troops have been fighting on the front line, he is regarded as one of the most culpable war criminals of the conflict. Mladić despises politicians and indeed politics, but he is intelligent and ruthless enough to know that during times of conflict the military exercises enormous political influence. I have spoken to Serbs who have fought next to him and Croats who have fought against him and all agree that he is an exceptionally effective and brave commander on the field. But he is also opinionated to an extent which easily puts him beyond control, not only of the civilian command. By giving succour to Babić, he became one of the major obstacles to the deployment of a United Nations' peace-keeping force in the disputed areas of Croatia.

While waiting to see the General, I pass the time studying the exceptionally detailed military map of the Krajina area which hangs in the office of Mladić's secretary. It is produced for the Yugoslavs by the British Ordnance Survey and pin-points even the smallest building in the most remote village. Finally I am ushered into his office together with Lazar Macura, now the Minister of Information and an adviser to Milan Martić, the peasant cop turned Interior Minister. Contrary to my expectations, I am not confronted by a tight-lipped and drawn schemer unable to contain his contempt for foreign civilians. Ratko Mladić is stocky and energetic. He wears a soft hat which covers a thinning but dignified spread of grey hair. His big eyes twinkle with mischief while the grip of his hand is as firm as his conviction is unshakeable. From the beginning of our two-hour discussion, it is clear that he will be setting the agenda and delivering almost all the reports. Indeed after my third question, punctuated by long soliloquies from the soldier of experience, he winks at me and in jovial honesty barks: 'You ask a lot of questions, my English friend!' Before I can answer he continues: 'By the way, why did you all turn out to be such cowards, following the Germans' recognition of Croatia like spineless animals?'

It is mid-morning, but as is my wont on the first morning following my arrival in a town like Knin, I am suffering from a slight hangover. Mladić, never quite able to discard a roguish smile, commands a minion to fetch coffee and refreshment. A few minutes later, the minion pours the coffee while Mladić distributes his home-made *rakija*. As he does, one of my companions, also still coming up for air from last night, issues a polite refusal. The General is momentarily perplexed and then humorously angry, 'For a moment,' he booms, 'I thought you were going to refuse my home-made. Which is very funny, you know, because nobody refuses my home-made.' Our hangovers thus forced into oblivion, we raise our glasses and down what is undoubtedly one of the best home-mades I have ever swallowed.

Mladić talks much about himself. His father was killed in 1945 while attacking the village in Bosnia where the Croat fascist leader, Ante Pavelić, was born. Mladić is a Serb from Bosnia whose consciousness was branded for life by the inferno of the Second World War and the National Liberation Struggle in Bosnia. His antipathy towards Germany and Croatia has remained with him ever since. For him, the creation of an independent Croatia is the natural revival of a German compulsion to rule Europe. This, he explains, is why the English were making such a mistake by recognizing Croatia. 'Munich,' he said, 'is being repeated all over and this time at the expense of the Serbs. But we will not roll over.' His phobia of Germany is shared by many Serbs. From early on in the conflict, Serbia became convinced that Croatia's bid for independence meant that the Germans had begun the establishment of the Fourth Reich. Eighteen months ago, General Mladić and Margaret Thatcher would have found each other ideal dinner partners because of their common fear of German expansionism. One of the great curiosities of the Yugoslav conflict is how soon after the fighting began, Margaret Thatcher became one of the most rabid supporters of Croatian independence, thus backing Germany's major foreign policy goal in Europe in the second half of 1991, which first the British and later the American establishments fought against tooth and nail.

After showing us a variety of weapons which he had personally confiscated from defeated Croat and Slovene fighters, General

Mladić, who was clearly enjoying his captive audience, chuckled as he prepared us for a tape recording of a recent telephone conversation between himself and the head of the Croat Interior Ministry (MUP) force in the nearby port of Split, one of the most militant homes of the Croatian Democratic Union. Although neither was expecting to talk to the other, it emerged almost immediately that the two were acquaintances of old:

'Is that you, Mladić?'

'Yes it is, you old devil, what do you want?'

'Three of my boys went missing near . . . and I want to find out what happened to them.'

'I think they're all dead.'

'I've got one of their parents on to me about it, so I can tell them for certain that they're gone?'

'Yep, certain. You have my word. By the way, how's the family?'

'Oh, not so bad, thanks. How about yours?'

'They're doing just fine, we're managing pretty well.'

'Glad to hear it. By the way, now I've got you on the line, we've got about twenty bodies of yours near the front and they've been stripped bare. We slung them into a mass grave and they're now stinking to high heaven. Any chance of you coming to pick them up because they really are becoming unbearable . . .?'

This camaraderie between the opposing merchants of slaughter was one of the most horrifying phenomena I observed during the war. Although the Split commander was a Croat, Mladić certainly felt as much affinity with him as he did with anybody else in a war. He felt especially affronted by outsiders. Negotiations with European Community monitors were almost more than he could bear. His reasoning was understandable: the EC operational monitors were military intelligence officers. Even though they were confronted with a difficult and dangerous job (as the shooting down of the helicopter with five monitors in it demonstrated), they were still offered the once-in-a-lifetime opportunity of poking around every nook and cranny of another country's territory while large amounts of the regional military capability were operational.

Later Mladić revealed how he was fighting not just for Serbia but for decent living. He was not ashamed, he said, that he had stayed true to his wife and family throughout his career. Loyalty and fidelity to his family and soldiers as well as conviction provided General Mladić with his strength and motivation. He would not answer directly a question concerning the deployment of the United Nations' peace-keeping troops according to Cyrus Vance's conception of the ink-blot. He merely pointed out that 90 per cent of the army in Krajina were local people who you could not withdraw from the region. He also said that if the army were to leave Krajina, the people would flee before them. He added that the army would never desert its foundation. General Mladić did not stay in Krajina. In early May, he was appointed head of the forces of the Serbian Republic of Bosnia-Hercegovina. I greeted the news with considerable apprehension, as I knew that if the Serb army in Bosnia-Hercegovina intended to lay waste to large parts of the republic, then General Mladić was the man to carry this out. My worst fears concerning his efficiency and ruthlessness were confirmed.

After my audience with Mladić, I went idly in search of the Knin generations which, unlike the General, did not grow up with a consciousness stained by the violence of the Second World War. I strolled into the town's most popular café, the Premier. Having been inundated with traditional Serbian music for many days now, it was almost unsettling to hear mid-Atlantic English echoing through the bar. There was much talking and it was hard to distinguish whether the clientele was listening to a radio or a tape. After I sat down, I was quickly corrected by a quintessentially Serb waitress, her pearl-black eyes beaming down at me from a great height. 'It's television,' she said, 'MTV,' her dead voice immediately deflating the drama of her appearance. After several conversations with the youth of Knin, I noted how many of the women found the struggle with Croatia to be an unnecessary irritant. Instead they talked about how they would like to leave Knin and see other countries, not just in Europe but in Asia and America. This apparent uninterest in the war was by no means the response of young Serb women everywhere, but despite its central role in the conflict, it must not be forgotten that Knin itself experienced very little of the war and unlike many areas, the economic hardship caused by the fighting was initially hardly noticed in this town. It was never opulent and after it was cut off from its natural economic supply lines in Croatia, these were replaced by the endless lorries trundling backwards and forwards between Knin and the most prosperous regions of Serbia. Apart from the cars of a few mad journalists like myself, these lorries and JNA tanks were the only vehicles which ran over the roads from Bosnia into Knin for much of 1991. In contrast to their female partners, the Knin boys were full of crude anti-Croat talk with the undercurrent of violence forever bubbling up to the surface. Speaking to people from their thirties onwards, I found that the women had lost their independent position, mirroring instead the resolute rejection of Croatia that was universal among men of all ages.

As I say my private goodbye to Knin, it looks as desolate as when I first saw it. I understand the historical grievances, the cultural divisions and the political struggles. But as this harmless little railway junction recedes into the middle of nowhere, I am still frustrated by my own inability to determine whether Knin is the victim of the grandiose stupidity and callousness which swill around the corridors of power in Belgrade and Zagreb. Or whether this wilderness with nothing to recommend it on the surface was merely waiting for the chance to exact revenge for its social, economic and political inferiority complex.

2 BELGRADE, MARCH 1991:

Dress Rehearsal – Serb Eat Serb

By the beginning of 1991, Serbia had become known as the 'Land of Mordor' among foreign journalists in Yugoslavia, thus honouring J. R. R. Tolkien's dark vision of a fallen kingdom. Elections in December 1990 had conferred a dubious democratic legitimacy on the presidency of Slobodan Milošević. His victory at the polls had deepened fears among Serbia's fragile liberal establishment that this 'Emperor of the Night' would now go on to fulfil the bleakest of the prophecies which had multiplied since September 1987, the month in which Milošević carried out a political assassination on his erstwhile mentor, Ivan Stambolić, thereby assuming the leadership of the Serbian Communist Party.

The drive towards war in Yugoslavia could not have been as dynamic as it was had it not been for the extraordinary personality of Slobodan Milošević, the most paradoxical of dictators. He is a man without passion, without any real nationalist motivation (although on the surface, he appears to wallow in it), and he is a man who has never shown any affection or regard for the masses upon whom he depends for support. Yet he is without doubt the single most influential post-war politician in Yugoslavia after Tito. Indeed there is a strong, rather depressing case for suggesting that Milošević may leave a deeper impression on history than Tito. Whereas the Partizan leader succeeded in ending the mass slaughter of Croats and Serbs born of the complex conflict which developed among the ruins of monarchist Yugoslavia during the Second World War, Milošević has invoked those spirits of violence and unleashed them to turn the sleepy backwater which the post-war Balkans had become into the pathologically unstable region that it was for the first half of the twentieth century.

The Seventh Session of the Serbian League of Communists' Central Committee in September 1987 was transformed into Serbia's

Night of the Long Knives when Milošević sank his teeth into the reputation of Ivan Stambolić. By denouncing the Serbian leadership's policy on Kosovo, Milošević also consigned the consensual politics of Tito's Yugoslavia to the historical dustbin. Until 1987, the Titoist balance went through a variety of modifications, substantial and superficial, but its fundamental premise was the maintenance of a relatively weak Serbia at the expense of autonomous republican centres. Despite this, Tito could not afford Serbs to feel excluded. This imperative ensured the relative strength of Serb politicians in Croatia, Bosnia, Vojvodina and Kosovo, as well as at a federal level. As a whole, the system could only function with two absòlute political taboos: overt nationalism and the active participation of the masses in politics. It was these two taboos which Milošević smashed in 1987.

The whipping stick which he used at that Central Committee plenum was the situation of the Serb and Montenegrin minority in the province of Kosovo, where a large Albanian majority lives. By affording Milošević their support, the Central Committee members raised a nationalist demand to the top of the agenda in Serbia, the republic which lay at the political and geographic centre of the old Yugoslavia. This was a challenge to all other republics: their choice was to recognize Serbia's seniority within Yugoslavia and by implication the dominance of a Serbian-dominated unitarist state, or to respond with a nationalist agenda of their own. The Slovene bureaucracy, under barely resistible pressure from an organized and exceptionally articulate opposition, was the first to rise to the challenge by issuing a trenchant attack on the repressive and centralist tendencies of the federal Yugoslav structures. Milošević's tactical call for justice for the Kosovo Serbs placed a profound strain on the map of a unified Yugoslavia and soon this tired document began to tear along nationalist lines. The frightening complexity of Yugoslavia's ethnic composition, which had been largely forgotten over forty years, began to reveal itself.

By 1989, powerful nationalist sentiment was stirring throughout the Yugoslav republics. In part, this was a nervous reaction to the centrifugal forces throbbing vigorously inside the Serbian vortex. But it also reflected the strength of regional and nationalist forces throughout Eastern Europe as one-party rule began to break down.

In Yugoslavia, the revival of violent, intolerant nationalism had begun before the collapse of communism had been predicted elsewhere in Eastern Europe. Without question, it was Milošević who had wilfully allowed the genie out of the bottle, knowing that the consequences might be dramatic and even bloody.

With the exception of Montenegro, Milošević was universally loathed outside Serbia. At first, not even the Serb communities in Bosnia and Croatia invested any particular hopes in him. The Serb communities in Croatia, for example, have never felt any great sympathy for the situation of the Kosovo Serbs who were the main instrument which Milošević used to attain power. Attitudes towards Milošević inside Serbia have always been complicated. By raising the flag of Serbia's ancient obsession, Kosovo, he won considerable sympathy among nationalist intellectuals guided by the novelist, historian and erstwhile dissident, Dobrica Ćosić. Ćosić and some like-minded academics from the Serbian Academy of Sciences had been behind a notorious document called the Memorandum which was published in 1986. This bitter attack on the Kosovo policy of the then Communist authorities anticipated the atmosphere of national intolerance which was about to smother reason in Yugoslavia. The Memorandum both prepared the ideological ground for Milošević by focusing public opinion yet more tightly on the Kosovo issue, and indicated to this ambitious *apparatchik* that there was a real base among intellectuals for a nationalist assault on the leadership of the Serbian League of Communists.

But the coup against Stambolić was not the end. Milošević was concerned to extend his power still further beyond the borders of Serbia. To do this, he broke Tito's Second Commandment by widening the nationalist debate to include the Serbian masses, a move fraught with incalculable danger for the Balkan peninsula. He organized a series of demonstrations in Serbia, in Kosovo and in the northern Autonomous Province of Vojvodina, where a substantial Hungarian minority lives. These were bizarre manifestations which perfected the fusion of communist, Serbian and Orthodox Christian iconography. Above all, the hundreds of thousands of Serbs who came to worship at this movable temple gave homage to Milošević, whose stern but flap-eared visage and shaving-brush hair-style became the central artefacts in this new religion.

Although the new Serbian leader gave vent to latent nationalist sentiment, he also actively encouraged the hysteria by establishing a 'demo network'. Unemployed young men were paid to travel around Serbia, Kosovo and Vojvodina to participate in these rallies. Firms were also encouraged to support the demonstrations financially. Some firms from the republics of Bosnia and Macedonia were forced into the scheme with considerable reluctance. The demonstrations were part of a well-organized plan, designed to intimidate the non-Serb peoples of Yugoslavia, instil among Serbs the idea that their fellow Serbs were being widely discriminated against, but on a higher political plane, to underline Milošević's determination to mark his territory as the undisputed master of post-Titoist Yugoslavia.

In Vojvodina, the followers of the 'anti-bureaucratic revolution', as Milošević named the crashing wave he had generated, succeeded in forcing the resignation of the incumbent government. To be sure, this body comprised self-seeking time-servers, but at least they did not carry the nationalist virus. In Montenegro, Milošević succeeded in destabilizing the republican government, whose successor adopted policies much more sympathetic to Belgrade.

The climax of the demonstration movement was the celebration planned for the 600th anniversary of the Battle of Kosovo on 28 June 1989. On this day in 1389 the forces of Serbia's medieval kingdom were defeated by the Ottoman empire, thus opening the long chapter of servitude in Serbian history, but also the long struggle for national statehood. Why the Serbs celebrate this as the greatest day in their history is a mystery to the rest of humanity, but celebrate it they do.

Prishtina, the capital of Kosovo and centre of the Kosovar Albanians, is a sad mixture of shanty-town poverty and pompous monuments to the architectural philistinism of the party bureaucracy, which in the 1970s and 1980s frittered away substantial development funds on civic buildings of no real benefit to the people of Kosovo. On 28 June, Serbia's most sacred day, Vidovdan, 1989, Prishtina was its usual sticky, shabby self as hundreds of buses pulled out of the town. Within minutes, the buses were bogged down in a viscous sea of Serb peasants who had come to pay homage to their dead of 600 years ago. Their accents revealed the

34

sing-song rhythm of Vojvodina, the long drawl of Užice or the grammatically precise language of Serbs from eastern Hercegovina – not to mention the smooth, central-Canadian dialect of Toronto and the piercing tongue of the Melbourne Serbs. The final path to the meadow of Gazimestan was a heaving mass of ordinary folk, for whom Cecil B. de Mille would have died. Of course, the festivities included a number of regional types of Serbian dances, the *Srpsko Kolo*, Serbian songs, readings from nationalist literature, backed by choruses sporting traditional dress, tutus and some garments whose style and cut were so peculiar as to render their origin unintelligible. The colourful dresses were worn by an unlikely mixture of communists, Orthodox Christians and monarchists with one thing in common – they were all Serbs.

The Field of Blackbirds, as the Serbian settlement of Kosovo Polje is known in English, was turned into an infinite expanse of Serbia's imagined glory, dominated by one image over all others – Slobodan Milošević. This gross display of Serbiana, in the heart of an area populated largely by Albanians, did not go unnoticed in the rest of Yugoslavia. Milošević's speech was carefully measured and not hysterical – but it contained some unmistakable warnings: 'Six centuries [after the Battle of Kosovo Polje], we are again engaged in battles and quarrels. They are not armed battles, but this cannot be excluded yet.' His message to the Slovenes, Croats, Moslems, Albanians and Macedonians was clear: 'Look with what ease I can mobilize over 1 million Serbs.' Gazimestan was the opening move in a rather chilling numbers game in which the players bluffed about how many of their people they could afford to lose before it would begin to erode their political power.

Because it was officially billed as a Yugoslav celebration, Gazimestan was also attended by the state President, the Slovene Janez Drnovšek, the Prime Minister, the Croat Ante Marković, and his compatriot, the Foreign Minister, Budimir Lončar. It is hard to imagine anyone looking more unhappy and embarrassed than Drnovšek, who was forced to stand at Milošević's right hand throughout this appalling nationalist display – the President of Serbia seemed determined to humiliate this polyglot, liberal and rather decent President of Yugoslavia. As an outsider, I had to conclude that his success was consummate.

And yet, despite this adoration among the Serbs, Milošević is in certain respects a reluctant dictator. True, his low, rolling voice is seductive, but he is none the less a disappointing and ineffective public speaker. His style reflects the cold and unfriendly aura which almost everyone who meets him detects. He has few if any friends, while his wife, Mirjana Marković, a lecturer in sociology at Belgrade University, is reviled by many who know her. She shares with him a fanaticism which would seem much more at home in the Hungary or Czechoslovakia of the early 1950s. In 1990, she became a founder member of the League of Communists – Movement for Yugoslavia (SK – PzJ), the so-called Generals' Party, which was devised by hardline army officers as a way of keeping the flame of their privileges alive at a time when the dawning era of pluralist democracy threatened to extinguish it. If Milošević and Marković were to profess any genuine ideology, it would not be Serbian nationalism, it would be Balkan Stalinism. He is a product of the communist bureaucracy whose authoritarian traditions fitted snugly with his own behavioural patterns.

As a politician, there is nobody who can compete with Milošević in the Balkans. As the events of the next few years would show, when on his home territory, Milošević could dance in circles around some of the world's most senior diplomats and statesmen. His success lay in the shameless exploitation of the most effective tools of Balkan politics: deception, corruption, blackmail, demagoguery and violence. As president of Serbia, however, Milošević was always careful not to bear apparent responsibility for any particular policy. When he devised and executed complicated political manoeuvres (for example, the arming of Serbs outside Serbia), he did not reveal his plan in its entirety to any other individual. An army commander would be apprised of one aspect, while a paramilitary leader or local potentate would be entrusted with another piece of information or task. In stark contrast to President Tuđman, Milošević had no trusted advisers who would guide him through protocol or awkward constitutional situations. He formulated all major policies himself. When accused by domestic and foreign politicians of having instigated a particular policy, he would simply point out that as president, he enjoyed few if any executive powers, so he could not accept responsibility. What is most remarkable is how over the next five years, Milošević failed to realize any of his announced intentions. He gave Slovenia the green light to leave Yugoslavia, thus facilitating the federation's demise. He later gave up his theory that all Serbs should be allowed to live in one country, selling his little minion, Milan Babić, down the river in the process, and he formally renounced territorial claims on Bosnia by defining the mini-Yugoslavia comprising Serbia and Montenegro. In the process, he succeeded in devastating his country. None the less he has demonstrated a remarkable political longevity. It was not until the imposition of United Nations' sanctions on the rump Yugoslavia at the beginning of June 1992 that Milošević weakened probably beyond the point of his long-term political survival.

During 1990 and 1991, the discussions between the presidents of the six Yugoslav republics became the central forum through which the country's disintegration would be regulated. Milošević's tactics at these meetings were clear. He would not accept the transformation of the Yugoslav federation into a loose association of sovereign states because this would substantially weaken the unitarist predilection which he and his allies in Serbia and the Yugoslav People's Army (JNA) shared. Following Tuđman's victory in the April elections, Milošević was increasingly willing to raise the spectre of the right of all Serbs to live in a single state, should Tuđman attempt to take Croatia and its 600,000-strong Serbian minority out of Yugoslavia. Milošević's chosen weapon, the Serb minority in Croatia, was a dangerous club to brandish. The two presidents, Milošević and Tuđman, began pulling and grabbing this excessively sensitive group of people like two small children arguing over a toy. Every time Croatia and Slovenia pushed their claims for independence, Milošević simply said that Croatia could go but without the regions where Serbs live.

Milošević frequently exasperated Slovenia's politicians during these meetings, but the threat under which they lived was not nearly so disturbing as that which he hung over Croatia's head. The implication was that Serbia would simply not tolerate Croatia's secession. In the Croat election campaign and even more so after the victory of Tuđman in the elections of April 1990, the obsessive need to create an independent nation state to fulfil the thousand-year-old dreams of the Croat people now dominated political debate in Croatia. It was clear, particularly after the first armed clash between the Serb paramilitaries in Knin and the Croat militia, that the two republics, Serbia and Croatia, were on a collision course that would result in war unless one of them backed down. In order to avoid armed conflict, Milošević would have had to discard his insistence on the maintenance of a tight Yugoslav federation, while Tudman would have had to show a greater willingness to negotiate with his Serbian minority. Neither president revealed the necessary statesmanship. There can be no doubt that from an early stage, Milošević was well-prepared to accept war as a solution to the Yugoslav problem. According to Croat politicians close to Franjo Tudman, the Croatian President believed quite mistakenly well into June 1991 that the army would not prevent his attempts to establish Croat national power in all areas of Croatia, including those dominated by Serbs.

Once it was clear that war was a real possibility, Milošević still faced two tedious related obstacles which he had to overcome before he could accelerate his preparations for the struggle. These were the democratic elections in Serbia and the appeal of opposition to Serbia's nationalist and democratic constituencies. As the League of Communists' structure in Yugoslavia dissolved during 1989 and 1990, the calls for a multi-party system throughout the country became irresistible, even for the mighty Milošević (all the evidence suggests that if Milošević could have retained one-party rule, he would have done).

Most political forces to emerge in Serbia in 1989 and 1990 were laced with a powerful nationalist toxin. Initially, these were all clumped together in a taut, concentrated ball of nationalist malcontents waiting to exploit the uncertainty and confusion which the introduction of a pluralist system and the reconstitution or dissolution of Yugoslavia would bring. Balkan malcontents being what they are, this ball of nationalism exploded and spawned a number of smaller formations, which expended considerable energy squabbling among themselves before they launched their emotive appeals to the Serbian public.

The tight ball yielded to a variety of extremist organizations, including the Serbian Radical Party (SRS) of Vojislav Šešelj, the self-proclaimed leader of the Chetniks in Serbia, and the Serbian

National Renewal (SNO), formed by Mirko Jović, a peculiar psychopath from Stara Pazova, a town in the south of Vojvodina. The military wing of Jović's organization, the *Vitezovi*, or 'Knights' of Serbia, had been employed to play Serbian knights in the film *Battle of Kosovo*, which was released to coincide with the 600th anniversary. Within a year, these men, together with the *Beli Orlovi* ('White Eagles') of Dragoslav Bokan and the followers of Arkan, a mafia-style criminal wanted in Sweden and under suspicion of having committed such crimes as murder and extortion in other European countries, would be fighting with real weapons, committing some of the most frightful crimes of the Yugoslav war in the process. The revival of the Serb nationalists, the Chetniks, has been one of the most hideous and frightening aspects of the collapse of communism in Serbia and Yugoslavia. This breed, which finds nurture in the perpetration of unspeakable acts of brutality, encapsulates all that is irrational and unacceptable in Balkan society. The thought patterns of the Chetniks are not peculiar to Serbia, but only here have they been allowed to fulfil their sick potential with no barriers.

Initially, Vuk Drašković, the leader of the Serbian Renewal Movement (SPO), was considered another of these dangerous, rightwing madmen. With his distinctive long hair and flowing beard, which inevitably raised the comparison with Jesus Christ, Vuk Drašković fascinated the people of Serbia, not to mention foreign journalists. A novelist and former journalist himself, Drašković renounced Yugoslavia from the start in favour of his conception of a Greater Serbian state. He preached a gospel of Greater Serbia. His initial message was greeted with a chill by liberals as he appeared to be an even more frightening manifestation of Serbian nationalism than Milošević. He spoke of expelling all Albanians from Serbian territory (which means from Kosovo) and he had an equally antipathetic attitude towards the Moslems of Bosnia and the Sandžak. Later on, however, Drašković revealed a genuine commitment to dialogue for solving constitutional and political problems. Not perhaps the consummate politician and lacking the liberalism of a part of the Belgrade intelligentsia, he has none the less evolved a principled stand against violence. Along with the Democratic Party (DS), which projected a centre national image, Vuk (he is invariably referred to by his Christian name in Serbia) and the SPO developed into the main anti-Milošević movement in Serbia.

The DS was stricken by a severe identity crisis from its inception. One section of the organization wished to present itself as a European liberal party, but in the heart of the Balkans this is a tall order if you are also aiming for electoral success. Not only had the poisoned atmosphere of intolerance, which Milošević had spread throughout the republic, imposed the imperative for a nationalist agenda on almost all parties; in addition, many DS members felt themselves to be Serbian patriots who would not allow themselves to be outdone by the flaming rhetoric of Drašković and of those further to the right: Šešelj and Jović. After a process of purging and splitting, the Belgrade professor, Dragoljub Mićunović, emerged as a centrist leader, flanked in ideological terms to the left by the energetic Frankfurt School student leader, Zoran Đinđić, and to the right by the composed and intelligent Vojislav Koštunica.

So although to the outside, Milošević may have appeared the toast of Serb nationalists, as the elections approached, he and his Socialist Party of Serbia (SPS) were also perceived by many Serbs to be incorrigible communists. Try as he might, he could not shake off the epithet 'Red Bandit' among a substantial part of the population.

In almost all respects, the state in Serbia was synonymous with Milošević's Socialist Party of Serbia, which in turn had offered the old bureaucracy and its dependants a new lease of life in rather ill-fitting democratic clothing. Naturally, this influence over state institutions entailed significant benefits for the Milošević campaign. Even so, his reluctance to call the elections was conspicuous. When no longer able to postpone Serbia's first multi-party elections, December 1990 was chosen as the date. The opposition seemed ill-equipped to halt the roll of the mighty bureaucratic juggernaut. With no money, very little access to the media and a catastrophic lack of experience, the Socialist Party's opponents looked a shambles, offering as much resistance to Milošević as David did to Goliath – only Goliath had the sling. There were signs, though, that this delicate plant, which had only just sprouted, had unnerved Milošević, whose dictatorial paranoia doubtless sowed seeds of uncertainty even where the soil was barren. The introduction of democracy involved a new set of rules of which he was not sure, even though the experience gained in the ruthless Machiavellian world of communist politics was certain to come in handy.

Anticipation surrounding the December elections was considerable throughout Serbia, but especially in Belgrade which boasts an important liberal tradition. Serbia's cities were unrecognizable among the forests of paper which the SPS had appropriated to smother every lamp-post and every hoarding available. The party's electoral promise was simple: *Sa nama nema neizvesnosti* (With Us There Is No Insecurity). Confronted with unknown organizations promising new-fangled, cosmopolitan solutions propped up by a ruthless market economy, Serbs, it was thought, would recognize the SPS to be a sturdy raft on a stormy sea of uncertain future. In order to reinforce his message, Milošević was still conveniently in absolute control of television. Access to the air waves was systematically denied to the opposition parties until a short time before the elections. Even then, their appeals were buried away on obscure Channel 2 slots, which could not be received throughout the republic. In a further insult, each party was given the same amount of air time on television so that the Rock 'n' Roll Party, for example, received the same amount of time as the Democratic Party or the Serbian Renewal Movement. Given this hollow manipulation of the democratic process, there could only be one outcome of the elections in Serbia. Even so, only 48 per cent of the Serbian electorate voted for the Socialist Party. Milošević had, naturally, anticipated this eventuality by taking a leaf out of the British electoral book and designing a system whereby he would still enjoy absolute political control with less than 50 per cent of the vote.

The masses spoke and the Emperor could accept his crown bedecked with the dazzling jewels of democracy, which in theory should bestow respectability on him and his counsellors in the most noble courts of Europe. To stiffen the backbone of the SPS victory, Milošević cruised home in the presidential elections. Many people were sceptical about the results, even allowing for the institutional advantages which the SPS had guaranteed for itself. Milošević won not only in his industrial strongholds, he also won in the central Serbian towns where Drašković and other non-socialist parties were expected to build on the intra-war monarchist and anti-communist tradition.

*

Thus was the rule of evil perpetuated in Mordor. Serbia and its capital were beginning to change. Officially, Milošević clung to a Titoist rhetoric, for the maintenance of a federal but unitarist Yugoslavia. Milošević and his acolytes continued to trumpet the virtues of the old Yugoslav order in an attempt to claim the diplomatic heritage of the Titoist state. A new, restructured Yugoslavia, which offered Tito's peoples their desire for independence, while at the same time recognizing the inextricable ethnic and economic bonds linking them all, would have been by far the most preferable outcome of the talks between the six republican heads and federal organs. But Milošević's conception envisaged little if any change in the division and spread of power. By March, this Serbian intransigence had hardened, and the equally determined logic of independence in Croatia and Slovenia had chewed up most other political options. Differences still existed within Croatia and Slovenia, and between Slovenia, Croatia, Bosnia and Macedonia, but all were united in their condemnation of Milošević's unitarist Yugoslavia which was driven by a volatile fuel containing a high octane mixture of Serbian nationalism and authoritarianism. It was about this time that in Croatia, but particularly in Slovenia, the movement towards the new unitarist Yugoslavia proposed by Milošević was given the derogatory name, Serboslavia. Nowhere was this celebration of intolerance more evident than on the streets of Belgrade.

Throughout forty years of communist control in central and south-eastern Europe, Belgrade had always offered a ray of optimism. Together with its sister cities in the federation, Zagreb, Ljubljana and Sarajevo, it boasted a lively cultural life, a relatively high standard of living and an electric cosmopolitanism whose absence elsewhere in Eastern Europe left the capital cities drab and suffocating. Belgrade was famous for its excellent film and theatre festivals, for its riverboat restaurants with their superb cuisine and energetic musicians and dancers. Together with Zagreb, the Yugoslav capital produced some of the finest rock music in Europe during the 1970s and 1980s. Belgrade had always been an exciting and welcoming city in spite of the fact that it lacked all architectural charm and suffered from some of the grimiest levels of pollution Eastern Europe could offer.

But by the beginning of 1991, a process which degraded Belgrade

was well underway. The city was being abused by the new mono-
lithic culture of nationalism which had begun its reign of terror,
imposing its primitive values throughout Serbia. From my early
youth, I have always found the romantic and dramatic use of
Cyrillic script in East European political iconography quite compel-
ling. But throughout 1990, Cyrillic became the oppressor in Belgrade. Latin script was replaced wherever it stood by modern
Serbian Cyrillic and by the older Serbian Cyrillic based on Old
Church Slavonic. At a demonstration called to support the maintenance of Yugoslavia in front of the federal parliament, the *Skupština*,
in Belgrade, I witnessed how one demonstrator was attacked and
his placard trampled into the ground because he had written Yugoslavia in Latin script. The signs around Belgrade University cele-
brating the anti-Stalinist egalitarianism of its former students were
swamped by the plodding but intimidating banality of phrases like,
'*Ovo je Srbija*' ('This is Serbia'). The market around Zeleni Venac, a
busy knot of semi-legal traders, had its roof restored with a pretty
patchwork of red and white diamonds. As soon as it was unveiled, a
campaign was launched to have it torn down as for Serbian nationalists the roof resembled the red and white chequered shield, Croatia's
central heraldic symbol.

Ice-cream stands had been swept aside by virtually toothless
young men with long hair, beards and denim jackets all selling the
bile of Chetnikdom: T-shirts with the words 'Freedom or Death'
curled around a skull and crossbones or proclaiming, 'Ravna Gora
(the Chetnik training camp) – camp of Serbia's heroes', not to
mention the endless stream of Chetnik and nationalist songs on
tape. The tune which had been on all the nationalists' lips since
Kosovo Polje was '*Ko to kaže? Ko to laže? Srbija je mala*' ('Who
dares say it? Who dares lie about it? Serbia is a small country').
Selling their wares on the street like this, the Chetniks and other
assorted extremists looked pathetic and harmless, merely lowering
the tone of Knez Mihailova, the long and rather elegant shopping
boulevard in the centre of Belgrade. But in Serbia, and in the
Balkans as a whole, including Croatia, fascist scum does not simply
surface occasionally before sinking again as it does in the democracies
of the West. The nationalist sinews in this region have been exercised
and strengthened by centuries of violence and uncertainty. All those

I talked to on Knez Mihailova had the same urgent, if poorly articulated messages: Serbia had been drowned in a sea of Communism, Serbs had been driven out of their homes by Albanian terrorists, and now Serbs in Croatia were being threatened with a revival of Ustasha terror. Only a merciless campaign of unity could prevent the demons of history, supported by Serbia's traditional Western enemies (by which they meant Germany), from staining the land with Serbian blood by dealing a fatal blow before they could rise. When these men on Knez Mihailova began to appear, I knew, however absurd it seemed at the time, that these were disturbing harbingers of chaos.

These people were, however, of the opposition and initially they were friends neither of Milošević, nor of the army, nor of the Yugoslav state. They had been stifled along with liberal dissent for many years and inasmuch they were authentic victims of communist repression. Their attempts to disseminate propaganda proved to be an exceptionally difficult struggle as from the beginning of his reign as Serbia's strongman, Milošević had paid the closest attention to the media in his republic. For much of the 1970s and 1980s, Serbia had boasted some of the finest publications and journalists in the socialist countries. Indeed, *Politika*, the largest circulating newspaper in Yugoslavia (most of it in Serbia), was one of the best dailies in Europe, virtually uncensored and with an unrivalled network of correspondents in the countries of the Warsaw Pact. Its staff flaunted a gritty independence in the face of a crusty Communist Party bureaucracy. As soon as he came to power, however, Milošević identified two main targets among the Serbian media: the first was *Politika*, the second, Radio Television Belgrade. He ordered a thorough purge of both organizations which was duly carried out within the first year of his taking office as head of the Serbian communists. Interestingly, he did not destroy all the media in Serbia, only those whose influence extended the furthest and who would be important should the narrow cadre politics of the communist era expand into a movement of masses. *Politika* and RTV Belgrade became hollow vessels which Milošević's bureaucracy filled with seductive nonsense, designed to manipulate and feed the gullible and disoriented Serbian people with a diet of suspicion and intolerance. The role of television during the elections had been especially tendentious.

Initially it was assumed that, following his defeat at the elections, Vuk Drašković, Milošević's strongest opponent, was politically washed up. But his entire party, the SPO, was deeply aggrieved by the election campaign and few people believed that the result was authentic. Nobody really doubted Milošević's victory, but many doubted its extent. Despite that victory, the SPS, Milošević and the socialist media barons could not resist crowing over the opposition's defeat and much air time was allotted to vilifying the SPO, the DS and Vuk Drašković in particular. The most important vehicle for this campaign was the main television news, *Dnevnik II*, which is probably RTV Belgrade's most infamous product. It was the repeated snide attacks on the SPO and the DS, broadcast by *Dnevnik II* and repeated in various newspapers, that lit the fuse which eventually exploded on 9 March. The SPO, still smarting from defeat but absolutely convinced that the SPS's victory was dishonourable, decided to mount a campaign for reform of the media in Serbia.

On 16 February 1991, *Dnevnik II* broadcast a commentary of Slavko Budihna which accused the SPO and Drašković of maintaining secret contacts with Tuđman's Croatian Democratic Union (HDZ). Vuk was furious, demanding an immediate right to reply and additionally, on 20 February, announcing 'the storming of the TV Bastille' on 9 March. In particular, the opposition sought the head of RTV Belgrade's director, Dušan Mitević.

The countdown to confrontation began. The official media hurled their thunderbolts of abuse from their olympian offices while plucky Vuk and an ever increasing number of opposition groupings stood firm by their resolution to hold the demonstration. The Interior Minister then banned the event, which Vuk had announced would begin on Republic Square in the heart of Belgrade and then head for Takovska street where the television headquarters is situated. The Interior Ministry did say that the opposition could hold a rally on Ušće, the large area of grassland by the confluence of the Sava and Danube rivers, but opposition and government alike were well aware that this would castrate the demonstration. One by one, the opposition parties announced their solidarity with Vuk's movement. Leading opposition MPs sought an urgent meeting with the President to avert a crisis, but they received a curt refusal from Milošević.

Serbia's complex, schizoid political constellation was further distorted by events, a week prior to the demonstration, in Pakrac, a mixed town of Serbs and Croats in western Slavonia some sixty miles east of Zagreb. Serb and Croat militiamen exchanged automatic gunfire as both sought to take control of the municipal assembly and the police station. The situation calmed after the intervention of the army and a stand-off between Zagreb and the federal Presidency which had ordered the deployment of troops. In one of the Yugoslav media's all too frequent examples of hysterical reporting, Belgrade Radio broadcast an account of the events given by a Montenegrin journalist, Dragan Pavičević. He reported baldly that Croatian police had killed six Serbs. This was sheer nonsense, but once the news spread around Belgrade, it temporarily raised tension to a dangerous level. Although Vuk consistently proved his commitment to democracy, Pakrac ensured that the forthcoming demonstration would not only be an attempt to prove who was the most democratic, Milošević or the opposition, but who was the most patriotic.

The great day came. Both sides were highly excitable and both were warning of blood and conflict.

At the time, the majority of Serbia's Interior Ministry forces were wasting their lives in Kosovo, which had by now become one large militia camp, empowered to administer the decaying colonialism of Serbian rule in the province. During the week prior to 9 March, large numbers of police buses and transporters trundled back and forth between Prishtina and Belgrade as Milošević prepared to confront the Serbian government's most powerful enemy – ordinary Serbs. Opposition activists from many parts of Serbia, noticeably from Drašković's stronghold in Šumadija, central Serbia, also swelled Belgrade's population. On the eve of the demonstration, the bloated police force spread its girth around the major entrances to Serbia's capital. Their thick blue coats, which are cut so inelegantly that their owners appear restricted to slightly comic, robotic movements, would swing out of the darkness and into the murky light of orange phosphorous which demarcates the periphery of Belgrade. Cars were searched, drivers questioned. Some were turned back, some were arrested if weapons were found. Not surprisingly, the police extracted as much capital as possible from SPO activists found allegedly carrying guns. By now the air was bristling with anticipation as Belgrade began to resemble a town under martial law.

At 10.30 the next morning, the SPO issued a statement which warned of a 'catastrophe', adding that 'there could be tragic consequences for which only the authorities could be held responsible.' The young men who were drawing ever closer to the centrally located Republic Square were not common or garden demonstrators from the 'freedom and peace' school – they included a large number of Serbian nationalists from the towns and villages of the Serbian heartlands. Throughout the morning, Serbia's police began taking up position around Republic Square and, in smaller groups, near many key installations in the city – not surprisingly a large contingent were directed to Takovska where they were allotted the unenviable task of defending the 'Bastille'. They were all equipped with gas masks, truncheons and riot shields while the tortoise-like movements of Armoured Personnel Carriers and water-cannon could be detected in the background. At 11.30, half an hour before the demonstration was due to begin, the police who had separated one large section of the gathering crowd in Republic Square from another behind Knez Mihailova, the shopping boulevard, were caught badly off balance when a group of opposition warriors surged through the cordon at the top of Knez Mihailova.

This was the signal for the onset of the opening bout of unrest which at the time appeared to be complete chaos but in retrospect was a gentle warm-up. Half an hour of tear-gas, pincer movements, stone-throwing and hand-to-hand combat culminated in the demonstrators overpowering a police transporter. Immediately, the front line of the opposition took up the cry, 'Ustasha, Ustasha' followed by, 'Go to Kosovo' and 'Go to Pakrac', for what offended many of these young Serbs most was not the violence of the state but the fact that the Serb state would perpetrate violence not on Albanians or Croats but on Serbs. What staggered most witnesses was the tenacity and courage of the crowd as the police exhumed a mighty array of exhibits from the bowels of the repressive state apparatus. None the less, after fifteen minutes of bitter exchanges, these shock troops of Belgrade's finest turned and fled. The triumphant demonstrators

atop the captured transporter planted a huge Serbian flag embla-
zoned with the great Serbian symbol: the symmetrical cross surrounded by CCCC. The raising of the flag brought a hysterical
roar of approval from the crowd as though the battle had been
won. The day would show, however, that the battle had only just
begun.

At midday precisely, Vuk Drašković, whose authority was rising
to newer, more mythical heights with every minute, strode onto
the balcony of the National Theatre as our eardrums cracked to the
cry of his name in the vocative case, 'Vuče, Vuče, Vuče'. This in
turn gave way to the challenge to Milošević which would echo
around Belgrade for the next week, 'Slobo–Saddame', the Iraqi
leader's name also being granted the vocative for the purposes of
metre.

After Vuk had spoken for some time, the police returned with all
the vengeance they could muster from Francuska street, from
Makedonska street, Vase Carapica street and 29. Novembar street.
They started by hurling tear-gas canisters into the centre of the
crowd, reinforcing this by driving water-cannon through the main
body of the demonstrators. Using horses and truncheons and firing
automatic weapons into the air, they assaulted anybody who got in
their way, launching Belgrade on a trajectory of uncontrollable
violence which lasted two days. The police resembled the riot troops
of communist Czechoslovakia whose brutality had provoked the
revolution in November 1989. The signal difference in Belgrade was
the target – it was not the Gandhi-like students and writers of
Prague but young Serb nationalists whose automatic reaction to
violence was to respond in kind. In addition, the police action
ensured that many of the demonstrators were bottled into a corner
and had no option but to fight their way out. Demonstrators who
fell into the hands of the police were greeted by blows to the head,
stomach and genitals. Police vehicles were literally ripped apart by
the demonstrators who had developed within the space of half an
hour into a psychotic mob. Armed with iron bars and stones, the
unrest swept through Belgrade city centre as shops and offices on the
main boulevard, Terazije and Maršal Tito street, lost windows and
doors. Battles were fought outside the Serbian parliament, outside
the television headquarters and then down Knez Miloš street.

By the church of Saint Mark near the television headquarters, a group of police offered a peculiar ideological explanation of the demonstrators: 'They're a bunch of committed Chetniks and Ustashas. Blood's going to flow here and we'll destroy them.' One of the mob mistakenly ran into this group of police and the largest militiaman crashed down his truncheon over his head. Completely unconscious, with blood streaming out of his head, the young man was thrown by the police into the back of an ambulance.

When the fighting reached Knez Miloš, police began drawing their pistols and firing. The gangly eighteen-year-old student, Branivoje Milinović, who according to his parents had no interest in politics whatsoever, had arrived in the centre from his home across the Sava in Zemun in order to buy some music cassettes. Inadvertently turning into Knez Miloš from Maršal Tito, a police bullet hit him straight in the head, tearing off much of his skull. For four years, Slobodan Milošević had been exciting Serbs with tales of the terror and discrimination that they faced. The first Serb to die in political terror since his rise to power was murdered by Serbian police working in the name of President Milošević. Elsewhere, a 54-year-old policeman, Nedeljko Kosović, also fell to the violence, presumably at the hands of a demonstrator.

Glass, smashed concrete, bent traffic lights, tables, chairs and headless and limbless mannequins had transformed the centre of Belgrade into a shambolic, decayed urban wasteland. To complete the imagery of violent disintegration, tanks of the Yugoslav People's Army rolled onto the streets wagging their gun barrels at recalcitrant groups of youths. The Army had been mobilized by a string of telephone calls instigated by the Secretary of the collective State Presidency on the instructions of its Chairman, President Borisav Jović, the primitive Serb who responded to Milošević's every political whim with alacrity. Jović just scraped together a telephonic majority of Presidency members facilitating the military's show of force. This was the first open move in a week of shadowy but significant stratagems undertaken by the JNA.

Hundreds of people were injured, and over 100 arrested, including Vuk Drašković. Studio B, the superb independent television and radio station responsible for the most precise documentation of 9 March, and Youth Radio B92 were taken off the air by the Interior

49

Ministry. The opposition and the authorities slept uneasily as Serbia braced itself for its most chaotic week since the war.

Student City lies over the Sava from Belgrade's centre, in New Belgrade. This is a flat area largely colonized by rickety high-rise buildings which went out of fashion in Western Europe in the early 1970s but which remained an unshakeable commandment in the bible of Eastern Europe's town planners. These sit rather uneasily with the wide, squat structures of the Yugoslav federation building, which is the other major resident of New Belgrade. On 10 March, students emerged from their crumbling dormitories and in a fit of spontaneous outrage began to march that late Sunday afternoon towards the town centre. As they passed the various ministries and the ugly and pompous Palace of the Federation, their numbers grew as little columns fed themselves into the central falange. The horns of taxi drivers (the most militant anti-Milošević group of all) squeaked with hysterical delight at the spectacle.

'I'm from Kosovo, studying engineering here,' one tall, bespectacled student with a slight lisp explained to me. 'Milošević talks about Kosovo, but never does anything there. He talks about democracy, but spits on the people. Everyone in the world believes Serbs are causing all the problems in Yugoslavia and now we have to show the world that true Serbs love freedom, democracy and peace.' The young man echoed a disturbing paradox which underlined all the March events – Serbs, who often evince an inflated sense of their importance as historical defenders of European culture, were increasingly perplexed by the isolation which was folding around them as the sound of war closed in on Yugoslavia. '*Govori srpski da te ceo svet razume*' ('Speak Serbian so that the whole world can understand you') is one of the Serbs' favourite, if rather mystifying, sayings.

Serbia's identity crisis notwithstanding, all the students I spoke with seemed to dance with self-confidence, convinced that they were about to fashion history after their ideals.

They approached the Sava largely unaware that they were treading in the footsteps of the 1968 generation whose students shook the 'Red Bourgeoisie' of Tito's Yugoslavia whilst simultaneously bridging the ideological gap separating the students of Prague and Paris.

Just as Tito's militia awaited the revolutionaries of 1968 on a bridge across the Sava, so did the front line forces of Milošević's mutants, so-called because of the hideous form which they assumed with their gas masks on, gather to welcome the students of 1991 on the western edge of the Bridge of Brotherhood and Unity. The students squeezed onto the bridge from the road. Some began to suffocate before the column began moving forward slowly but with determination. I was in the middle suffocating with them and decided to fight my way through to the front and through the first, thin line of police. At this early stage of the evening, a press card still carried some authority.

After a rather confused discussion, the students decided to edge their way forward to the other side of the river. Three-quarters of the way across the bridge, a brace of gas canisters were launched, landing just in front of the confident marchers and signalling the return of chaos. I slipped down the bank on the eastern side to avoid the gas, and the fighting began. As I attempted to return up the bank, I was stopped by a militia man. 'If you go back there, I'm going to kick your motherfucking arse, motherfucker,' he warned me. My press card had suffered a dramatic depreciation in the space of an hour and was now of as much value as a used bus ticket. I crept round the back and up to Brankova street near Zeleni Venac from where I could hear the groans, cracks and explosions of a second violent riot. Where these demonstrators in the centre of town had appeared from, I had no idea, but for the second time in as many days, rebellion was shaking Belgrade.

It was by Zeleni Venac that I bumped into Zoran Đinđić organizing his student battalions. Đinđić was in his element – a leading and respectable DS parliamentarian, he had never been able to discard his Marcusian memories gained as a disciple of the Frankfurt School. This evening he could cast caution and ideology to the wind because this was the night of student power. Sandy-haired and with John Lennon type glasses, Đinđić cut a stylish, romantic figure – this was his night. He explained to me hastily how a battle was raging near Republic Square. From all around, the insidious fumes of tear-gas were working their way into the back of our throats while sound of water-cannon and gunfire could be heard echoing from every direction. I decided to risk running up to the Hotel

51

Moskva which separates Terazije and Balkanska but has entrances on both. Just before the front door on Balkanska, a gas canister exploded five yards away from me and a jet of poison shot into my face. I staggered into reception where the disoriented but ever helpful Moskva staff sat me down and revived me with water.

After another hour and a half of fighting, a group of several hundred students planted themselves in the middle of Terazije around the Česma drinking fountain. There are many drinking fountains around Belgrade, several of them, like the one on Terazije, decorously constructed. This one was erected in 1860 to celebrate the return of Prince Miloš Obrenović to Belgrade from exile. Around this tall, rather curious monument a large chunk of the students prepared to settle down for the night, surrounded by some 500 well-armed policemen. Đinđic, who continued to monitor, direct and inform the opposition headquarters of the evening's developments, went down to negotiate with the police. 'Look, people,' said one exasperated commander, 'we're only carrying out our orders. Look, we came in from Kosovo last night. One of my boys has just collapsed unconscious through exhaustion. What are we supposed to do?' he enquired despairingly.

The police warned that they had orders to attack if the students did not disperse but at about 4.30 in the morning they withdrew except for a few officers who merely continued to observe. It was a bitterly cold night but the spirits of those around the monument were soaring. 'We've seen them out,' one told me, 'this is now our country.' As the morning drew on, this new land of student optimism attracted hundreds and thousands of settlers. By midday, tens of thousands of people were listening to speech after speech which students began to deliver spontaneously. This was the origin of the student parliament in Belgrade which turned into a week-long vigil, as mighty a symbol of democratic desire as all the demonstrations in Leipzig, Prague and Timisoara. At its height, over half a million people controlled Belgrade's main thoroughfare and on many occasions it seemed that this volcano of discontent would erupt with such fury that the lava would engulf Milošević and his corrupt bureaucracy, the very agent which had aroused it from slumber.

Terazije – all it represented and all that surrounded it – was a last opportunity to muzzle the dogs of war in Yugoslavia. Only one outcome could guarantee this – the fall of Milošević. But the heroes of Terazije pulled back when standing on the brink of success.

Terazije was transformed during this week into the largest public tribune erected in the Balkans since the war. Throughout Belgrade there were a myriad centres of political activity: the Serbian parliament, the federal Presidency, the trade union organizations of *Politika* and RTV Belgrade, and the headquarters of the main political parties. But they were all driven by the awesome social power which the Terazije tribune was generating like a massive political turbine. Speakers ranged from unknown students through famous actors, peace activists, lawyers, workers, opera singers, restaurant owners to historians. Playing the best role in his career was the dashing MC, Branislav Lečić, who, curiously, had starred alongside the Vitezovi in the *Battle of Kosovo*. Lečić directed the first two days of the meeting during which the students and popular tribunes attempted to wrench politics away from the petrified institutions of the state. Even before the Sunday night was out, the students formulated eight demands which became the basis of their political programme for the next week:

1. An end to the repressive measures of the unconstitutional state of emergency.
2. The freeing of all those arrested during the demonstrations on 9 and 10 March.
3. *The uncovering of those responsible for all bloodshed and repressive measures.* [My italics – M.G.]
4. The resignation of Dušan Mitević, Sergej Šestakov, Predrag Vitas, Ivan Krivec and Slavko Budihna [Milošević's media barons].
5. An end to the monopoly of the ruling party of the mass media and a guarantee that the Independent Television Station, Studio B, and Youth Radio B92 be allowed to work unhindered.
6. Access for Independent Television Studio B to RTV Belgrade's technical facilities.
7. The resignation of the Minister of Police [sic], Radmilo Bogdanović.

8. The immediate convening of an extraordinary session of the Serbian parliament.

During the first two days, speaker after speaker urged the students to hold their ground until all these demands were fulfilled. Although the police were able to block the arrival of many students from other parts of Serbia into Belgrade, large sympathy demonstrations were reported from Niš, Kragujevac and Novi Sad. The demonstration on Terazije expanded by the hour and as it did, the demands of the students were met one by one.

The first was the convening of the Serbian parliament although it was called as a scheduled and not an extraordinary session. All of a sudden, the Socialist MPs were willing to discuss the opposition's demand for a new press law and other constitutional issues. These parliamentarians, whose activities were being broadcast live for the first time without any breaks for sensitive discussions, proved themselves to be monstrous clowns with little if any understanding of parliamentary procedure. The SPS MPs found it hard to contain themselves, fulminating against the students as anti-Serbian, pro-Albanian scallywags. The event was not without its lighter side. At three o'clock in the morning, one ageing SPS MP, Branko Lazić, hogged the floor for some ten minutes as his colleagues were falling from their desks with exhaustion. As the waves of revolution were lapping at the shores of state outside the parliament, he announced in all seriousness that instead of discussing the item on the agenda, he wanted to tell the House a fairy story about a man and his grandchild, but it would be 'a story with a sad ending'. At this veritably surreal juncture, his fellow MPs burst out laughing, no longer able to believe the farce being played out before them. The long-suffering Slobodan Unković, Rector of Belgrade University and the then President of the Parliament, buried his head in his hands and out of desperation blurted over the microphone: 'Oh my God, you Serbs are such a difficult people!' The whole of Serbia started laughing and since then Unković is known by everyone as 'the man with a sad ending'. The resolutions passed by parliament included a partial fulfilment of Student Demand Five, allowing the unhindered work of the Studio B and Youth Radio B92. The first part of Demand Five was never agreed to, but by the end of the week, the students had succeeded in extracting all but two demands, Three and Six, the latter being less important.

Although Milošević and the bureaucracy offered some resistance, the head of RTV Belgrade, Dušan Mitević, and his four cronies resigned, albeit with exceptionally bad grace. Radmilo Bogdanović, the Interior Minister and one of the least pleasant ministers in a cantankerous government, was also sacrificed. First Vuk and later the other demonstrators in custody were released and greeted with wild cheers on Terazije. The students and the united opposition began to believe that they were heading for a comprehensive victory. They should have been warned after Mitević's resignation. His replacement, whose appointment was announced almost immediately, was Ratomir Vico, a long-term political adviser of Milošević's and former journalist known for his hostility to Solidarność and other popular movements from Eastern Europe's pre-revolutionary past. The Mitevićes and Vicos of this world grow on trees in Serbia. Some oppositionists, generally those not sitting in parliament, insisted that unless Demand Three were understood to mean the removal from power of Slobodan Milošević, then the entire exercise from 9 March onwards would have been futile.

This point was reiterated on the Thursday, 14 March, when writers and intellectuals gathered for a passionate meeting, entitled *Anti-Politika* and chaired by the essayist, Aleksandar Tijanić. This was Prague, both in 1968 and 1989. The writers bemoaned the philistinism of Milošević and the bureaucracy, and some of their number also warned that the student demands amounted to a palliative which would not solve any of the underlying problems facing Serbian society and politics. These Cassandras pointed to the precedent of 1968, when Tito had embraced the revolutionary students following their brutal treatment at the hands of the police. He berated his 'evil counsellors' and by employing skilful tactics defused the student movement. This is what Milošević did in March 1991, even though he faced a much larger and more dangerous popular movement than Tito – and despite the fact that nobody had any illusions about 'evil counsellors'. Everybody agreed in March 1991 that the only man who could have insisted on such drastic repressive action on 9 and 10 March was President Milošević himself. When the students first raised the demand that those responsible for the bloodshed be exposed, many in Belgrade assumed that this was the signal for an assault on Milošević. They were wrong. Although the heroes of Terazije believed the day belonged to them, in political terms Milošević turned them into pulp using his uncanny ability.

The first political response to the weekend of 9 March was the holding of a rally on Ušće on the Monday, 10 March. As the Terazije parliament was attracting tens of thousands of participants by the hour, the Socialist Party was able to muster between 20,000 and 30,000 supporters (although the official media claimed that the figure was between 350,000 and 400,000). The Ušće rally relied upon old and faithful cadres of the League of Communists. It was one of the last opportunities for the weakening core of Partizan fighters to defend their struggle of the Second World War and the Yugoslavia which had been their prize. The average age of the demonstrators was over fifty and many were older still. Although they responded warmly to the ringing xenophobia and Stalinism which poured out from the platform with its enormous PA system and socialist realist placards, these demonstrators were sad, ordinary people whose political certainties had all but collapsed. They were clinging on to a Yugoslavia which had already expired.

It was during the rally that the SPS brought out its most emotive ammunition for the first time that week: the situation of the Serbs in Croatia. Dr Milan Babić sent a special message to Ušće:

The Serbian Krajina looks to you in Serbia for unity among the Serbian people . . . The Tuđmanites are triumphant. Mesić thanks his political ally, Drašković. What Franjo [Tuđman] and Stipe [Mesić] are unable to achieve, Vuk [Drašaković] does for them. Let us be as one – the Serbian people of the Krajina stands with the leader of all Serbs, Slobodan Milošević.

Less than a year later, Dr Babić would fulminate with all the hatred he could muster against 'the leader of all Serbs', but in March he was still paying off the hefty political bill which he had received from Milošević for supporting his activities in the Krajina. At the end of the meeting the apoplectic Minister of Industry, Dušan Matković, ordered his geriatric troops into action: 'There are 12,000 to 15,000 of them and 150,0000 of us. If they don't disperse, let's take them on.' Apart from being arithmetically dyslexic, Matković had apparently overseen that these tired workers and bureaucrats were already staggering home, their day's work already done by midday. The masses, it seemed, were not ready to defend the fatherland, so Milošević had to think of different options.

Milošević himself judged the political mood well. He could not disappear completely from public life, but by making strategic appearances and measured speeches, he ensured that hostility towards him personally was kept within limits which did not threaten. He saw to it that the anger was directed at individuals who were dispensable in their current function. When parliament was convened, Milošević made one of his rare appearances in the seat of Serbian democracy:

Serbia and the Serbian people are faced with one of the greatest evils of their history: the challenge of disunity and internal conflict. This evil, which has more than once caused so much damage and claimed so many victims, more than once sapped our strength, has always come hand in hand with those who would take away our freedom and dignity ... All who love Serbia dare not ignore this fact, especially at a time when we are confronted by the vampiroid, fascistoid forces of the Ustashas, Albanian secessionists and all other forces in the anti-Serbian coalition which threaten the people's rights and freedoms.

Milošević's forceful appeal to the threat posed by the enemy without paradoxically underlined the threat to Serbian unity which he himself caused. He already bore a heavy moral responsibility for the two Serbs killed on 9 March, but his refusal to accept any political responsibility for the extraordinary events two hundred yards away from the parliament building was breathtakingly audacious. Yet it was, in part, successful. Most people recognized the President's argument that the Terazije parliament was facilitating the plans of the Ustashas and Albanian terrorists, for the whitewash it was. Yet the thrust of popular anger was still being aimed at the dispensable individuals of Milošević's regime and not at the President himself. The students were determined that their original demands be met, but publicly they deferred to the President. As Dragana Topalović, the President of the Student Union of Student City, intoned from the Terazije platform on Wednesday, 13 March: 'We students demand that all of our demands be fulfilled, nothing more, nothing less. But let nobody demand the resignation of the government or of Slobodan Milošević.' On the same day in Zagreb, Milorad Pupovac, a Social Democrat leader in Croatia, who during the subsequent war became the most important representative of Serbs in areas under Croatian control, issued probably the most precise statement released during the March events:

The demands of the Serbian opposition and a great number of citizens of Serbia, notably the students and lecturers, represent a great hope for the development of democracy in Serbia and Yugoslavia, and a great step in the direction of the way out of the pat positions to which we, as citizens and peoples of Yugoslavia, have been led by policies formulated over our heads ... It is evident that the democratic consciousness of Serbia has overcome the national monolith ...

This decisive democratic demand must not and cannot be stopped by any force, still less by the blindness which claims that Serbs are only democratic if they are together and gathered around one leader and a single politics. Therefore we cannot agree with those representatives of the Serbs outside Serbia who ... blindly following the national monolith and the politics of one national leader, continue to support the policies of Slobodan Milošević. If these leaders do not understand immediately that the current type of nationalist politics in vogue in Yugoslavia is heading towards its end, so much the worse for them and, unfortunately, for those who still follow them.

It took a Serb in the Croatian capital to articulate that if Milošević survived March, the war could begin. The next week, an influential group of intellectuals launched a petition demanding that Milošević give up all his posts. The petition was, as far as it went, a success but because by then cars, and not students, were running up and down Terazije, the petition was more or less meaningless.

On one occasion, Milošević was confronted directly. This was during a meeting between the President and a delegation of students. In the delegation was a psychology student, Žarko Jokanović, and a talented young actor, Tihomir Arsić, one of the creators of a theatrical masterpiece called *Thus Spake Broz*, a savage and wonderfully comic deconstruction of Tito. Milošević said he was unable to respond to the student demands because as president these did not fall within his jurisdiction:

MILOŠEVIĆ: I repeat: Replacing the leadership of the television is not within my powers. I personally cannot do anything.

ARSIĆ: We didn't come to you personally, nor because of you personally. Personally you don't interest us. We came to you because you are President of the Republic . . . and if you will allow me to be personal, if I were you, I would find some discreet way of suggesting to those people in television that they resign even though it's not within my power, because there are people dying on the street. I'm sorry it turns out you are not able to do anything, but something tells me you're not quite as powerless as you make out.

JOKANOVIĆ: You have the powers of an American president, yet here you behave like the Queen of England.

Never has anyone had the gall to speak so forthrightly to Milošević as Arsić and Jokanović did on that March day in the President's own headquarters. Milošević was visibly irritated by the tone they struck and thereafter recoiled into his shell until the weekend, allowing other characters close to the government to take the flak which was flying from all sides.

The most comic figure to distract Serbia's attention from Milošević was Borisav Jović, President of Yugoslavia, and one of the most lamentably weak intellects to represent the Serbian cause throughout the Yugoslav crisis. Jović was leading Milošević's charge in the federal Presidency to have a state of emergency imposed throughout Yugoslavia during the week of the Terazije parliament. Having failed to gain the requisite support in the Presidency despite the energetic aid of the army leadership, Jović appeared on television on Friday evening and in a verbose and occasionally unintelligible speech announced his resignation. He explained that he had no wish to preside over the dissolution of the Yugoslav federation. Once the drama on Belgrade's streets had subsided, the federal parliament quietly refused to accept Jović's resignation. Jović accepted their refusal, gallantly staying on as state president, and until he was scheduled to hand over the office to Stipe Mesić, his Croatian counterpart in the collective Presidency, it was back to business as usual.

One irritating aspect for anybody trying to follow the disintegration of Yugoslavia was the constitutional jungle which governed the state. Not only was the 1974 constitution a worthless scrap of communist formalism, any definitive interpretation of its dubious provisions was rendered impossible by dint of decision-making procedures premised upon a series of contradictory clauses written into the Constitution to satisfy the country's various nationalities. After Jović resigned, people in Yugoslavia spent twenty-four hours working out what this actually signified. Eventually it became clear that his resignation was not valid until ratified by the federal parliament which, because of its majority of pro-Serb MPs, was as much an instrument of Milošević's policy as Jović himself.

While people from Ljubljana to Skopje were scratching their heads as to the significance of Jović's gesture, Milošević appeared on Serbian television and delivered an extraordinary speech. Galled that the Presidency would not agree to the Serbian plan for the imposition of martial law in the country, President Milošević announced that 'Yugoslavia has entered into the final phase of its agony. The Presidency of the Socialist Federated Republic of Yugoslavia has not functioned for a long time, and the illusion of the functioning of the Presidency of Yugoslavia and its powers, which in reality do not exist, has since last night finally expired.' Elsewhere in his speech. Milošević said that 'the Republic of Serbia will no longer recognize a single decision of the Presidency under the existing circumstances because it would be illegal.' At the same time, Milošević ordered the mobilization of reservists in the Serbian police force and the immediate formation of additional militia forces. Later on, especially during the war, Milošević would insist on the sanctity of the Yugoslav federation and its Presidency. Milošević, who had so often gained capital from his Yugoslav patriotism, demonstrated with this speech that he was nothing but an opportunist.

While this drama was being played out on the main stage, in the bowels of the Yugoslav theatre, more sinister discussions were underway. The only information which emerged from the meetings of the Presidency were short and invariably obscure statements which referred to how 'the collective head of state has considered the socio-politico-security situation in the country and would be undertaking the necessary measures to settle the disputes and calm the general situation.' Behind this gobbledegook, the Serbian leadership through the agency of President Borisav Jović and General Blagoje Adžić, the operational commander of the JNA, were cajoling the other members of the Presidency into agreeing to a state of emergency and the imposition of martial law throughout the country. This they failed to achieve, leading to a rethink in the Serb strategy now being developed by Milošević, Jović, Adžić, increasingly the Defence Minister, General Veljko Kadijević, and above all the mastermind of the military party, SK-PzJ, the former Defence Minister, retired Admiral Branko Mamula.

The Prime Minister, Ante Marković, called an emergency session of the cabinet to discuss the growing chaos in Belgrade and its implications for the security of Yugoslavia. The only cabinet minister, General Kadijević, whose presence would have been essential at this session, was missing. Kadijević had never missed a cabinet meeting and his absence generated a plethora of rumours about his health. It later emerged that on the 10th and 11th, Kadijević made a secret trip to Moscow where he held negotiations with the then Soviet Defence Minister, General Dmitri Yazov. The two of them sealed an arms deal worth $2 billion for which the JNA would receive helicopter gunships, rocket launchers and tanks. Two days before the attempted coup in the Soviet Union in August, the Romanian Defence Minister arrived in Belgrade for talks with the JNA leadership about the transport of these weapons across Romanian territory. The deal, it is believed, was never honoured because of the coup's failure. As the subsequent weaknesses of the JNA operations in Croatia were to prove, the material would have aided the military leadership in Belgrade considerably.

That failure notwithstanding, the March events had cemented the alliance between the JNA and the Serbian leadership, by no means as firm as people imagined up until then. If Milošević wished to retain power in Serbia and if the JNA leadership wished to hang on to its privileges in Yugoslavia, it would be necessary to act fairly soon. Croatia and Slovenia were preparing to hand them the excuse on a plate. Once the conflict began, the struggle of the bureaucracies would become a Serb–Croat war.

3 JUNE–JULY 1991:

State of Independence

Even in the worst circumstances, the beauty of Prague can alleviate pain. In late May and early June 1991, the full majesty of the city is on display. The setting exaggerates the promise of the Conference on a European Confederation sponsored by the guest of honour, President François Mitterrand, with some coy support from his Czechoslovak counterpart, Václav Havel. As Havel must know, the actual project itself is doomed from the start. Not that he cares unduly – the French President has cobbled together the idea of a European Confederation as a sop to East European countries. It is a potemkin village, the façade maintaining the fiction of European unity, while disguising the strict upstairs–downstairs relationship of the European Community and the supplicants from Eastern Europe on the inside. Thus the participants' a priori knowledge that the idea is stillborn, combines with the magic of Prague to generate an absurdly buoyant mood – this is a delightful freebie for those taking part.

A large number of movers and shakers from the world of European foreign policy fills a few rooms of the ghastly Palace of Culture (one of those rare buildings in Prague without a soul). Their task is to consider the best design for the fictional European Confederation. The Palace of Culture has one redeeming feature, a resplendent view of Prague across the valley separating Vyšehrad from Nové město and beyond to the Hrad, the presidential castle. Only one group of people seemed not to be enjoying the jovial proceedings. Instead its members appeared infected with a virus which trapped the victim in a state of permanent depression – these were the Yugoslavs, at the time still comprising Slovenes, Croats, Serbs, Macedonians, Albanians and the other passengers on board this ramshackle bandwagon of nations.

The first Yugoslav with whom I talked in Prague was Mate

Babić, professor of economics at Zagreb University and a former Deputy Prime Minister responsible for the economy in the Croatian government. Babić was most engaging. He was the first, but by no means the last, who described from the inside how President Tuđman attempts to run the budding state. If Milošević is the 'Emperor of Mordor', Tuđman is the Red Queen from *Alice in Wonderland*. The Croatian President is capricious and self-willed, dismissing every piece of legislation proposed by Babić and other economic experts. Although he was distinctly no friend of Milošević, Mate Babić admitted frankly that Serbia had gone further down the road to privatization than Croatia. Tuđman, he insisted, was consciously blocking Croatia's progress in this direction. Let it be remembered that according to President Tuđman, Croatia's moral superiority over Serbia lay in its fervent commitment to free-market economics. Babić suggested that Tuđman's main economic strategy involved maintaining the privileges of those members of the communist nomenclature who had declared themselves in favour of his party, the nationalist Croatian Democratic Union (HDZ). In addition, Tuđman had received substantial financial backing from the Croat *émigré* community ($4 million for the HDZ election campaign alone), which was being paid off in a variety of political and economic currencies.

Elegantly, Babić mapped out one of the powerful undercurrents which had been steadily eroding the foundations of the Yugoslav state since its inception in 1918. The European Community, he pointed out, had emerged initially from a series of trade agreements between Germany and France, which then expanded into other areas and to other countries. Its bureaucracy has doubtless taken on a life of its own since then, but the EC still reflects the objective economic and social interests of its members. Yugoslavia, he continued, was constructed in the wake of the Great War as a political imperative without regard to the region's economic requirements. In the post-war communist federation, the imbalance between Slovene sophistication and the developing-world conditions prevailing in Kosovo, southern Serbia and Macedonia could only be rectified by massive state control of the economy. This created resentment in the prosperous north, the fruits of whose productivity were transferred to the dusty climates of the south where they rotted in the sun. Above all, a taut mistrust grew up between Slovenia and Croatia, where a more industrious work ethic was the tradition, and Serbia, the borderland of the Ottoman empire's corrupt economic values. Being inextricably involved with the Serbian economy, which appears to be fuelled by lotus leaves, had a damaging long-term effect on the Croat and Slovene economies. When the political decay in Yugoslavia accelerated, following the multi-party elections in the republics, the economic tensions ensured that this mistrust would deepen.

There are some important caveats to Babić's economic theory. Firstly, there were influential trends in both Croat and Slovene society which supported the Yugoslav idea in the nineteenth and early twentieth century – many of the leaders of the national revival movements saw union with the other southern Slavs, the Serbs in particular, as the only guaranteed escape from Austro-Hungarian or Italian hegemony. Although their motivation was primarily political, they also believed that independence in a southern Slav state would reduce the economic tutelage imposed by Vienna and Budapest. The poorly-constructed southern Slav state cannot be written off merely as a Greater Serbian machination and the many attempts to do so in Croatia over the past two years are a reflection of a lack of historical maturity. Secondly, the relative prosperity of Slovenia, in particular, and Croatia as well, depended to a great extent on the unfettered access which they had to the large markets of Serbia, Macedonia and Bosnia. Slovenes are now realizing that they are rarely competitive in European markets. As a consequence, Slovene businessmen began pouring back into Serbia for business purposes less than a year after the declaration of independence in 1991 which Serbia had publicly denounced. Although political relations between Serbia and Slovenia were frozen, business between them boomed as never before. Despite his pessimism about developments in Croatia and Yugoslavia, Babić's style was upbeat and entertaining.

The following day I spoke to Srđa Popović in one of the Palace of Culture's subterranean grottos. The gloomy artificial lighting competed with the sour chicory coffee, but neither could dampen my excitement at meeting Popović. Here was the most famous human rights lawyer in Belgrade and the head of the European

Movement in Yugoslavia. He was also the moving spirit behind
Vreme, the Belgrade magazine which was founded just in time to
prepare for the war and which has since developed into one of the
finest news publications in Europe. *Vreme*, which means 'time',
gathered some of Serbia's most accomplished journalists in order to
provide a record of the collapse of Yugoslavia which was free from
the prejudice which Milošević and the Serb nationalists demanded
of their publications. The work of three journalists on its staff has
had a particularly powerful impact on our understanding of the
disintegration and the war in particular. Miloš Vasić uncovered a
treasure-trove of information about military affairs which provided the insider's guide for understanding how the Yugoslav
People's Army (JNA), in particular, developed its strategy. Stojan
Cerović delighted all his readers with sketches of the insane figures
who peopled the former Yugoslavia's political landscape, encapsu-
lating the very essence of each character in two lucid pages.
Roksanda Ninčić kept people abreast of the endlessly devious
political twists and turns which enabled the Serbian leadership, in
particular, to survive the consequences of its catastrophic policies.
Whilst it is true that the majority of Serbs was influenced above
all else by television, no other republic in the former Yugoslavia
enjoyed such a thorough, intelligent and sane publication as
Serbia, thanks to *Vreme*.

Popović was, and is, one of Europe's great liberals. His public
profile was well complemented by his personal style. Tall, with a
long, handsome face, Popović spoke with a deep, gritty voice that
shuddered with authority. As we sat down, I told him that I
found it slightly ironic how the conference participants were pon-
tificating about the desirable route to European unification just as
one of the Balkans' deepest wounds was about to split wide open.
Despite his congenital optimism, Popović's eyes looked serious
and worried: 'I don't think Europe quite realizes the potential for
violence in Yugoslavia,' he said, 'and it could be about to start
any time now, probably around the declarations of independence.'

A few days later, I was in Belgrade. Before the declarations of
independence, I had decided to travel to some of the areas of

Yugoslavia whose fate, inasmuch as it was known at all, was being clouded over by the burgeoning conflict between the Serbs (a.k.a. Yugoslavs, Serbo-Bolshevnik-Chetnik terrorists) on the one hand, and the Croats and Slovenes (a.k.a. fascist-secessionist-Ustashas) on the other. Belgrade itself was a mess. The opposition was broken and Milošević was in full control again. The media devoted most of their coverage to attacking the perfidious secessionists, Slovenia and Croatia, stressing thereby the position of the defenceless Serbs in Croatia who were already, it was claimed, having to defend themselves against the dark, genocidal urges of the Croats. RTV Belgrade had begun the dress rehearsal for its forthcoming performance as a demonic chorus whose chief function was to encourage the audience to bay for blood. Early on in the war, a surprisingly broad spectrum of people in both Croatia and Serbia singled out Croatian Television (HTV) and RTV Belgrade as two of the most culpable war criminals of the Yugoslav tragedy.

Belgrade was sticky and depressing and I was soon heading south for Kosovo. The main motorway in the south of Yugoslavia ends close to the major southern Serbian city, Niš. As one turns right for Prishtina, the capital of Kosovo, one sees the first road sign for Athens and Thessaloniki. The temptation to cast caution to the wind and continue on to Greece is enormous. With an almost audible unwillingness, the car swings to the right towards the dingy southern Serbian town of Prokuplje on the first leg of a cracked and rotten road which ends in Prishtina.

What hope remains for Kosovo? There is nothing about this territory to recommend it except for many of the Albanian intellectuals who live there and some of the little restaurants close to the ghastly Grand Hotel. The best of these is without doubt Allo, Allo, named in honour of the sitcom (probably the most influential British import throughout Yugoslavia) and home to one of the juiciest *ćevapčići* in the Balkans. Served with freshly chopped chives, raw onion and biting-hot peppers, these little rolls of minced meat covered by a bun are the staple diet in many parts of the country. The Grand Hotel itself is an unmistakable monument of late Titoism in Prishtina. It was constructed in the 1970s at a time when the federal government in Belgrade pumped endless funds into Kosovo in the hope of curbing unrest among poor Albanians in the region.

These monies fell into the hands of the Kosovo League of Communists bureaucracy, largely Albanian, whose ideal of infrastructural renewal was to erect many grandiose buildings in the capital. Such white elephants, however, should have been built after investment in jobs and primary requirements, such as improved road and rail access to Kosovo. Of the many pompous buildings which litter the centre of this provincial backwater, the Grand Hotel takes pride of place as the most ridiculous of all. True, it does obviate the need to stay in the Hotel Božur, which makes the House of Usher look inviting, and it did once provide a meeting place for many young people, Albanians and Serbs alike, but those days are long gone.

The Grand Hotel, thirteen decaying stories high, is now one of the most important operational centres of the Serbian police in Kosovo. Previously, the hotel was run by Albanians, who, despite the Stalinist repression which functioned in Kosovo, were interesting sources of information. Over the past three years, all Albanians working in the Grand Hotel have joined the tens of thousands of their compatriots who have been made redundant by the Serbian authorities. Belgrade has transformed Kosovo into a squalid outpost of putrefying colonialism. It must be said that the Serbian personnel in the Grand Hotel have improved the efficiency of the establishment. Most of the clients, however, are now employees of the Serbian Interior Ministry. Sitting in the moribund bar of the Grand, I struck up a conversation with a Serb who told me quite openly that he was working for police intelligence. He continued that he had just finished a spell working with Serb organizations in Croatia but that he had been redeployed as there were fears of unrest among the Albanians.

Most of the Grand Hotel was full of special police on duty in Kosovo. Their presence was an unnecessary burden on the Serbian tax-payer (among the top victims of the Yugoslav war) but essential for the authorities to maintain the fictional threat posed by hordes of alleged Albanian rapists and murderers. At night the Serbs would take over most of the establishments lining the Korzo. The Hotel Božur and its restaurant was a pot of sugary chauvinism around which the Serbian flies buzzed all night. Exceptionally loud Serbian music would boom out of gargantuan speakers while the lyrics were mouthed by drunken, aggressive louts. This scene of naked philistinism rammed home to the Albanians how politically powerless they were. And indeed as the struggle between Serbs and Croats intensified and war fever rose, the international community became decidedly less interested in the issue of the Kosovo Albanians.

The Serbs serving in Kosovo understand their role within the framework of colonialist rule. The Serbs living in Kosovo are genuinely frightened, victims of their perception of Albanians as terrorists, which may be a self-fulfilling prophecy if Belgrade refuses to acknowledge the Albanians' right to self-determination. But the uncertainty of the Serb minority in Kosovo is prolonged by Belgrade as an instrument to justify the exercise of the repressive state apparatus against Albanians. The vocal backing which Serbs outside Kosovo give to Belgrade's policy is born of prejudice and ignorance – it is striking how few Serbs from outside Kosovo have ever visited the region. Few appear capable of avoiding the pejorative term *Šiptar* (derived from the Albanian word for Albania, Shqiptar, but insulting when used in Serbo-Croat instead of the standard *Albanac*) when referring to Albanians. In the Serbian parliament, even the most liberal members will stress their patriotic commitment to the maintenance of Serbian rule over Kosovo. Any validity in the Serbian argument that Kosovo is the cradle of their civilization is lost both by their refusal to apply this criterion to other regions and by their demonization of the Albanian population and the bald abuse of the basic human rights of the Kosovar Albanians.

Although excluded from the official organs of power in Kosovo itself, the Albanians do now have their own political structures. In addition, they have developed a social and economic system which functions with absolute autonomy from the official structures which had excluded them. This has given the Kosovars a self-confidence which was lacking in the past under Communism. It has also bestowed considerable authority on the political leaders in Kosovo, notably the great unifier of Kosovars, Ibrahim Rugova, but increasingly the boy wonder of Kosovar Albanian politics, Veton Surroi.

On this occasion in June, ten days before the independence of Slovenia and Croatia, I sat with Veton at a café on the Korzo which by day is not dominated so ostentatiously by the Serbs as it is by night. He is a short man but one who, despite the cultivation of a designer stubble, is incapable of looking shabby or casual. People are surprised that this skilled, urbane polyglot is only just over thirty, as he is a cunningly aware politician. The warm, pleasing sun glowed across Veton's contented face as he assured me that there will be no war in Croatia. 'Nobody wants it and they will find some way around it, you can be sure,' he said. (Six months later, on Christmas Day in fact, I asked Veton again what he thought would happen, both in Croatia and in Kosovo. He laughed heartily, 'Why bother to ask me?' he boomed. 'The last time you asked me something like that I told you there wouldn't be a war in Croatia!') Despite Veton's conviction that there would be no war, he was dressed for our coffee in a khaki-shaded suit. 'Who knows?' he chuckled. 'Maybe I will have to become the Commander-in-Chief of Albanians in Kosovo.' Veton was joking, but I felt that the mischievous twinkle hid a serious intention. Indeed in his khaki outfit, with his dark glasses and his stubble, Veton had almost begun to resemble the popular image of a guerilla leader. If fighting begins in Kosovo, few Albanians there enjoy the authority, the intelligence and the ability to organize as Veton does. In contrast to all other national groups in Yugoslavia, however, the Kosovar Albanians do not have firearms. This will guarantee an uneasy peace for some time unless Kosovo becomes caught up in the southern Balkan storm which civil war in Bosnia still threatens to stir up.

One other development had had a significant impact on the Albanians since I was last in Kosovo in early 1990: the revolution in Albania itself. The end of Stalinism in Albania had produced a euphoria among Kosovo Albanians that unification was now imminent and inevitable. Few yet appreciated the depth of the trauma experienced by most people in the Republic of Albania as they slowly awoke from the clammy nightmare of Hoxhaism. The Albanian revolution was accompanied by the rapid atrophy of the social infrastructure countrywide, such that living standards had dropped below the level at which normal social psychology begins to function. To a large degree, this has led to the temporary suspension of nationalism as a pertinent ideological motivation among large sections of the population in Albania. So miserable is their situation that they regard the Kosovars, whom they have

hardly known over the last seventy years, as witless but comparatively well-off outsiders who deserve to be plundered. The resentment towards Kosovars in Albania is only matched by the deep
shock which nationalists in Kosovo have experienced when they
observe for the first time just how completely Enver Hoxha destroyed any consciousness in Albania, political or national. None the
less, in the long term, Albanian nationalism is likely to be a factor
contributing to the instability of the southern Balkans and in the
summer of 1991 I could begin to feel its excluding influence in
Kosovo. Even if the lack of firearms meant that we would be
spared a war between Albanians and Serbs, the pain of Kosovo,
already intense, always seemed able to worsen.

The Šar mountains with their crystal streams and rich vegetation
grant glorious relief from the two pained Albanian communities
they separate: the Kosovars to the north and the Albanians of
western Macedonia to the south. For a brief half-hour, I can escape
the ceaseless tales of misery and repression and, fortified by my
small break, I cruise into the bustling market town, Tetovo, in an
optimistic mood. It is axiomatic, not just in the Balkans, but among
most European minorities that each national group believes its
experience of repression to be more intense than any other. This
phenomenon breaks down even within national communities. Observe the western Macedonian Albanians. By the summer of 1991,
the Albanians here are without question the most prosperous of the
three compact territories on which Albanians live. Just a few yards
down from Tetovo's rather unappealing main square, which is
badly scarred by the poorly-tempered knives of socialist architects,
is the Albanians' lively market. Both the quality and variety of the
produce are unrivalled anywhere in the former communist regions of
the south Balkans. Indeed they now organize regular supplies of
food and medicines for deprived Albanian villages and towns in
Kosovo. Economic life in Tetovo is clearly dominated by Albanian
entrepreneurial spirit and the ethnic Macedonians play only a peripheral role. True, they do not have full access to the organs of
power, but the harsh repression of the pro-Serb communist leadership in Macedonia has been rapidly eroded since the elections of
1990. And yet the Albanians here seem almost unwilling to shake

off that past, insisting that their fate remains more terrible than that of the Kosovar Albanians, despite the common knowledge that to the north their compatriots are kept in check by one of the most militarized police forces in Europe. Despite their moaning, it is a relief to be in a relatively peaceful corner of the Balkans.

Twenty-five miles to the east of Tetovo lies one of the least-appreciated capitals in Europe. Skopje is the administrative, economic and cultural centre of the republic of Macedonia. Although in the meantime Macedonia has disengaged itself from the Yugoslav federation without blood being shed, it has, at the time of writing, yet to win recognition from the European Community or the United States because of Greece's hysterical objection to Macedonian statehood. The creation of such a state, the Greeks say, is an affront to the tradition of Hellenic Macedonia and it implies a plan of territorial expansion. The Slav Macedonians, poor and small in number, have been branded as ruthless expansionists by three of their four neighbours, Serbia, Bulgaria and Greece. Relations with the fourth neighbour, Albania, are comparatively good although the fate of the western Macedonian Albanians is a thorn in the side of their development.

The Macedonian question, which so terrorized southern Europe in the first fourteen years of this century, comprises two elements which paradoxically run parallel and concurrently. The first element comprises the various perceptions of Macedonia's neighbours. Except for the most extreme nationalists, Serbs have, by and large, come to accept the Titoist solution which afforded recognition of the Macedonian nation, within the boundaries of Vardar Macedonia, roughly corresponding to the republic's present borders. Some political currents in Serbia still maintain Vardar Macedonia is southern Serbia, as the territory was officially known in the inter-war years. To the east, Bulgaria has recognized the Republic of Macedonia as an independent state but still refuses to acknowledge the existence of a Macedonian nation. Greeks show the least willingness to compromise of all – neither the Macedonian nation, nor a Republic of Macedonia can exist because Greece has exclusive historical and territorial rights over Macedonia. These attitudes, which range from grudging tolerance to a hostile campaign directed against the Macedonian state, are leading to the suffocation of this small but vital square of territory which provides a land crossing, east and west and north and south, across the Balkan mountains.

The depth of suspicion felt by Macedonia's neighbours has in part been reached because of the existence of Macedonian minorities, notably in Bulgaria and Greece. The largest lives in Bulgaria. No government in Sofia, however, is prepared to concede that they are anything other than Bulgarians. Macedonians speak a language which is very close to Bulgarian. You may find many areas, both in Macedonia and Bulgaria, where the peasants do not really know whether they are Macedonians or Bulgarians (and in some places they think they may be Serbs). In Greece, the authorities refuse to recognize the existence of a minority, referring to it instead as the community of Slavophone Greeks. It is this historical, linguistic and national confusion that has contributed to the ease with which Macedonia's neighbours have until now been able to exclude the people and territory from the map of the Balkans. Because of these sensitivities, Macedonia is only viable if it is confined to present borders. The Macedonian government and the Macedonian parliament in a new Constitution have conceded this, and even the less pleasant nationalists who are grouped in the powerful VMRO – DMPNE Party have dropped any territorial claims. Still the Greeks are not satisfied, preferring instead to prolong the misery and instability of Macedonia as a stateless territory.

Macedonia has been demonized by its neighbours to such an extent that the innocent visitor arriving from Greece or Bulgaria may imagine Skopje to be inhabited by a sub-human species. In fact, if one had to choose an interior city in the southern Balkans to live in, Skopje would come out on top with ease. The city displays some poignant reminders of how its bulk was obliterated by the earthquake in 1963. The façade of the former railway station in Skopje still stands with the clock which indicates unflinchingly that the time is ten to five, the moment when the earthquake struck. But the old town with its Ottoman-like bazaar has been rebuilt – it is less authentic than many markets in the region but it still provides the outsider with a genuine sense of the Orient.

In the early summer, Skopje is glorious, particularly if your guide is Sašo Ordanoski, one of Macedonia's youngest but most influential journalists. Everybody in Skopje knows Sašo and is always delighted to talk to him, except, of course, those who fall foul of his electrifying pen. Together we visit the opening of an exhibition within the decrepit castle walls which overlook the city. Macedonia being a small place, anyone who is anything is there and within the space of five minutes, Sašo has introduced me to the man writing Macedonia's constitution, the Minister of Health and Vasil Tupurkovski, the Macedonian member of the Yugoslav Presidency.

Before the disintegration of Yugoslavia began properly, Tupurkovski was hated by the Croats and Slovenes for once having accused them of forming an 'unprincipled coalition' against Serbia within the Central Committee of the Yugoslav League of Communists. Throughout 1990 and 1991, his maverick role in the Yugoslav Presidency earned him the bitter and unforgiving dislike of a large part of Serbia's political establishment. But for those who needed to understand what was going on in Yugoslavia, his frankness and warmth were indispensable. Nobody exposed the pomposity and self-importance of Yugoslavia's establishment better than Tupurkovski, whose drooping moustache and bulbous shape, squeezed into T-shirts in the summer and woolly jumpers in winter, always placed the futile, vengeful discussions of the Presidency in their proper, absurd context. Tupurkovski may have been the most relaxed member of the Presidency, but there was nobody among that motley crew with as much commitment to peace, as much intelligence, and as much concern for ordinary people as he regularly displayed. He expended enormous energy in attempts to mediate in the Serb–Croat conflict and his clipped and clear interviews were refreshingly free of dotty rhetoric.

This particular encounter with Tupurkovski was the most informal meeting I enjoyed with him and we merely exchanged a few pleasantries. So exceptionally relaxed was the atmosphere atop Skopje's castle that for once, nobody had the slightest intention of discussing politics. The event took place against a background of spectacular fireworks, while the music was provided by one of the many Macedonian rock bands who, since the collapse of communism, have devoted themselves almost exclusively to the cult of Alexander the Great. Alexander lived before the Slavs had settled in Macedonia, but he remains an important foundation stone upon which Macedonian nationalists build their myths. Despite the significance which the musicians invest in their songs, it is impossible not to giggle at these ridiculous ensembles who look like the mutant children of an unholy union between Jethro Tull and Deep Purple and sound even worse as they offer their cacophonic homage to Alexander up to the bright, summery Macedonian skies. Their performance is worthy of the Balkans' endemic passion for nonsense.

There are two enormous open-air complexes in Skopje where Macedonian youth dream away their summer nights. Inside there are discos, cafés and bars – all open air, all marvellously relaxing. Among the fragile high-rise buildings which sprang up around Skopje following the earthquake, tacky little cafés sell some of the finest frogs' legs in Europe. For centuries, the Macedonians have survived thanks to the trade possibilities which their geographical position affords them. From Western Europe to the Orient, and from northern Europe to southern Europe, you have to pass through Macedonia if you travel by land. This tiny territory, which includes some of the oldest and most remarkable shrines of the Orthodox Church, has been blessed and cursed by its geography. As Sašo and I enjoy its succulent fruits, we sit and discuss the futility and the inevitability of the coming war. Sašo insists that Macedonia will be able to avoid involvement in the war but he despairs of the Macedonian leadership's ability to steer the republic towards stable statehood, and he warns of the deep dishonesty which plagues Macedonian society. I express my fears that war will sweep over Macedonia after the Serb–Croat conflict triggers a chain reaction in Yugoslavia and the Balkans. Despite our worries, Sašo and I enjoy ourselves to the full, probably the last time that either of us will for many months. Those three lazy days in Skopje still feel like a celestial gift, a last reprieve before witnessing the concentrated bestiality of the war. On my last evening, Sašo and I sit in the garden of Georgi Marjanovski, a professor of law and one of Macedonia's great liberals. We talk in the darkness, listen to the crickets who click their legs in time with a festival in the distance, the full-blooded celebration of a Romani marriage in Europe's gypsy capital. If the fire of prejudice could be doused with a potion of tolerance, the Balkans would be the most wonderful region in the world.

*

I had last been in the Croatian capital at the beginning of May, soon after the incident in Borovo Selo. Twelve Croat policemen and three Serb civilians had been shot dead in this small settlement just three miles north of a town called Vukovar in eastern Slavonia, in what many Croats said marked the beginning of the war. I had made a fairly close examination of the Borovo Selo incident and my findings suggested to me for the first time that the Serbs and the army were not the only ones preparing for and even trying to provoke armed conflict. Although I had always considered the HDZ a dangerous organization, I believed Milošević to be the evil genius of the Yugoslav crisis. Borovo Selo was to instruct me in the ways of Croatian nationalism which, when activated, proved a formidable counterpart to its Serbian opponent.

The Serbs in Borovo Selo, an insignificant suburb of Vukovar whose inhabitants were in the main employed by the Borovo shoe factory, were known to be especially hostile to the HDZ and the new government in Zagreb. The Croatian Interior Minister at the time, Josip Boljkovac, was a cautious man who worked hard to preserve the delicate peace which had existed between Serbs and Croats, with a few nerve-racking interruptions, since the first armed conflict in Knin on the weekend of 17 August the previous year. With Boljkovac's knowledge, an agreement was struck between Zagreb and the Serbs in Borovo Selo that no Croatian policemen would enter Borovo Selo without the express approval of local Serb representatives and that no violence would be used. This had originally been discussed at a meeting between the erstwhile Serbian Interior Minister, Radmilo Bogdanović, and Boljkovac which they had held in the town of Bačka Palanka, just across the river from eastern Slavonia, in Vojvodina. Ignorance was not an excuse for Borovo Selo. There is no doubt that the incident raised the violence of the conflict to a new level, resulting in a complete breakdown of trust between Serbs and Croats in the Vukovar–Vinkovci region, thus clearing the ground for one of the bloodiest and most inhumane struggles of the entire conflict.

On the night of Wednesday, 1 May, two Croat policemen in a police patrol car were arrested by Serb irregulars from Borovo Selo. According to the Croat Interior Ministry, their car and a second police vehicle were fired on by automatic weapons when they entered the village. The federal Interior Ministry, however, said that they were in civilian clothes and that at the exit of Borovo Selo, one had fired at random with an automatic weapon while the other tore down the Yugoslav flag which stood at the edge of the village. They were fired on by Serbs and then arrested.

Prior to this incident the situation had been relatively calm, although the Croats had complained to Serbia and the federal Interior Ministry about two provocative visits, one to Borovo Selo, the second to a neighbouring village, Jagodnjak, made by Vojislav Šešelj, the Serbian Chetnik leader, Milan Paroški, a Serb nationalist MP, and the shady character, Stojan Cvijan, the man in the Serbian cabinet responsible for 'relations with Serbs living outside Serbia'. The Chetniks, with the tacit backing of Milošević, were clearly stirring up anti-Croat sentiment in Borovo Selo although | the hard-line policies of the regional HDZ had already fertilized this latent hatred. But despite the best efforts of the Chetniks and the HDZ, the tension around Borovo Selo had receded until the two members of that untimely patrol were arrested on 1 May.

The following day the Vinkovci Chief of Police, Josip Đaja, ordered twenty of his men into Borovo Selo to investigate the arrest of the two patrolmen. The buses in which the Vinkovci contingent travelled were greeted by a deadly outburst of automatic fire from Serb paramilitaries – 150 Croats were then sent in as reinforcements from Osijek. But they were unable to fight their way through and it was left to the army to divide the two warring sides. This terrible incident claimed the lives of twelve Croat policemen and three Serb civilians. A few days later, Croatia's Deputy Interior Minister, Slavko Degoricija, showed photographs to the press which he said were three dead Croats returned by the Serbs from Borovo. The men had been badly mutilated after death – one had an arm chopped off, the skin on the second man's back had been comprehensively flayed, while the face of the third had been thoroughly gouged. It was an abominable reminder of the foul traditions from the Second World War that awaited Serbs and Croats if fighting broke out. But Degoricija also admitted that 'it is said that Borovo Selo was a mistake of the Vinkovci and Osijek police. Now we can confirm this, although I must say that these same police had reached agreement a few days before with political activists of Croat and Serb parties ... in particular the SDS (Serbian Democratic Party in Croatia) that things would not be solved by force.' Degoricija also said that he did not specifically order the twenty Croat police into Borovo Selo. This was done by Josip Đaja, who would have been well aware that there was an agreement not to send police into Borovo Selo without the permission of Serb leaders in the village.

Some have expressed the opinion that the twelve Croat police killed in Borovo Selo (there were also twenty wounded) were sacrificial lambs whose deaths would then justify still tougher repression by the Croat Interior Ministry. The trail of decision-making stops before it reaches Zagreb, ending instead at the door of local Croat forces in eastern Slavonia who seemed determined to raise the temperature of conflict as a preface to driving the Serbs out. Chetnik and Serb government-sponsored groups were already infiltrating the Serb communities in Croatia and supplying them with weapons but at the same time, militants in the HDZ, together with even more extreme Croat forces, were distributing weapons and intimidating Serbs by bombing their homes, restaurants and shops.

Most disturbingly, the local HDZ government had willingly, on instructions from Zagreb, begun sacking Serbs from a wide variety of jobs purely because of their nationality. The Croats argued that because Serbs in Croatia had been unfairly favoured under communism, they would now have to make way for Croats. It is certainly true that Serbs had enjoyed privileges in Croatia under communism. But the solution offered by the HDZ, which was to sling out Serbs willy-nilly, was no solution at all, it merely exacerbated national tension. Contrary to the propaganda put out by Zagreb, the HDZ did not restrict these redundancies to public administration – there are documented cases of Serbs losing their jobs in tourist firms, in restaurants, in private companies, in the health service and in education. Borovo Selo was a disaster for the social fabric of eastern Slavonia. From that day on, prejudice and violence rose along an exponential curve until the pent-up hatred of the region exploded in July and August. Given the delicate balance which existed in eastern Slavonia at the time, the dispatch of Croat Interior Ministry forces into Borovo Selo was an unnecessary provocation, neither the first nor the last.

Returning to Zagreb from Belgrade, a few days before the declarations of independence by the Slovene and Croat parliaments in mid-June, I travelled along the *autoput*, which is not just the link between the capitals of Serbia and Croatia, it is also the main trunk route for traffic travelling from north to south Europe and on to the Middle East. Insofar as hostility did develop between Croatia and Serbia during Titoist Yugoslavia, it was revealed in the great saga of the *autoput*. The single-lane version of the road, which was officially entitled Brotherhood and Unity, was constructed during the 1940s by participants in the most famous *radna akcija*, or 'voluntary work brigade', of the post-war period. The workforce was comprised largely of enthusiastic students, drawn from all over Europe and sympathetic to the Yugoslav model of socialism, and political prisoners culled in the main from the Croatian and Serbian bourgeoisie. As one well-known commentator on Yugoslav affairs, Dennison Rusinow, remarked perceptively if unkindly, this explains the road's atrocious quality.

In the early 1960s, as the transfer of labour from north to south led to large divisions of workers trundling back and forth along the *autoput*, it was decided to expand the single lane into a two-lane motorway. The chief beneficiary of such an expansion was Serbia. However, because of Croatia's curious shape, all but seventy-five miles of the 250-mile drag lay in Croatia. Zagreb argued that the bulk of the financing for the extension should come from Belgrade's budget because the Serb economy would benefit most from the expansion, while Belgrade insisted that any building on Croat territory should be funded by Zagreb regardless. Over almost three decades, the two sides fought bitterly over the financing of every kilometre. The Croats built eastwards some sixty miles, the Serbs westward about forty, leaving 150 miles of the most dangerous single-land road imaginable. Every summer the Yugoslav media was full of horrific accidents in which over-laden lorries would collide head on with over-filled buses, squeezing families of Turkish *Gastarbeiter* in their Transit vans in between. Every summer, traffic jams of up to sixty miles in length would ensnare rich, sweltering

Germans and Swedes en route to Greece in Mercedes and Volvos, along with the less wealthy Turks whose whole material history would bulge out of their beat-up Opels and Fords.

Finally, in 1989, Yugoslavia secured a financial package from the European Community which guaranteed the completion of the *autoput* as a modern motorway. Too late! At the time of writing it has been impassable for over six months, chewed up first by columns of tanks and transporters, and then by mortars and howitzers.

In early June 1991, however, it was still functioning. Indeed, it had never been more interesting. Frightened off by the growing reports of armed conflict in Yugoslavia, the German tourists, most Turkish *Gastarbeiter* and almost all foreign lorries had given the *autoput* a wide berth, preferring instead to take ferries from Italy to Greece or to drive via Hungary to Belgrade and then down south. Soon after the end of the Serbian part of the motorway, I saw for the first time the road sign '*Republika Hrvatska*', bedecked with the Croatian insignia, standing clearly and defiantly by the side of the road. I almost jumped from my seat. One of the extraordinary aspects of federal Yugoslavia was that although almost all journalists, diplomats, academics and even Yugoslavs knew in theory where the borders between the republics were, these were never marked and few people could ever say for certain when they were close to the long stretches of republican borders, whether they were in Serbia, Croatia or Bosnia. In addition, the national composition of each region was not very important under the Titoist system, a matter of idle interest perhaps, but nothing more. Now, all of us studying Yugoslavia, for whatever purpose, were frantically trying to identify the national make up, not just of regions but of towns and villages. In one small town on the border between western and eastern Herce-govina, I was even shown a crude sketch outlining the national make up of a single street, one part of which (Croat) was considering declaring autonomy from the Serb majority – like *Passport to Pimlico* with guns! The other foolproof method of identifying border crossings between Serbia and Croatia was provided by the local police force. On my drive to Zagreb from Belgrade, I was stopped at the end of the Serb motorway by police easily recogniz-able as Serbs by their red star with five points (*petokraka*). A mile later, the car was being searched by members of the MUP RH (the

Interior Ministry of the Republic of Croatia) who proudly bore the red-and-white chequered shield of Croatia on their caps.

The empty roads and the glorious sunshine could not disguise the spread of Yugoslavia's gun culture – Croatia was now loaded, its inhabitants thought primarily of guns. Soon after entering Croatian territory, breathtakingly tall pine trees arch above to create a curious natural tunnel on a road which stretches in a dead-straight line beyond the horizon. The only break in the trees, which flank the road for many kilometres, is provided by a couple of service stations, where in normal times the *Gastarbeiter* stop for leisurely picnics. These service stations are hidden from sight, however, until you reach them, so it was a shock to see not a single *Gastarbeiter* but instead a little colony of armed Croats – police with their automatic weapons, civilians with fingers on their shotguns.

For the moment, they remained exceptionally polite to foreigners. Serbs travelling through the roadblocks which appeared just before and after the pine avenue were subject to the most thorough searches and occasionally humiliating treatment. One only needed to travel off the *autoput* a few miles to find roadblocks manned by Serbs, clothed in a variety of disturbing uniforms and, of course, armed to the teeth. For the moment, the Serbs, too, were polite to foreigners, but it was most inadvisable for Croats to attempt to cross such a line. Shootings, beatings and kidnappings (particularly in the regions of Krajina, Banija and eastern Slavonia) were perpetrated by both sides regularly. Passing through these areas, it was now crystal clear that war was approaching with great speed. In the field, both sides were ready, waiting and apparently wanting to blow each other's brains out.

The *autoput* is flanked by a variety of monuments to fear. To the north are tragedies still fresh or about to happen. Soon after entering Croatia, there are signposts to Vukovar (which lies next to Borovo Selo), Vinkovci and, a little later, to Osijek. These were peaceful regions during the Second World War which in 1991 were infected by the virus of war in a curious way, as we shall see. Ninety miles further on, the historical tragedies lie to the south. The flat lands of central Slavonia are suddenly broken by the stark protrusions called the Kozara mountains. Now part of Bosnia, the Croat Fascist government surrounded and occupied Kozara in June

1942 after a massive operation including the Ustashas, Italian, German and Hungarian armies. A certain Kurt Waldheim played a modest role at Kozara as a junior intelligence officer. Ten thousand Serbs, refugees and Partizans, including 4,000 children, were captured after Kozara; almost all were slaughtered in one of the most bestial rituals performed by the insane Ustashas.

Kozara is followed swiftly by Jasenovac, again to the south, the most dreadful Ustasha extermination camp whose facilities were grim even by the standards of Axis Europe. Immediately after the Second World War, the Titoist authorities proclaimed that a million lives, mostly Serb, had been lost at Jasenovac. The figure was a gross exaggeration, although few Serbs will admit this even when confronted with evidence to the contrary. The most accurate figure ascertained by independent Croat and Jewish scholars puts the number of Serbs, Jews, Gypsies and members of the Croat opposition killed at Jasenovac at about 200,000. It may seem insensitive to discuss figures, but the Serbs and Croats themselves use Jasenovac numbers as a political whipping stick. Whatever the truth, the memory of Jasenovac is never far from the consciousness of Serbs living in Croatia. As a consequence, one of the cardinal errors committed by President Franjo Tuđman after his election was to ignore this memory. A gesture of reconciliation by Tuđman for the wrongs committed by the wartime Independent State of Croatia against the Serbs in Croatia (as symbolized by Jasenovac) might have created a very different atmosphere when negotiations between the HDZ and Serb representatives took place in the summer of 1990. Croats I spoke to on this issue argued that as Milošević had expressed no regrets over the death of thousands of Croats at the hands of the communists after the war, Tuđman should not feel compelled to apologize for the crimes of the Ustashas. This argument does not hold, especially for an administration which claimed, as Tuđman's did from the moment of the HDZ's election victory, that it was among the most democratic in Europe. The Ustasha crimes took place on Croatian territory in the name of the Croatian people. President Tuđman was elected as a representative of the Republic of Croatia and his duties were exclusively to the population of this territory. What Milošević did or did not do has no relevance. Tuđman should have felt naturally compelled to assure the Serb population in Croatia that his government had nothing to do with the dark side of Croatia's history, and an unambiguous expression of regret on the subject of Jasenovac would have provided proof of such a commitment.

I turn off the traumatic Road of Brotherhood and Unity with its monuments to the fratricides of the past and of fratricides yet to come, and arrive in Zagreb.

By now Zagreb and Belgrade feel like the capitals of different countries. There are still many people in Croatia, in Serbia and above all in Bosnia who consider themselves Yugoslavs. But for most Croats and Slovenes, Yugoslavia is part of a history which can never again be resurrected. The Croatian capital is without doubt of Central European, Habsburgian pedigree, whose population is experiencing the same mixture of liberation and uncertainty as the peoples of Budapest and Prague when they broke free from the fetters of 'actually existing socialism'. Zagreb is urbane, petty-bourgeois, although not quite as eerily Austrian as Ljubljana and other Slovene towns. Even though brutal gun-fights and nationalist killings have been reported as near as twenty-five miles from Zagreb, the population seems more interested and excited by the impending declaration of independence. Defiant symbols of Croatian statehood bedeck the central square, formerly Republic Square, now renamed the square of Ban Jelačić, the nineteenth-century Croatian military leader whose features bear an uncanny resemblance to the academic Slaven Letica, one of President Tuđman's most colourful and entertaining advisers. A voluminous Croatian flag, recognizable by the chequered shield, is draped limply over the huge statue of Ban Jelačić. Along with drink cans containing 'Fresh Croatian Air – to open when homesick or in need of freedom', street traders tout maps of Greater Croatia including much of Bosnia and parts of what is now Serbia. Inset proudly next to the map is a photograph of Ante Pavelić, the Ustasha leader. After intense lobbying by the Jewish and Serbian communities, the Zagreb authorities banned the sale of this map, although I subsequently saw it on sale in Osijek, Karlovac and Split. A few weeks later, the socialist mayor of Vienna, Helmut Zilk, as well as MPs from the Austrian Greens, would passionately demand recognition of Croatia in front of St

Stephen's Cathedral in Vienna, while official stewards at the demonstration sold photographs of Ante Pavelić and his map for 100 Schillings each.

Just as Serbia drowned in the four Cyrillic Cs, so was the chequered shield of Croatia rammed down the throat of Zagreb. Shopkeepers had plastered over every window in the town the appeal 'God Protect Croatia', while fly-posters detailed how to join Zagreb's unarmed (underlined and in bold) civil defence. Stressing the absence of weapons was guaranteed to ensure nobody would sign up. On housing estates, the word Chetnik began to appear on the doors or beside the doorbells of Serbian families. Although some 200,000 Serbs lived in Zagreb, they had become disenfranchised from society, just as the Croats in Krajina had been.

The greatest pomp was reserved for Croatia's parliament, the *Sabor*, and the Banski Dvor (the Court of the Ban), the official residence of the President of the Republic of Croatia. The two buildings are separated from each other by the rather unappealing church of St Matthew on Radić square. The government buildings are all in the old town, a raised area above Republic square which in parts can rival Prague in beauty. After the Serb members of parliament (with the exception of those still operating in the former Communist Party, the Party of Democratic Changes) had walked out of the *Sabor* for good, its proceedings took on an increasingly triumphalist, Croat nationalist tone. It never assumed the nauseating sycophancy which characterized many of the debates held in the Serbian parliament, but it frequently resembled a madhouse whose inmates displayed a tendency towards the rhetoric of violence or, more frequently, unfathomable insanity. After a particularly crass provocation by some Serb militants in eastern Slavonia, one deputy of the HDZ lost his ability to speak, so deep was his outrage. After about thirty seconds of spluttering and spitting, he suddenly blurted out the phrase '*Pasulj, pasulj, pasulj!*' ('Beans, beans, beans!'), a mysterious reference to the staple diet of many Serbian peasants. After expressing his anger at the Serb provocation in the only way apparently open to him, he stalked off the podium to mild applause and solemn head-nodding from the floor.

One of the first measures undertaken by President Tuđman on assuming office was to create a ceremonial guard for the Banski

Dvor. There is nothing that he enjoys more than to be photographed receiving a foreign dignitary surrounded by this platoon of over-dressed hussars. The presidential obsession with symbols and proto-col hints at a deep insecurity which all leaders feel throughout the region of central and south-eastern Europe. While state symbols are by no means absent in Western Europe and the United States, nowhere is such attention given to detail as in the Balkans. Tuđman was himself a military historian who became fascinated by the heraldry of Croatia, so it was no surprise that he let his imagination loose once he was elected to office. But his obvious delight in the paraphernalia of statehood is shared by many of his compatriots. Throughout 1990 and 1991, the Croatian flag, and above all the chequered shield, flooded all communities in Croatia until in certain areas, Serbs tore down what they believed represented a fascistoid, anti-Serb ideology and began replacing it with their own, equally exclusive symbols.

That Croatia was losing territory, partly because of this euphoric celebration of the national identity, did not seem to have really penetrated the consciousness of most Zagreb Croats – independence was but a few days away and after that, the organs of the new Croat state would re-establish order from Borovo Selo to Knin. That, at any rate, seemed to be the general mood in Zagreb. But as Ivan Bobetko, a hard-line HDZ MP who was military commander in the front-line town of Sisak, angrily informed the *Sabor* a few days after independence: 'The war looks very different in Sisak than it does to you gentlemen sitting here!' This misplaced triumphalism was encouraged by the government but above all by President Tuđman who, as evidenced by many statements, suffered from an illusion that the Yugoslav People's Army would not intervene if Croatia and Slovenia proclaimed their secession from the federation.

As the *Sabor* prepared to declare independence, there were still a few Croats who believed in a Yugoslav solution to the problem, but their numbers were declining day by day. One morning just before the war, I sat in the Dubrovnik café overlooking Ban Jelačić square, talking and listening to a group of Yugoslavs telling jokes. Veton Surroi was in Zagreb to appear on talk shows and discuss the situation in Kosovo with the Zagreb Albanians. Next to him sat Milorad Pupovac, a remarkable lecturer in linguistics at Zagreb

University. With finely drawn features, yet frail-looking, Pupovac emerged during the course of the conflict as the undisputed leader of the urban Serbs in Croatia. His commitment to rational political solutions aimed at minimizing violence and discrimination earned him the crude opprobrium of the Croat establishment, which never relinquished its self-appointed right to select puppets as representatives of the so-called 'loyal Serbs'. On the other hand, the Serb aggressors in Krajina, eastern Slavonia and, of course, Belgrade detested Pupovac as he preached not a gospel of fire, brimstone and armed resistance but one of peace and reconciliation. To my left was Žarko Puhovski, a professor of philosophy at Zagreb University, and one of Croatia's most engaging political thinkers. Rastko Močnik, a sociologist from Ljubljana, was one of the spiritual movers behind the Slovene Spring of 1989 who refused to be seduced by the nationalist hot air which had made giddy many of Slovenia's finest dissidents. Between Močnik and Puhovski was a member of Montenegro's Liberal Party which is a defiant combatant of the pro-Serb chauvinism of Montenegro's ruling party, the socialists (a.k.a. communists). This group was living proof of Yugoslavia's intellectual vitality – their virtual exclusion from politics by state authorities and a militarist mentality, however, bore testimony to the complete collapse of rational politics in Yugoslavia and its constituent republics.

The most striking manifestation of this collapse was the homogenization of consciousness among Croats and later among Serbs (although in Serbia the process was never as complete as it was in Croatia). This was fascinating to observe, if ultimately incomprehensible and distressing. Croats and Serbs argued endlessly with me as to why Serbs and Croats, respectively, were congenital monsters. They would cite history, religion, education and biology as reasons, but nobody could ever convince me why a Serb or Croat was *per se* good or *per se* bad. Throughout the campaign, nobody was able to convince me either that Serbian aggression against Croatia was justified or that the Croatian leadership had acted properly in deciding to leave Yugoslavia without taking into account the needs and fears of its Serb minority. Because of my belief that both Milošević and Tuđman were responsible for the war, I was accursed in both republics. In Serbia, unknown people telephoned me at my hotel at three o'clock in the morning and screamed at me for 'supporting the irredentists and Ustashas'. They have also never forgiven me for what I have written about Kosovo in the past. In Croatia I was denounced as a 'Chetnik-lover upon whom revenge would be wrought'. On the whole, Croatia's case was presented with considerable sympathy in the West European media. Those of us who were not uncritical of Tuđman's programme were subject to ever more poisonous attacks as the war spread. Most shocking of all were the people I had known for many years from left and liberal circles in the United Kingdom who had fallen under the spell of Croatian nationalism. These people demonstrated their consistent solidarity with a small-minded, right-wing autocrat as a consequence of losing the ability to argue rationally. In extreme situations, nationalism appears to neutralize that part of the mind which is able to fathom complex equations. Instead, action is motivated by a single Leninist principle: 'Those who are not for us, are against us'. Or as George Orwell paraphrased it in *Animal Farm*: – 'Four legs good. Two legs bad!'

In late 1990, the Slovene government decided to take out political insurance against the failure of talks between the presidents of the six Yugoslav republics: Kučan (Slovenia), Tuđman (Croatia), Milošević (Serbia), Izetbegović (Bosnia), Bulatović (Montenegro) and Gligorov (Macedonia). These had been instigated in order to draw up a new Yugoslav order at the highest level which would take into account national aspirations and the collapse of one-party rule. Slovenia, which was bound to Yugoslavia by markets but less by blood or by political inclination, was unable to disguise its impatience with the idea of any Yugoslavia even before these talks were really underway. In December 1990, the government in Ljubljana held a referendum on independence from Yugoslavia which predictably won an overwhelming majority. The talks of the six clan chiefs foundered on the rigidity of all participants except for the Macedonian and Bosnian presidents, whose realism was matched only by their powerlessness. Milošević's obstructive tactics were an especial stumbling block to progress during the negotiations. The war in Croatia had a variety of complex causes but one of the most important was this combination of Slovene uncompromising self-interest and Serbian inflexibility which began the process ending in war between Serbs and Croats. Although Tuđman's ultimate goal was clearly the creation of a Croat state, he did keep open the option of a new Yugoslav community until the Slovenes suddenly began a gallop towards independence. Once it was clear that the Slovenes were serious about jumping ship unilaterally in June 1991, Croatia knew that for tactical reasons it must follow the Slovene timetable. If trouble broke out, the theory went, then two republics would be better equipped to tackle it than one. Apart from ignoring the fact that there is no permanence in a Balkan alliance, this policy also misunderstood the very different nature of the struggle for Slovene independence and the struggle for Croatian independence. To equate the two, as many Croat politicians including the President did, was blithely to ignore the central feature of Croatian politics – the Serbian question.

Tuđman's dismissal of the Serbian question as somehow irrelevant was, and still is, quite baffling. At the time of writing, UN troops are attempting to complete their deployment in the disputed territories of Croatia where Serbs form the majority. Croatia may have gained recognition as an independent state under Tuđman but it has got no closer to solving the cause of the war, the Serbian question. In the absence of a solution, Croatia will remain a crippled state, unable to control a third of its territory and economically unviable.

The date for the declaration of Slovene independence was set as 26 June 1991. Because the Slovene break had been well-flagged, the overwhelming majority of journalists had travelled to Ljubljana that week. I was much happier positioning myself in Zagreb for independence. I knew that in principle Milošević had accepted the idea of Slovene independence. Indeed, it was no secret that with the doggedly intelligent politicians of Slovenia removed, Milošević would find it much easier to apply pressure on Croatia.

In the days preceding the independence declarations, a real sense of urgency and crisis had spread through the organs of federal Yugoslavia in Belgrade and elsewhere. The man who chimed the bell loudest and longest was Ante Marković, the federal Prime Minister, who is a Croat. His frenetic appeals to the Croats and Slovenes not to leave Yugoslavia heralded the final chapter in a political career which was very well-intentioned but, if we take survival to be the most important aim of the Balkan politician, exceptionally poorly executed. Marković had been responsible for a heroic and successful battle against inflation in Yugoslavia which he reduced from 2,500 per cent to between 1 and 2 per cent in the first half of 1990. He then set about implementing a series of market reforms intended to modernize the Yugoslav economy and prepare it for an association agreement with the European Community. His programme began its downward slide after he had curbed inflation, for although Marković is a pleasant, highly likeable man, he none the less succeeded in alienating almost every other actor in the Yugoslav drama. By June 1990, he was hated or spurned by everybody except for a number of foreign missions in Belgrade, who still believed, in spite of overwhelming evidence to the contrary, that federal Yugoslavia would somehow be unaffected by the Slovene and Croat independence declarations. Marković's most serious problem was his inability to understand that economic reform alone could not solve the Yugoslav crisis – you had to search for a political consensus as well.

Slovenia and Croatia were suspicious of Marković because of his determination to keep the coffers of the federal government well stocked with coins culled from the two northern republics. After Milošević's ascent to power, Serbia resented any interference from Marković against its attempts to centralize the republic, while in December 1990, the Serbian government was caught with its fingers in the federal till, literally appropriating billions of dollars which did not belong to it for Serbia's exclusive use. The only people who maintained tolerable relations with Marković were the generals and the army chief-of-staff. Until they struck a tentative agreement with Milošević in March 1991, they worked closely with Marković, who still paid their wages. Fatally, Marković appeared not to notice when his relationship with the army soured.

By the time he travelled to Zagreb to address the *Sabor* on Monday, 24 June, Marković was a figure of ridicule throughout Croatia (among Serbs and Croats alike). His last minute appeal to the Croats to rethink their policy of independence (or dissociation as it was euphemistically called at the time) was met with such derision by MPs at the *Sabor* that Žarko Domljan, the speaker of the *Sabor*, who can hardly be charged with being a moderate, had to intervene angrily so that Marković might speak. That day, Marković cut a pathetic figure, but he issued an unambiguous warning to both the Croats and the Slovenes: 'The federal government will counter unilateral secession with all available means.' The warning fell on deaf ears.

Everybody still anticipated that the Slovenes would be the first to declare independence on 26 June but it was the *Sabor* who surprised the world by voting in favour of Croatia's independence at just before six o'clock in the afternoon on Tuesday, 25 June. The vote was followed by a rousing bout of self-congratulation. President Tudman applauded wildly from the podium while tears rolled down the cheeks of some nationalists overcome by the state of independence. The Croats' glorious moment was followed by a rather tuneless rendition of *Lijepa naša domovina* (Our Beautiful Homeland), which had now officially replaced *Hej, Sloveni* (Hey, Slavs) as the national anthem in Croatia. The Slovenes, whose noses had clearly been put out of joint by the Croats' decision to pre-empt their declaration of independence, hastily followed with their independence that evening and a wild, public party ensued in Ljubljana. By contrast, the Croat preparations for independence were furtive. The Croatian authorities had held their referendum on independence but a month before the declaration to catch the slipstream of Slovene secession. Here, there were no elaborate celebrations, merely a rather tasteless and self-congratulatory reception at Zagreb's Intercontinental Hotel for President Tudman and his supporters. The noise was still enough, however, to wake the demons of civil war from their 46-year-old hibernation.

Before the Croat leadership had recovered from its independence hangover on the morning of 26 June, the forces of the Martićevci had begun a serious offensive a mere thirty-five miles from Zagreb in the town of Glina. The Martićevci, the largest paramilitary force among Serbs, had launched a surprise attack on the Glina police station where Croat police were holed up. Glina is an instructive example of the complexity of the Serb–Croat conflict. It is a charming town, resting in a gentle, shaded valley between two ranges of hills, which were Partizan strongholds during the Second World War. Much, but not all, of the fighting in 1991 took place in areas where the Partizans had fought a guerilla war against the Ustasha state exactly half a century before. Glina is just in the region known as Banija, which borders Kordun to the West. It is close to the village, Topusko, which was the regional Partizan headquarters during the Second World War and from where the Kordun and Banija Partizans spread into the surrounding hills. In this region the Partizans were nationally mixed – by the end of the war, 60 per cent of the guerillas were anti-fascist Croats. In 1991 it was a simple battle between Croats and Serbs – journalists came across mixed marriages in Banija which had been split by the war. One female Croat soldier on the front line south of Sisak (the Croat headquarters for Banija) told reporters how she had joined the National Guard when her husband signed up for the local Serb paramilitaries. She explained without bitterness how she was now firing at her husband. Many mixed marriages have been wrecked by the war, although I observed a general pattern in the crisis areas of women assimilating the national consciousness of their husbands: Croat women espousing the Serb ideals of their partners and Serb women denouncing Serb aggression against the homeland of their lovers.

The national make up of the forces in Kordun and Banija in 1991 provides an important counter-weight to the frequently articulated argument that this was not a nationalist war but an ideological one. With a few freakish exceptions, Croats made up the forces in the north while Serbs from all over Serbia, Croatia and Bosnia comprised the troops to the south. When the Yugoslav People's Army became heavily involved, this equation was complicated somewhat because of the presence of all Yugoslav nationalities in this conscript force. Even within the JNA, a process began early on in the conflict involving the steady reduction of non-Serb nationalities in the officer corps, which was predominantly Serb and Montenegrin in the first place.

Supporters of Croatia's cause claimed that the war was between Milošević's Bolshevism and the free-market, democratic spirit as embodied by Franjo Tuđman. Serbs countered this by saying that the war had begun with the onset of genocide against Serbs in Croatia which prefaced a fascist offensive in the Balkans, executed by Tuđman's Ustashas (many Serb leaders were absolutely convinced that the Tuđman administration was fascist) on behalf of their paymasters in Europe, the Germans. Both these theories are constructed from a series of half-truths, cemented by a low-grade mixture of myth and legend. On the field in Glina and elsewhere in Kordun and Banija, Serbs were shooting Croats and Croats were shooting Serbs. The cultural and political splits within the Serb and Croat communities had an enormous impact on the intensity of the struggle, as we shall observe later, especially in eastern Slavonia. Anybody who doubts the deeply nationalist aspect of this war has clearly never been anywhere near the battlegrounds.

I had been to Glina in September 1990 after the Croatian Special Police force had raided the town and attempted to disarm the Serb police reservists. Instead of scenes of destruction, I was greeted by a quiet country town blessed with scores of trees whose brown and green leaves provided enough shade to cool a hot autumn sun but not enough to extinguish its pleasant, yellow light. Its air of rural harmony deceived. In the wake of the incident with the Specials and Serb civilians, nobody at the police station or at the Serb cafés along the high street wanted to talk to me. They snarled and grunted, betraying a mixture of suspicion, fear and aggression. Finally, I found one young Serb who explained much about these small mixed or predominantly Serb settlements which are squeezed into Croatia's ethnic twilight zones. He took me down a side street, avoiding groups of more than three people, to a small café. We sat outside and he began to talk – there was almost no need to pose any questions. He spoke very softly and frequently turned his head to see if anyone was listening or watching us too intently. Occasionally he mumbled but his message was clear.

Like the majority of Serbs in Banija, he considered himself a social democrat and had voted for Croatia's former Communist Party, the Party of Democratic Changes (SDP). At the time of the election in April 1990, he had not believed the national question to be of central importance. Of much greater concern, he continued, was the fate of the few large companies which dominate Banija's economy and whose future looked uncertain. There was no inclination in the town itself to secede from Croatia and considerable pride that the Serbs here had backed a multi-national party, the SDP. Following the incident in Knin a month before, however, strains emerged between the Serb-led SDP in Banija and the largely Croat leadership in Zagreb which, the Serbs felt, was too ready to back nationalist positions of the HDZ and Tuđman. But the collapse of confidence in the SDP was not the decisive factor in Banija. Rather, it was what he perceived to be the determination of the Croat authorities to assert their control through regular shows of police force in the region. The Glina Serbs believed that the government in Zagreb was subjecting a relatively peaceful area to Knin-style pacification tactics.

This was accompanied by regular doses of Croat triumphalism in the form of flags, symbols and songs. The red and white chequered shield (*šahovnica*) is one of the oldest Croatian symbols. Unfortunately it was also used most prominently by the Ustashas. In 1990, the *šahovnica* was used to replace the principal Yugoslav symbol, the red star. Serbs in Croatia view the red star not just as a communist symbol but as a sign legitimizing their equal status with Croatians, and they believed that the ubiquitous presence of the *šahovnica* underlines that loss of equality. Serbs believe they fought two world wars in order to preserve that equality and now the separatist will of the Croatian government is attempting to strip them of their hard-won prize. It does not matter how close to the truth this is. It does not matter that Tuđman's government was not a fascist one – the point is, enough Serbs believed it to be so and Tuđman bore a considerable responsibility for not allaying the fears of what is historically an almost psychotic part of the Serbian nation's make up. Croatia had no hope of leaving Yugoslavia peacefully (regardless of the help received by the local Serbs from Belgrade) without striking a deal with the Serbs in Krajina, Lika, Kordun, Banija, western and eastern Slavonia.

Serbs in Glina had particular memories which their elders nurtured. In 1941, some 800 Serbs were massacred in Glina's Orthodox church, while later, over 1,000 more lost their lives on the outskirts of town. The memory of Croat atrocities in Glina remains vivid. My friend told me he thought that in Krajina, there was a deeper sense of hostility between Serbs and Croats. He agreed that this existed in Banija, too, but that it was not so developed. I thanked my friend and asked him for his address and phone number. He mumbled an apology to the effect that life was simply becoming too dangerous and he hoped I would forgive him. He drifted into the dusk before I could try and persuade him otherwise.

At the same time as Zagreb had been attempting to impose Croatian political authority on Glina, Babić had been sending emissaries from Knin in an attempt to undermine the social-democratic forces in Glina in favour of the militant Serb nationalist line. The Serbs in Glina resisted Babić's bloody entreaties until June but by then they felt that they no longer had a choice – it was Croats or Serbs, and they were Serbs.

The return to Glina on 26 June was sad and sobering. Driving from Petrinja, the car developed a disturbing low growl which seemed at first to herald a flat tyre. It was soon evident that the road was suffering from damage inflicted very recently by a column of tanks. This noise would later become a useful early warning signal of military activity. After crossing a number of Croat check-points on the road from Petrinja to Glina, we were greeted by tanks of the JNA at the northern entrance to the town. It was a scorching day. My colleagues and I were already sweating from the drive, but as we approached the army check-point just past the Glina road sign, our pores opened still wider – the turret of a Yugoslav-made T-55 swivelled round and aimed its barrel straight at me and my friends. The tank had no intention of shooting as I was conversing with two soldiers but it was the first time that I had personally been confronted with the arrogant aggression of ballistics. In the next few months, I would face many similar encounters, but I would never get used to them. For somebody who is by nature a committed coward, the Yugoslav civil war would test my nerves to the limit. The first soldier, a recruit, muttered under his breath that the fighting had been heavy and that at least three Croat police were dead. 'It's quiet now but very tense . . . ' He was interrupted by a gruff, booming voice: 'What d'ye think you're doing here. Clear out.' The rookie smartly shut up and disappeared. I asked his commander whether we could go into Glina. 'You're not going anywhere except back from where you came. And you are not going to cross my line in a million years.' The commander was nervous and unhappy but he would not say any more.

A local Croat signalled to us that he knew a way into town and we were soon travelling in a three-car convoy along a stone road that threw up so much dust that within five minutes the car and all its inhabitants were coloured grey. At one roadblock, manned by the most primitive Croat peasants carrying shotguns, the local people tried to prevent three of us, including myself, from travelling on as they found the word Belgrade in our passports on the stamps issued at Surčin airport. Anything vaguely Serb was hostile in their eyes. Their world had been turned upside down and they could no longer trust anyone. After some ten miles skirting around Glina, our ghostly convoy was flagged down by a group of Croat police and civilian volunteers. They explained that this western entrance to Glina was completely blocked by JNA tanks with particularly hostile crews on board, but we could drive a little further on and try from the south-west. We gave a lift to one of the men. 'My brother's a policeman in Glina and I must go in there to get him out somehow. They think he's been wounded,' he explained, anticipating the tens of thousands of dreadful personal tragedies which were soon to descend on this blighted country. 'Relations between us [Croats and Serbs] have always been bad here. The Serbs ran the local [Communist] Party, the local factories, the local police. Now they have lost this in democracy and they're going to fight to keep their privileges.' This was an honest man. Like most of the fighters on both sides, he had been pulled into conflict unwillingly – his version of the truth was as convincing as that articulated by my young Serb social-democrat friend inside Glina nine months prior to this.

Soon after dropping him off at the south-western entrance, two young women wearing overalls and in hysterics walked up from the town. They were in tears and almost completely incoherent, talking as fast as they could of shooting, of a body with its head blown off and of the police station. The incessant crackle of automatic gunfire in the distance provided a powerful chorus of warning to their urgent appeal against us entering the town. We soon found the leader of the HDZ in this predominantly Croat village on Glina's outskirts. She was a competent woman who explained to us that the Martićevci, who had been hiding in the hills overnight, swarmed into Glina and attacked the police station in a merciless operation. After several hours of fighting, the JNA arrived in force from Petrinja. The army had slowed down the bloodshed but their presence partially guaranteed the territorial gains of the Serb militia. This was a pattern that would be repeated. In the initial stages of the war, the army frequently kept the casualties to a minimum but they invariably shored up Serb advances. Co-operation between the Serbs and the JNA varied greatly from region to region. During the first phase of the war in Banija, the army's role was relatively benign.

On the return to Zagreb, we were stopped three times at Croat roadblocks. At the second, a hysterical old man leapt out of the forest waving his shotgun directly at our heads. His comrades calmed him down after we had proved we were unarmed. The old man was drunk. Inebriated gunmen were an especially nasty hazard which journalists had to face on all fronts. They were common to both sides. It had been an exhausting trip to Glina. As we cruised back into Zagreb, one thought projected itself with crystal clarity above a cerebral haze: 'The war has begun.'

On returning to Zagreb, it became clear how out of touch Croatia's capital was with the war that was bubbling and spitting but twenty-five miles away. It was also still difficult convincing the outside world that bloody civil war was imminent in Europe. Most journalists were in Ljubljana for the independence declaration and so the war in Banija was given short shrift. Less than twelve hours after my return from Glina, they seemed to be vindicated when the JNA moved to secure Yugoslavia's Slovene borders which the Slovenes said they would now be administering. The government had passed a resolution which would 'ensure the immediate execution of federal regulations during the crossing of state borders on the territory of Slovenia (the Croatian government had not ordered its forces to take over borders, in contrast with the Slovene government) ... The unilateral acts of Croatia and Slovenia are neither legal nor legitimate and the consequences of these acts are unconstitutional ... In carrying out federal regulations concerning the crossing of state borders, the Federal Secretariat (of Internal Affairs) will co-operate with the Federal Secretariat for National Defence *as to how the border units of the JNA should be deployed* [my italics – M.G.].'

A few days later at a press conference in Belgrade, Ante Marković denied giving his permission to the Defence Minister, General Veljko Kadijević, for the use of military force. Yet with the constitutional Commander-in-Chief, i.e. the Yugoslav collective

Presidency, not functioning, the Defence Ministry, subordinate to the Prime Minister, was obviously the only body able to mobilize the troops. The government statement above seems fairly unambiguous that Marković had given his approval. Following this denial, Kadijević launched a bitter attack on the Prime Minister, accusing him of lying and shirking his responsibility. The attack on Slovenia was the last nail in Marković's coffin. During that press conference in Belgrade, he was so busy denying everything that one journalist remarked aloud: 'Don't ask me, I'm only the Prime Minister!' The joke was lost on Marković but not on anyone else.

The army had moved towards all Slovene border posts, initially crushing resistance but soon coming up against tougher, more committed units of the Territorial Defence (TO) who were clearly prepared for a fight. I watched the 'ten-day war' largely through a televisual haze, trying to reconcile my memories of this placid little country with the senseless, albeit measured, destruction taking place there. I drove into eastern Slovenia several times to watch the tenacity of the TO members and the confusion of the conscript soldiers. On one border between Croatia and Slovenia which is just twelve miles from Zagreb, soldiers' heads bobbed nervously up and down out of the tank turrets to see whether the vehicles passing contained Slovene military personnel. But they seemed uncertain about their role. When I asked them what their function was, they pushed me away nervously and told me to continue my journey. A few miles further on, I was greeted by two enormous German lorries which were bombed out and now being used as barricades on the Zagreb–Novo Mesto road. The Slovene TO would not reveal whether they had been commandeered first and then bombed out or vice versa. However, near the Italian and Austrian borders, the TO confiscated the vehicle keys and passports of foreign lorry drivers (mainly Turkish) in order to use the lorries as barricades. The lorries were strafed by the Yugoslav air force and several foreign lorry drivers died.

The JNA operation in Slovenia was a limited one. Twenty thousand troops were stationed on Slovene territory but only 2,000 were deployed in the attempt to secure the borders for the federal government. Many of these were brought in from the Varaždin, Zagreb and Karlovac barracks, all bases in Croatia. The Slovenes suffered few deaths before General Kadijević decided that the JNA would give up Slovenia and, in accordance with the Brioni Accord negotiated by the European Community, the army relinquished its grip on the new country. A few months later I spoke at length to retired Admiral Branko Mamula, the moving spirit behind the *SK – Pokret za Jugoslaviju* (League of Communists – Movement for Yugoslavia). Mamula's influence over Kadijević was considerable. The Defence Minister did not take any significant decision without first consulting Mamula, and the retired Admiral had nothing but praise for Kadijević. 'Kadijević made one very big mistake with which I disagreed,' Mamula told me. 'He decided to let go of Slovenia. I protested but he insisted. After that happened, it was clear that we had lost Yugoslavia.' Mamula implied that it was difficult to justify a war in Croatia in the name of Yugoslavia once you had capitulated to Slovene independence demands. The war lost its Yugoslav character and assumed a strong Serb–Croat one. This greatly troubled the many JNA officers (including Croats, Slovenes, Moslems and Macedonians) who believed in maintaining the integrity of a Yugoslav state but who were disturbed by the idea of fighting for a Balkan state dominated by Serbia.

Aside from the exceptional organization and motivation displayed by the Slovene TO and the government in Ljubljana, this is the central significance of the war in Slovenia. By forcing the independence issue, Slovenia bears some indirect responsibility for the war in Croatia. Once Slovenia insisted on breaking up Yugoslavia, the accumulated tensions in Croatia had to express themselves through violence. Yet on a political level, the Slovenes may well argue that as an essentially homogenous ethnic territory with nation state aspirations, there was no justification for it to remain in an unstable Yugoslavia merely because Croatia had a range of potentially violent problems. Slovenia could act as a catalyst but it could never generate massive instability in the Balkans. In June 1991, only the Serbs and Croats were capable of that, and following the declaration of independence by the Croatian *Sabor*, it was exactly what they were about to do.

4 JULY 1991–JANUARY 1992:

The Twilight Zone

A tank races through the main thoroughfare of a busy city, smashing buses and other vehicles in its wake. A desperate, angry man manoeuvres his *Fića* into its path before leaping out of the way. The *Fića*, a tiny bubble-like Fiat 126 manufactured under licence in Yugoslavia, resembles a dozy hedgehog crossing the street. The armoured monster runs headlong into the *Fića* chewing up every metal part as if it were flesh and blood, dragging the remains for a hundred metres before spitting the carcass onto the pavement.

During the 'ten-day war' in Slovenia, this most memorable image which blitzed the televisions of the world was actually recorded in Osijek, the eastern Slavonian capital which lies thirteen miles west of the Danube, Croatia's border with Serbia. So confusing were the wars on the disputed territories of Croatia and Slovenia that several international television networks decided against explaining that this was not Slovenia but Croatia, as they reasoned that trying to differentiate between the two conflicts would be beyond the viewer's comprehension. When the war broke out in Slovenia, many Europeans became acquainted with this small pocket of the Alpine lowlands for the first time.

But a different war in Croatia was well under way before the Yugoslav People's Army (JNA) and the Yugoslav state effectively capitulated to Slovenia by signing the Brioni Accord. This agreement, which acknowledged Slovenia's liberation from the control of Belgrade, was preceded by a burst of chaotic diplomatic activity organized by the European Community Troika of foreign ministers: Jacques de Poos from Luxembourg, Hans van den Bruk from the Netherlands and the colourful chief of Italy's diplomatic corps, Gianni de Michelis. These three swept into Belgrade and Zagreb two days after the fighting began. On their heels was a gaggle of journalists, all based in Brussels, who had travelled on the European

Community aeroplane. The culture shock they experienced was visible on their drawn and confused faces. After all, they had just dropped in on an absurdist Balkan nightmare from the clinical corridors of Brussels. The three foreign ministers negotiated with Slobodan Milošević and General Veljko Kadijević in Belgrade before talking to President Tuđman and the Slovene President, Milan Kučan, in Zagreb.

The discussions in Zagreb only finished at three o'clock in the morning whereupon a press conference was held in Banski Dvor, the official seat of President Tuđman. The three foreign ministers looked pleased with themselves, especially Gianni de Michelis who believed he understood the Yugoslav situation much better than his eleven European Community peers. Tuđman looked of another world with his distinctive physical tics having shifted into over-drive. Milan Kučan, exhausted from running a war, emerged from his BMW with the complexion of a wraith surfacing from his subterranean den. I cornered de Michelis who told me triumphantly that the Troika had sorted out the entire problem and the fighting would stop the very same day.

Another two days later, the Troika returned. Not unpredictably, the fighting had not died down, it had intensified. This time de Michelis was no longer wearing his mask of confidence. He now realized that all his theoretical understanding was of little value in a country where deceit is the most common political currency. For Balkan politicians, it is axiomatic that the only truth is the lie. Throughout the Yugoslav crisis, both Presidents Tuđman and Milošević, not to mention scores of lesser figures, committed themselves solemnly to accords and agreements whose provisions they would openly flaunt the following day. To his credit, de Michelis had only needed forty-eight hours to appreciate that this was how they behaved. The Italian Foreign Minister assured me that on the occasion of the second press conference at Banski Dvor, the Troika had reached full agreement with all leaders. 'That's what you told me last time,' I reminded him. 'Yes,' he countered in desperation rather than triumph, 'but this time we've got it all down on paper!'

Although there were some further hiccoughs, the work of the Troika mission eventually flowered into the Brioni Accord. This stipulated the withdrawal of all Yugoslav army units from Slovenia, thus implying that international recognition of southern Slavdom's small Alpine protrusion would soon be granted. But although the Croats were party to the negotiations which led to Brioni, the agreements therein left the issue of Croatia entirely open. Thus while this initial intervention of the European Community was not without value as it ended the war in Slovenia, it none the less failed to address the central issue of the Yugoslav crisis – Croatia. The essential problem of a Yugoslav state lies in the numerical and political dominance of Serbs over Croats; the essential problem of a Croatian state lies in the numerical and political dominance of Croats over Serbs. In order to secure peace in the Balkans, this conundrum must be solved along with two others: the constitution of Bosnia-Hercegovina and in Serbia, the political status of the Moslem, Albanian and Hungarian minorities in the Sandžak, Kosovo and Vojvodina, respectively. This is not merely a pragmatic response to the problems of Yugoslavia – national and ethnic minorities provide a highly sensitive detonator of war during a period of immense political instability. The failure to solve the problems surrounding minorities, which by definition question territorial integrity, is behind the fighting in Croatia, Bosnia, Moldova – Trans-Dniestr and Nagorno-Karabakh. There are dozens of other nationalist disputes fermenting in Eastern Europe and the former Soviet Union. In order to find a long-term solution for these problems, a normative system must be developed and applied to these regions. At the moment, the international community lacks this and is also short of resources. However, the efforts of the European Community and the United Nations in Yugoslavia and Nagorno-Karabakh indicate that it is not entirely lacking in motivation. The more these disputes develop into open warfare, the more urgent the need for a systemic approach to these problems becomes, but given the pressures which are determining foreign policy development in the USA, Europe and Japan, it is unlikely that an international political model for combating nationalist instability will be created.

Neither Croatia nor Serbia featured centrally in the Brioni Accord. So instead of understanding the wars in Yugoslavia as part of an integrated complex, the European Community embarked on a policy of localized solutions in the Balkans which have neither stopped the violence nor resolved the underlying causes of that violence. The Slovene issue was admittedly the one political problem which could be solved in isolation (although the question of Slovenia's economic relations with the other republics remains unanswered), but the success of the Brioni Accord was understood by the European Community (especially the German political establishment) to mean that it could promote piecemeal solutions to the Yugoslav crisis – a grave error.

During Slovenia's ten-day war, three regions in Croatia experienced a critical upsurge in fighting between Serb irregulars and the JNA on the one hand, and the Croat police and the republic's embryonic army, the National Guard, on the other. The first was on the border of Lika and the Dalmatian hinterland. It was in the region, near the small village of Lovinac, that the first massacre of innocents was uncovered when the rotting bodies of five Croat civilians were discovered in some bushes by a passer-by. The dead men, who included one in his seventies, had been kidnapped and tortured by Serb irregulars (the vile Chetniks had achieved considerable success in infiltrating this region) before their bodies were dumped not far from where they lived. The centre of fighting in this region for much of the war was Gospić, a mixed Serb–Croat village which was to experience destruction and trauma akin to that which Vukovar would later suffer.

The second region was Banija. After the battle of Glina, Serbs and Croats began fighting from village to village. The strategic goals were Petrinja, with its large barracks and its control of the entrance to Banija, and Sisak whose oil refinery bestows substantial economic significance on the town. Despite heavy fighting, relatively little territory was to change hands in the period following the battle of Glina. This reflected a critical aspect of the first five weeks of war in Croatia – in certain areas (notably Krajina, southern Lika and Dalmatia), Serb paramilitary forces and the JNA worked hand in glove. In other areas (northern Lika, western Slavonia, Kordun, Banija and partly eastern Slavonia), the army saw its role not as a combatant but as a peace-maker. Even after it became clear that the army was operating as a full combatant in certain areas, President Tuđman and his adjutant Stipe Mesić (theoretically still the President of Yugoslavia) stressed a commitment to work with the army. Popular hostility to the JNA was considerable and it was vigorously articulated by MPs in the Croat parliament, the *Sabor*. But Croatia's leaders frequently expressed the desire to cooperate with the JNA. On 2 July, for example, the Deputy Prime Minister, Franjo Gregurić (who later became Prime Minister), said that Croatia 'does not want a war with the Yugoslav army'. He criticized the military operations in Slovenia but added that Croatian forces 'would not engage in armed actions' against the JNA.

The most serious fighting in Croatia during this first period flared in eastern Slavonia. During the war as a whole, this region suffered a terrible fate but it is one which explains a great deal about the Yugoslav crisis. My attention was alerted to the deteriorating situation by a grenade attack on the police station in Tenja which was perpetrated at the very end of June. On 1 July, my decision to investigate the regional capital, Osijek, and the surrounding district was accelerated by the murder of Josip Reichl-Kir, chief of police in Osijek, which lies just two miles from Tenja. Assuming the perpetrator to be a Serb, I was concerned that the incident would provoke heavy fighting. When I heard that the killer was a Croat and a former head of the Croatian Democratic Union (HDZ) in Tenja and that a leading HDZ member from Osijek and a Serb politician from Tenja were also killed my curiosity was aroused beyond the point of no return and I decided the same day to head for Osijek.

The Road of Brotherhood and Unity was now weirdly empty. A car or a truck would pass by every five minutes. This pattern was punctuated every half-hour by a sudden cascade of military vehicles either heading towards Slovenia or being deployed as reinforcements in the crisis areas of Croatia. Normal traffic between Serbia and Croatia had just evaporated, an early consequence of the economic war which developed between the two republics soon after the declarations of independence. The republican government in Belgrade insisted quite disingenuously throughout the war that the Republic of Serbia was a disinterested observer of the entire conflict. Although the government in Zagreb claimed from the beginning that Serbia was waging an undeclared war against Croatia, it was not in a position to order an attack on Serbia. So beyond its strategic goal of gaining international recognition, the only instrument with which Croatia could weaken Serbia was economic. Apart from no longer supplying parts for tanks and other weaponry from factories in areas under Zagreb's control, the most effective decision taken by the Croatian government was to cut the oil pipeline which supplies Serbia from the port of Rijeka. The markets of Serbia and Croatia are exceptionally interdependent and it was not long before some enterprising businesses were operating 'sanctions-busting' schemes across the territory of Bosnia-Hercegovina. To an important extent, however, both republics suffered greatly from the economic war. Nowhere was this more evident than on the ghostly asphalt of Brotherhood and Unity.

The Croat police checks were more numerous than they had been ten days before but they were still relatively lax until reaching the turnoff for Osijek. From then on, they cropped up every six miles. Most of the police were armed with Kalashnikovs, probably from consignments shipped illegally through Hungary. Notwithstanding European Community and United Nations sanctions, Yugoslavia boasts the most porous borders in Europe thanks to a conspiracy of geography and corrupt neighbours. Rarely has there been such a honeypot for international arms dealers as Yugoslavia at war. At this early stage, Croatia was still arming itself, and the Serb forces enjoyed an enormous advantage in the amount and variety of hardware they possessed.

It was a glorious early summer's evening as I travelled the thirty-five miles north from the *autoput* to Osijek. The Croat police and their motley irregular colleagues toting shotguns were both friendly and helpful. From the beginning, ordinary Croats seemed to understand instinctively that it was important to be open and friendly with the foreign press. Without doubt, this led to a positive presentation of the Croat cause in Western Europe and the United States. The Serb government, the JNA and many ordinary Serbs close to the fronts were dismissive and hostile towards the foreign press. About two months after the war in Croatia began, the Serbs began to appreciate that this was a serious error. Both sides were quick to denounce foreign journalists who did not represent them as morally infallible but at least the Croatian authorities afforded one the benefit of the doubt to begin with. I passed through the roadblocks with friendly waves to speed me on my way.

In the orange glow of evening, Osijek assumed dramatic contours which were defined more precisely when a long convoy of camouflaged lorries with open backs drove by, each with a heavy-duty machine-gun secured to the bed. Attached to each gun was a young man clothed in the makeshift uniform of the National Guard. In a theatrical, almost recidivist display, the novice gunners swivelled their deadly toys from side to side aiming at imagined aircraft. Outside Osijek's police headquarters, the lorry drivers performed a gratuitous, motorized war dance. After this criss-crossing, tyre-squealing performance, they parked in a well-choreographed move which left two lorries splayed out from the pillars of the police station's front entrance, gunners alert. To their side, the six remaining lorries were parked in two lines of three with guns covered, but still projecting a fearful symmetry.

A group of soldiers waited expectantly at the imposing neo-classical entrance of what was now called the General Staff Headquarters. A minute later a much smaller group led by a small, slightly balding man with a resolute gait strode towards the pillars. As far as the young rabble was able, it stood to attention. From close up, the small commander with steel-blue eyes resembled a poor country cousin of Hannibal Lecter as portrayed by Anthony Hopkins in *The Silence of the Lambs*. This was my first glimpse of Branimir Glavaš, HDZ fanatic, military fantasist and, eventually, commander of the National Guard in the Osijek region. Adored by many Croats in eastern Slavonia, he was viewed nervously by Tuđman in Zagreb because of his ruthlessness, his ambition and his unpredictability. The Serbs created monstrous fighting units such as the White Eagles, the Arkanovci and Dušan the Mighty. Croatia had, among others, Branimir Glavaš, a serial killer in fatigues.

Osijek's police station is just a few metres away from the main square, which is now named after Croatia's most influential leader of the nineteenth-century national revival, Ante Starčević. On the west side of the small square is the city's ugly red-brick cathedral whose neo-Gothic spires contributed to the general sense of foreboding. Behind Starčević square on the bank of the Drava river, just ten miles before it flows into the Danube, is the Hotel Osijek. The early 1970s tower-block design makes it look decidedly out of place in a town with few high-rise buildings, but with decent direct dial telephones in every room and cheap whisky readily available, it soon became a firm favourite with foreign journalists, who were its only guests until it was blown apart during an offensive two months later. The Hotel Osijek was without question the easiest target for the Serb artillery which was only separated from it by the river. Across the water lay Baranja, historically a Hungarian region, which was poorly defended by the Croats and gobbled up by the Serbs and the army in a matter of days during July.

The following day I sought out the editor of *Glas Slavonije* (Voice of Slavonia). During the communist period, Osijek had suffered from one of the most Stalinist communist leaderships, which had allowed UDBA, the Yugoslav secret police, a very loose rein. Under this regime, *Glas Slavonije* had degenerated into a dreary, sycophantic rag which, among journalists in Croatia, was a by-word for all that was bad under Titoism. This condemnation was all the more powerful as, in contrast to other East European countries, Yugoslavia boasted some of the finest European journalism for long stretches under the Titoist order. After the collapse of communist authority in Yugoslavia, a new editor, Drago Hedl, was appointed, and he set about renewing the paper with vigour, such that by the time that war broke out in Croatia, it was regarded as perhaps the finest regional paper in the republic.

Hedl, a poet and writer of children's books, was an exceptionally nice man. He explained that *Glas Slavonije* was denounced with equal vehemence by the Serbs fighting in the surrounding villages and by the HDZ, above all by Branimir Glavaš. He proudly showed me an advertisement paid for by the Osijek HDZ that they had carried the previous week. It was an appeal to all readers of the paper to boycott it. Drago said that since the HDZ had started the campaign to boycott the paper, its circulation had risen by over a thousand. Hedl was sympathetic to the Hrvatska Narodna Stranka ((HNS) Croatian National Party), which had actively campaigned among both Serb and Croat communities in the republic, retaining a decidedly liberal profile. The HDZ in Osijek, on the other hand, provided a good example of how the organization moved to the right the further it was from Zagreb.

Hedl was the first man to give me details about the killing of Reichl-Kir, a well-groomed and intelligent 35-year-old whose antecedents were German and Slovene although he considered himself a Croat. He was not, however, a member of the HDZ but had taken over the job as head of Osijek's police a year before at the personal request of Franjo Tuđman. Reichl-Kir was determined to stop distrust between Serbs and Croats from sliding into open hostility. For weeks before his death, he travelled tirelessly from village to village striking local deals to prevent the extremists in both communities assuming a dominant influence. Almost unbelievably, given his position and the atmosphere within which he worked, Reichl-Kir never carried a firearm.

The road from Osijek to Vukovar, both towns with majority Croat populations, is flanked by a dozen or so villages, all but one of which are dominated by Serbs. All these have Croat minority populations of varying sizes. The day before his death, Reichl-Kir had guaranteed the safety of Serbs from attack in one of these villages, Bijelo Brdo, in exchange for the Serbs taking down their barricades and allowing the normal flow of traffic between Osijek and the Serbian province of Vojvodina. The next day he led a team of Croats from Osijek in negotiations with the Serbs of Old Tenja. He and one of his colleagues drove with two Serb leaders into Osijek for clarification of certain issues, before returning to Tenja to sign a deal. According to Gordana Ajduković, a professor at the Osijek Faculty of Economics and adviser to the Serbs during the negotiations in Tenja, the agreement would have prevented the spread of war to the village. At the entrance to New Tenja (the Croat part of town), a former head of the HDZ in Tenja, Antun Gudelj, launched twenty-eight bullets from a Kalashnikov, into the Zastava in which Reichl-Kir was travelling. He was killed instantly along with his Croat adviser and one of the Serb leaders from Tenja. The second Serb escaped with light injuries. Although the incident took place a few metres from a police roadblock, Gudelj, who was politically close to Glavaš, executed a miraculous escape from the scene of the crime and has never been seen since.

The death of Reichl-Kir brought open war in eastern Slavonia one long step closer. Two days after his death, I drove to Old Tenja. At the entrance, a toothless and slow civilian guard waved down the car. My colleague, Alison Smale from the Associated Press, and I explained that we were British journalists who wished to talk to Serbs from Old Tenja. After a short wait, a group of friendly Serbs retrieved us and accompanied us into the village. For two hours I sat with Žarko, Batele and friends listening to their story. Žarko had been a factory inspector in Osijek, one of twelve, he explained. Six months earlier, he had been dismissed from his job for no reason. He had, of course, lost his job because he was a Serb. The Serbs clearly had an unfair advantage over Croats during the communist administration of Osijek, but the vengeful sacking of hundreds of Serbs by the state after the HDZ victory was perceived by the local Serbs to be a racist move. Because Tenja was so close to Osijek, a high percentage had been employed in the city and therefore a high percentage lost their jobs.

But further east on the road to Vukovar, there were other villages most of whose inhabitants worked the land. Their jobs were not under threat and so the sudden rush of redundancies was not responsible for the deterioration of Serb–Croat relations in these places. Again it is worth noting, in this region, the war was quite clearly nationalist in character. Through a variety of middlemen, Milošević gave particular encouragement to the Serb militias in eastern Slavonia because any territorial prize would include large tracts of fertile agricultural land. But the villagers who did much of the fighting were motivated not by a desire to enlarge Serbian territory but by a phobia concerning the Croatian state and the HDZ. Yet curiously, relations between Serbs and Croats in eastern Slavonia had traditionally been very good, even during the Ustasha regime. History indicated that it was most unlikely for vicious conflict to break out here. Something had happened to destroy the harmony in eastern Slavonia.

At the end of the Second World War, large numbers of *došljaci* (immigrants/settlers) were transferred from other parts of Yugoslavia to villages and towns in eastern Slavonia and Vojvodina. Here they moved into the homes of the large German community which had either evacuated the area or had been expelled. Many Hungarians had also left, especially from Baranja and Vojvodina. The Croat *došljaci* came largely from western Hercegovina while the Serb *došljaci* arrived chiefly from the Dalmatian hinterland or in shorthand, Knin. As Miloš Vasić, the phenomenal journalist from the Belgrade magazine, *Vreme*, put it: 'The communists took the most bitter fighters of the civil war and planted them in the middle of Eastern Slavonia, guaranteeing that when the hatred of the war was exhumed in 1991, it would spread to areas hitherto untouched by it.'

The Serb community in Tenja was one of the last among the dozen villages between Osijek and Vukovar to come under the poisonous influence of the nationalist Serb paramilitary organization. This is because they were almost all from old Slavonian families who sought no quarrel with old Croat families in the region. New Tenja was built after the war largely for the benefit of immigrants from Hercegovina, and although it may be coincidental that peace in Tenja became unsustainable when Reichl-Kir and his two co-negotiators were murdered, it is worth noting that Gudelj and Glavaš were both born in western Hercegovina. Bobota and Borovo Selo (the most militant Serb strongholds in the region) were populated chiefly by Serb *došljaci* and they were the first to declare their refusal to recognize Croatian authority. The tiny village, Klisa, which lies between Tenja and Trpinja was composed of only old families – even when the fighting was raging in Tenja, and Serb irregulars in surrounding villages were roughing up Croats and shooting at approaching cars, Klisa was an isle of tranquillity. Klisa was later drawn into the fighting, but there are several villages in eastern Slavonia (noticeably between Osijek and Našice) where, despite being on the doorstep of some of the most appalling fighting, not a bullet was fired during the war. Serbs and Croats continued living in harmony with one another throughout the internal events. In these villages, there were no *došljaci*, neither Serbs nor Croats.

Žarko and Batele introduced me to a Serb working in Germany who had just returned to Tenja for a visit. He was clearly deeply distraught. He had arrived two days prior to this and on the same evening a group of Croats had vandalized his brand new Volkswagen Jetta. All the glass had been smashed and the peripherals destroyed, but across the bodywork, the Croats had scratched and sprayed the words 'Long live the Ustashas and HDZ' adding some crude representations of the *šahovnica*. The Serbs in Tenja were genuinely frightened, and convinced they were about to be slaughtered. By the time I visited Žarko and Batele, the emissaries of Belgrade had begun to arm the Tenja Serbs, but until the death of

Reichl-Kir they had remained keen to keep open channels of communication. That was to change the Sunday after his murder.

It was a fresh, warm Sunday morning and I was on the verge of leaving Osijek and taking a leisurely drive back to Zagreb when I and my producer, Kirsty Lang, heard that fighting had broken out in Tenja. We travelled towards the northern entrance to the village from Osijek just by the housing estate known as 'Jug 11'. Less than a mile from the edge of New Tenja, we were stopped by the Croat police. They informed us that a bitter battle was being fought in the village and we would have to wait if we wanted to go on. This suited both Kirsty and myself admirably. We could observe from the columns of rising smoke and the frantic activity of the ambulances screaming in and out of the village that the situation was unpleasant. Half an hour after our arrival, two cars coming from Osijek packed full with National Guardsmen screeched to a halt by the barricade. The drug of armed conflict, which transmutes ordinary men to marauding Rambos, was clearly coursing through the veins of these fighters with their headbands, tattoos and their assumption of cool. From their midst jumped Commander Glavaš, smoking his familiar brand of cigarette, Croatia Tobacco. His sharp blue eyes were projecting a critical overdose of adrenalin. After talking to the police, Glavaš said to his men: 'It's a really nasty battle, we're going in,' and off the cars shot, weaving between the right-hand and left-hand lanes theatrically in order to avoid sniper fire. An hour later, a JNA Armoured Personnel Carrier sped out of Tenja to Osijek at about sixty miles an hour. The Croat police stepped out to wave it down but the APC simply accelerated. A figure popped out of the hatch and screamed: 'We've got wounded on board!' The Croat police, uncertain, like everyone, as to the role of the army at this point, let the APC go.

Two hours later, the army sent in substantial reinforcements through Old Tenja to stop the fighting. The Serbs stopped fighting immediately as the army guaranteed that they would lose no territory to the Croats. There were some brief skirmishes between the National Guard and the army. At one point, a JNA tank fired a grenade which flew over our heads and demolished a seventh-floor flat in a tower block just on the outskirts of Osijek. It emerged later that the flat belonged to a retired JNA officer!

Travelling into New Tenja, I saw a scene of unimaginable devastation: lorries lying on their side with whole axles blown away, a burned out transit van riddled with bullet holes and soaked in blood. Either side of the road, houses were bombed out or pitted with hundreds of bullet holes. By a small café, dozens of Croat National Guardsmen lay shattered from fighting, their faces blackened and their makeshift uniforms torn – some were nursing small wounds, some were drinking brandy and several just staring into space. 'We lost at least twelve in a house down the road. It was terrible. They got caught there and were just mincemeat.' I drove on towards the line drawn by JNA vehicles. As in Glina, the tank turret turned towards me and stopped. I carried on a little further to peer down a side-street on which lay a dead dog and a dead pig, the first of many.

The following day, I returned to see Žarko and Batele in the morning. This time I went across the lines – Žarko's name serving as a passport. Tanks and APCs lurked at the bottom of every street like overgrown reptiles. Just before I reached the headquarters of the Serb fighters, I observed that a wall was daubed with a huge Cyrillic acronym indicating the Serbian Chetnik Movement). Inside the local government offices, I met for the first time one of the most insane actors in this war, Nebojša Jevrić. With the hair and thin frame of a hippy and a shotgun slung over his shoulder, he introduced himself as a journalist from the Belgrade magazine, *Duga*. Whenever a new front was launched in this war, this mad scribe, who was given to issuing blood-curdling threats to his colleagues, would be there, hoping to kill Croats in order to add perverse colour to his pieces.

Žarko took me off to see the house where the Croat National Guardsmen had been surrounded. On the way, we had to dodge snipers until protected by a row of two-storey houses. From twenty feet, I saw a village shop, half-destroyed and scarred as black as pitch by artillery fire. Outside lay the body of a guardsman whose head and arm had been obliterated, apparently by the grenade he was trying to throw.

On the straight road from Osijek to Vukovar, the contours of a distant, dreamy mirage soon reveal themselves to be those of your worst nightmare. Four figures dressed in jeans stand with two Kalashnikovs apiece jutting from their hips, while their T-shirts are patterned with grenades. Trpinja is just past Bobota, the centre of Serb extremist operations in this strategic cluster of villages. The perversity of this war is demonstrated by the fact that Bobota is one of the five richest villages in Yugoslavia, thanks to the exceptional fertility of the land tilled by its inhabitants. Most of the houses have swimming pools, while Mercedes are dotted around the main road. It is no longer possible to travel to Bobota as all unidentified vehicles are fired on without warning. If Bobota is in an advanced state of war readiness, then Trpinja is well on its way. Jeans and designer shades complement the T-shirts of the keepers of Trpinja's gate who would strike terror into the hearts of mafiosi gunmen.

I and my two passengers are pulled from my Austrian-registered car. Our passports are taken from us and I am pushed against the wall where I answer questions with a gun to my stomach and one to my head. I explain I am travelling to Belgrade. One particularly unpleasant man, who is short of three front teeth, interrogates me while his larger comrades start examining the contents of the car in minute detail. For some reason, the villagers decide that a single cassette will provide proof as to our sympathies. Fortune has rarely looked down on me with greater kindness as the tape they chance upon is dominated by an interview in Serbo-Croat with Žarko from Tenja – they could equally have chosen an interview with Glavaš! After fifteen nerve-racking minutes, the toothless boss returns and pointing to the tape says: 'It's okay, he's one of us.' The biggest, meanest goon of all sits in the passenger seat of my car. Without looking at me, he says: 'Drive. Anyone takes pictures, I'll kill them.' After a minute, he starts talking in an unexpectedly conciliatory manner. 'I must apologize that we have to put you through all that,' he began, 'but you must understand that we no longer trust anyone here any more. We know that we will all probably die fighting to defend our village but we will never let the Ustashas take it.' I had no reason to disbelieve him. 'By the way,' he finished, 'if you had been German or Austrian, it would have been a very different story.'

By early July, a division in the European Community over its response to the Yugoslav crisis was already evident. Germany, supported most vocally by a broad political spectrum in Austria, had made little secret of its sympathy for Croatia and Slovenia. This was shared neither by the British Foreign Office, whose diplomats opposed Hans-Dietrich Genscher's efforts to recognize Croatia and Slovenia, nor by the State Department in Washington. The German and Austrian positions reflected both countries' economic, cultural and historic interests in the region, but in Serbia they were perceived to represent the imperialist expansion of a unified German state into Eastern Europe. Colloquially, Germany was now referred to in Serbia as 'The Fourth Reich', while many Serbs believed Tudman to be a German puppet whose ideology reflected a natural German inclination towards fascism. This was utter nonsense but it was nonsense which a large number of men with heavy weaponry believed, and so German citizens were taking a big risk by travelling around Serb areas. There was a parallel anti-British sentiment in Croatia, especially in the crisis areas, but it was slower to develop and never assumed the conspiratorial proportions that the Serb perception of the German position did.

Notwithstanding Serbia's exaggerated response, the German insistence on recognition was critically flawed. Eventually, Germany applied enormous pressure on the British and the French to accept EC recognition of Slovenia and Croatia. Recognition did not stop the fighting between Croat forces, on the one hand, and the JNA and Serb irregulars, on the other. The fighting was stopped in accordance with a ceasefire agreement negotiated by Cyrus Vance, the UN Special Envoy to Yugoslavia, contained in a broader framework which included the dispatch of UN peace troops to the disputed territories in Croatia. Not only did recognition fail to stop the fighting, it had no significant impact on the core of the problem in Croatia – the Serbian question. The issue which provoked war in the first place remains a matter of seemingly irreconcilable dispute. The Vance plan at least meant that the conflict in the crisis areas would be frozen until a proper political solution could be found. It places on the UN troops an unenviable burden of administering territories where there are mixed populations and two central authorities demanding the setting up of administrations which are mutually exclusive.

By the time such arguments reached the fighters in Trpinja, they boiled down to the fact that I was not German and as a result, I am still alive. I was allowed through the barricade at the other end of Trpinja with grace because I was accompanied by Mr Big who shook my hand and wished me and my passengers well.

On the outskirts of Vukovar, we stopped at a café – here were the same monsters with the same murderous intent as our inquisitors in Trpinja. The difference was, of course, that these were Croats who launched into a flavoursome attack on the Chetniks. The arguments were the same, the anger was the same, the irrational beliefs were the same – Serbs and Croats in the eastern Slavonian region were trapped in the logic of mutually assured destruction, although this still prepared none of us psychologically for Vukovar.

After the unnerving experience of Trpinja, Vukovar was a welcome sight. This was the prettiest of small Danubian towns characterized by a variety of rural and urban architecture with many attractive neo-classical pillars holding up the buildings in the centre. The townspeople were visibly nervous. Borovo Selo, the centre for Serb extremist operations, was but two and a half miles from Vukovar's centre, while the military could target the city from various directions with ease. Heavy artillery was positioned across the river in Vojvodina, to the south, to the north and to the south-west. Already Croatian access to Vukovar was limited to a tortuous route from the neighbouring town of Vinkovci nine miles away. Similarly, Serbs in Vukovar felt under pressure from the aggressive representatives of the HDZ controlling the town, especially the local Interior Minister, Tomislav Merčep, whose reputation for brutality grew as did the struggle, such that President Tuđman eventually decided to pull him out of eastern Slavonia because he gave the Croats such a bad reputation. Tuđman tried to do the same with Glavaš later on but failed because of Glavaš influence.

After our brief visit to Vukovar, we headed towards Vojvodina, passing through Šarengrad and Ilok. Three months hence, the Croat inhabitants of Ilok would be given an ultimatum by the JNA to evacuate their town, which is well known for the large number of wooden buildings. If they did not voluntarily join the hundreds of thousands of distraught Serb and Croat refugees who had already been chased from their homes, the JNA would bomb it from the air, from the Danube and from the eastern bank in Vojvodina. They left. After them, so did Ilok's Hungarians. As late as March 1992, the Slovak inhabitants of Ilok (Vojvodina and eastern Slavonia boast one of the densest mixes of Central European peoples) contacted the Czechoslovak ambassador in Belgrade in desperation as they were being threatened and cajoled by JNA officers to abandon their homes as the officers were planning to move Serb refugees into them.

Just outside Ilok on the Croat side of the 25. Maj bridge which spans the Danube and separates Slavonia from Vojvodina, a Croat policeman sat in his squad car, observing the two APCs and one tank which squatted on the Vojvodina side of the bridge. When I arrived in Belgrade, I turned on the radio to hear that a JNA tank had flattened the Croat police squad car on the western end of the 25. Maj bridge. The policeman was killed instantly.

There is a secret history to Vukovar before the siege of the town began in early August – there were considerable tensions in the town between Serbs and Croats, yet the details remain mysteriously vague. I only visited the town one more time. That was on the second day of the siege in early August. I travelled by Vinkovci in convoy with Marc Champion from the *Independent*. We arrived in Vinkovci which had itself taken a steady battering from the army and Serb irregulars stationed in a village suburb, Mirkovci. The air was clouded with the dull thud of regular artillery and tank fire, some of it landing on Vinkovci, most on Vukovar. At the press centre, we were told that the news from Vukovar was encouraging: two hundred soldiers had lost their lives in the first thirty-six hours of fighting. JNA losses throughout eastern Slavonia were exceptionally high during the fighting, but such a figure was a fine example of Croat wishful thinking. Marc and I were told we could travel to the tiny village of Bogdanovci, which is within one and a half miles of Vukovar, at our own risk. Here we could discuss entry to Vukovar with the local National Guard.

We arrived at this tiny village which was buzzing with National Guard activity. Enormous blasts from JNA tanks a few fields away accompanied our discussion with the local commander who said we could travel across the cornfields at our own risk. He would take us as far as the outskirts and then we would be on our own. At this point, a red Opel coming from Vukovar screeched to a halt. The driver said that the bombardments and the fighting around the barracks and the police station had intensified and that the situation had become exceptionally dangerous. Marc and I discussed the matter and decided against going to Vukovar – later on we admitted to each other how often and how deeply we regretted that decision. We had travelled to the edge of a crime without parallel in post-war Europe. It was our duty to report the precise details about Vukovar but we were too scared. Regardless of the complex causes of the Yugoslav crisis, the JNA and Serb irregulars must be condemned for the wholesale destruction of this town for no apparent purpose. The exhilaration of Serb fighters and many civilians at the news of Vukovar's liberation can be to an extent explained by ignorance. But anybody who believes that you can liberate a pile of useless ruins which you yourself have created needs remedial education in semantics.

I returned to Osijek many times in the next few months. In late August I travelled to Sarvaš, the last village to the north-east of Osijek which was still being contested by the JNA and the National Guard. As I drove out of Osijek, a light rain accentuated the cold, blustery afternoon. On the edge of the village was a Croat gun nest. They said I could go and look at my own risk. Slowly I drove through the village, seeing the now familiar patterns of destruction. One old woman wandered out into the front garden of her house, which was riddled with bullet holes. I reached the point of no return. This was the Catholic church whose spire had become famous after it was filmed being blown away by a mortar and cannon attack. Opposite the church was a shop and café, bombed and burnt to the ground. I got out and looked around. Dead pigs. In the distance, I could just make out the Serb-manned barricade at the other end of the village. A MiG jet swooped down low, crushing the silence and bursting my ear-drums. Terrified, I ducked and for a few seconds remained immobile with fear before leaping into my car. Gunfire burst out around me while grenades began falling. I revved the car and pulled out the clutch suddenly so that the vehicle would shoot forward unexpectedly. One spray of auto-matic fire caught the left-hand side of the car, whose fuel tank was mercifully on the right-hand side. I reached the Croat gun nest, where one soldier leapt out and asked if I was injured. I told him I was just shaken, upon which he screamed: 'Then just get out!'

A couple of months later after Sarvaš had become the last of these villages on the Vukovar road to fall to the Serbs, I visited Osijek airport which curiously was still under Croat control despite being surrounded by dozens of JNA tanks. The commander of the small National Guard platoon took me to the roof of the control tower building. From here, the strategic value of the villages became clear: Sarvaš, Bijelo Brdo, Vera, Trpinja, Bobota, Silaš, Celje (the one Croat village which had been thoroughly plundered by Serbs) and, finally, Tenja formed a huge circle around the airport. Through his binoculars, the commander showed me where the JNA tanks were hiding behind the cornfields and the trees which lined the villages. 'I've told the JNA that if they attack the airport, then we'll blow up all the jet fuel,' he said. Thereupon he brought out a map of the airport showing the extent of the underground fuel reservoir – this lay in channels under Bijelo Brdo, Bobota, Silaš, Celje and part of Tenja. 'If they attack, the fuel goes up and takes their villages with it,' he concluded. He then showed me the bombs which he had planted on the pump system. I was never able to establish whether this was a Croatian fantasy tactic or whether the jet fuel represented a real threat.

Within a month of the war's outbreak, Croats had become completely committed to the defence of their republic's borders as defined by Tito's Yugoslavia. The greatest political threat to Tuđman came not from the opposition, all of whom joined a new coalition government of Franjo Greguric, formed in August. It was the right wing of the HDZ which seemed concerned to undermine the President, who they believed was prepared to concede territory within the framework of European Community negotiations. Tens of thousands of Croat men had responded to the call-up which in some areas was compulsory. In contrast to the mobilization of reservists which was ordered in Serbia and Montenegro, the Croatian government found little if any resistance to its mobilization orders except, of course, among the Serb minority who were ordered to join the National Guard in parts of the republic. Not only were the Croats willing to fight, they fought exceptionally bravely and for the most part effectively, destroying a myth rooted in the Second World War that Croats are cowards who cannot recognize one end of a gun from the other. Where Croatia suffered serious defeats, it was not usually the fault of the fighters but of the military command structure which for a long time was notoriously poorly organized. Even after the various Croat forces had been placed under the unified command of the former JNA officer, General Anton Tus, serious logistical and tactical errors continued to be made.

The intense commitment felt by most Croats was best demonstrated to me by a surreal encounter during one of Zagreb's most vaunted air raids. Much evidence suggests that the air raid warnings were given in order to promote a war psychosis among Zagreb's population. If this was the aim, it was successful. One night, I was walking through the city centre in search of a drink with Hermann Tersch, the brilliant East European correspondent of *El Pais*. The sirens began wailing and within thirty seconds all the lights in Zagreb had been extinguished. The sky was overclouded, leaving Hermann and me completely blind – we could see literally nothing. After a long day, we were determined to find a drink. During the air raids, all restaurants and drinking establishments were closed down. However, Hermann has a robotic ability, enabling him to detect functioning watering holes in the most adverse conditions. Using his uncanny sixth sense, we felt our way to a small square just below Ilica street which leads on to Ban Jelačić square. Through an open gate and across a courtyard we crept along until we reached a narrow lane where stood an oasis of light in the black desert. In we strode to order our whiskies. Slowly scanning the bar, it became clear that this was the local frequented by the junkies of Croatia's capital. Every guest was drugged to the eye-balls. We saw one member of the National Guard slumped across his automatic weapon in a catatonic state. The guests may have heard the air raid warning but they had no intention, or were not capable, of taking any notice of it. Hermann and I struck up a conversation with a junkie, one of whose eyes appeared to have detached itself from the socket – it floated this way and that without any apparent coordination. Talking half in Serbo-Croat and half in English, this young man, who could not have been more than a few weeks away from a sad, self-inflicted death, just managed to get his message across to us. 'If they get the chance, the Serb Chetniks will kill us all. We must all fight the Chetniks to save our homeland. Our homeland is being attacked – you must tell the world so Croatia can survive.'

I was in Zagreb on another gloomy August day when a shooting incident took place involving Serb paramilitaries and the Bosnian police from Velika Kladuša, which is just across the Croatian–Bosnian border south of Zagreb on the edge of Petrova Gora, a range of hills which was among the most impenetrable Partizan strongholds during the Second World War. I decided to visit Velika Kladuša and the larger town of Bihać in Bosnia where there was a military airport and large JNA barracks to gauge the situation there. This involved crossing Serb–Croat lines just south of Karlovac. This proud military city had suffered some damage when shooting between the JNA headquarters and local Croat militia broke out, but it was generally still untainted by the fighting in August – Karlovac would be devastated later.

At the Karlovac town hall we were informed that the situation a mile or so out of town was unpredictable. Croat forces were in control of the road until just beyond the Kupa river which forms Karlovac's southern boundary. As we approached the Croat barricade, we joined a small queue of cars, filled with desperate people who, for some unfortunate reason, were destined to commute between the Serb-controlled areas and Karlovac. We were all waved through without difficulty. A mile further on, the straight road sinks steeply as it skirts the northern tip of Petrova Gora. The Serb front line was positioned by a lay-by next to an isolated house just beyond the dip as the road rises gently.

The Serb side of the border was a hive of operational activity as a crucial logistical process was under way. The JNA had decided to cut its losses and leave Karlovac where its men and equipment were under threat from the remarkably effective blockades which the National Guard had thrown up around them. In Varaždin, the JNA commander had surrendered the entire barracks and its contents to the National Guard which was able to begin the formation of its first tank and heavy artillery brigades. Two JNA barracks immediately south of Zagreb were threatened by the National Guard tactics: Jastrebarsko and Karlovac. The latter was evacuated first, while the former went in accord with a later agreement brokered by the European Community.

On the Karlovac front line, there were some large stationary JNA vehicles whose function appeared to be merely to intimidate rather than anything more sinister. The JNA took but a cursory glance at our papers but members of the Martićevci waved us into the lay-by where they were checking every vehicle and its passengers. With the usual swing of the automatic gun, we were ushered out of the car which was then thoroughly searched as we stood under the watchful eye of the barrel. 'Where are you going?' said the militia captain whose cap was adorned with the four Cyrillic Cs. 'We are travelling to see the Prime Minister of the Krajina Government, Mr Babić,' I lied, suspecting that there was little way they could have checked whether Babić was expecting us a hundred miles away. At that point communications among Serbs throughout Krajina and Lika were still poor. Babić was still the idol of all Serb fighters, such that if invoked with sufficient authority, his name alone could open doors. After staring at our passports for a minute, he returned them and with a nonchalant flick of his head muttered: '*Hajde!*' ('Get going!').

Although not especially fertile, the region is covered by rich grassland and deciduous trees. The hills look luscious but they also provide ideal hiding places for guerillas – Partizans swarmed throughout Kordun during the Second World War harrying the Ustashas. The Serb villagers of Petrova Gora provided them with shelter and food. Dotted around the Partizan strongholds were some Ustasha centres from where the Croats launched what were often futile forays against the Partizans. As we passed through the villages of northern Kordun, the Croat villages were easily identifiable. They were empty, a few windows smashed here and there, with only a single dead pig on this occasion. Most of the inhabitants had just run and left since the Martićevci and the JNA had secured their positions along this main road south. Every single road sign had the Serbian Cross scrawled on it or simply the words *Ovo je Srbija* ('This is Serbia'), written in Cyrillic. The Serb villages were easy to recognize because life continued in them as normal. This was an eerie pattern, indeed.

There were no other vehicles on the road except for a regular stream of empty tank transporters coming towards us while we overtook large numbers of personnel carriers and transporters loaded with tanks travelling south. Just below Slunj, thirty miles south of Karlovac, before one reaches the tourist attraction, the Plitvice lakes, the JNA has one of its largest installations in Yugoslavia. The army was shifting all its hardware from Karlovac to this base. How they were able to pass through Slunj, I do not know as this was one of the best-defended Croat towns of all. Their passage may have been negotiated as part of the agreement regulating the evacuation of Karlovac.

Halfway between Karlovac and Slunj, we were stopped by a Krajina patrol. We were directed into a lay-by. The two policemen behaved like traffic police. They were correct and thorough. But there were five Serb reservists from the JNA with them who had evidently been brutalized by the war. After we had gone through the initial interrogation, the first policeman walked off to radio something from his vehicle. One of the reservists with long, straggly hair was lying on a mound of sand. He stood up and, noticing Kirsty, he shouted: 'Leave the girl here.' I pretended not to hear but he approached the car with another vile-looking colleague. As an unpleasant smile began to crack the line of his face, he repeated: 'I said leave the girl here, motherfucker.' At this point the policeman returned from his car, handed back our passports and said: 'Get going,' before turning to the reservists and saying: 'Leave it out.' A woman was taking a big risk by crossing into occupied Krajina, peopled by war-mad, rapacious Serbian reservists.

We turned off just before Slunj on to the road towards Velika Kladuša which is in the north-western wedge of Bosnia. A few empty villages were sprinkled along this road until, to my great surprise, we came to one where a Croat flag blew defiantly from the top of the church. Below this sat a very old man but other than that the village appeared deserted. This was Cetingrad, a Croat nationalist stronghold. I asked the man if anything had happened in the village. He looked as if he had been brainwashed and he repeated a single phrase over and over, *'Ništa neznam'* ('I know nothing'). Before and after Cetingrad, I saw ten manned machine-gun nests – I no longer cared who they belonged to and whether they had seen any action. I simply smiled at all the gunners, hoping that they would not act hastily. It worked and with a great sigh of relief, Kirsty and I arrived in Velika Kladuša.

The return journey to Karlovac was similar but we succeeded in reaching Zagreb unharmed. A week later, two Polish journalists visited the mayor of Vrginmost, a village on the Kordun–Banija border. Although guests of the local Serb leader, they were picked up by a group of terrifying Chetniks in the village who took them prisoner, confiscated all their belongings including their car and threatened to kill them, before the Polish ambassador was able to intercede and save their lives. They were finally dumped at the army headquarters in Banja Luka, almost paralysed with fear. Kirsty and I were not only stupid, we were fortunate. Twenty-two journalists were killed during the first nine months of fighting in Yugoslavia, while four went missing presumed dead. From the beginning of the conflict, journalists were even prized targets. Some were killed by the JNA, some were killed by the Chetniks, some were killed by the Croats, some were killed accidentally by driving over mines. Journalists were fodder like the villagers and other innocents.

The posthumous mutilation of Croatian policemen in Borovo Selo provided a most public announcement that the forthcoming war would be grisly. Prior warning, however, did nothing to blunt the shock of being confronted with countless examples of unspeakable brutality.

The spiral of nationalist violence between Serbs and Croats began before the war. The HDZ's campaign of sacking Serbs was in some regions accompanied by the confiscation of rented accommodation. From about May 1991 onwards, Serb property, especially in the crisis regions under Croat control, became the target of regular bomb attacks while the Serbs who remained were frequently ostracized by the Croats. In Croat nationalist strongholds like Split, open intimidation was reported much earlier. Soon after the 1990 elections, right-wing organizations, such as the Ustasha Youth and the Black Legions, embarked upon modestly successful recruiting campaigns among the young and unemployed. Returning Croat émigrés, who had afforded the HDZ considerable financial help, contributed substantially to hostility towards Serbs. Some hardline émigrés, like the Canadian pizza-parlour owner turned Croat

Defence Minister, Gojko Šušak, exerted great influence on Croat government policies. As a rule, émigrés from Yugoslavia who were free to nurture their prejudices outside their home country were less forgiving towards their traditional enemies than those who were confronted with the delicate reality of relations between nationalities. Once the war began, every Serb in areas under Croatian control knew that he or she was under threat, particularly as the gruesome tales of Serbian atrocities against Croat civilians began to emerge from the shadowy kingdom of the Krajina.

The Serb 'émigrés' who encouraged a fanatical war were of a different kind. These were the 'Serbs from outside Serbia', meaning those Serbs who were from Croatia, Bosnia or elsewhere in Yugoslavia. Almost all those who bayed loudest for retribution against Tuđman's administration and the Croats in general hailed from outside Serbia. Milošević himself was raised in Požarevac in Serbia but he comes from an old Montenegrin family. The Operational Commander of the JNA, General Blagoje Adžic, was from Croatia where, during the Second World War, the Ustashas killed his entire family. The former Defence Minister, General Veljko Kadijević, was born to a Serbian father and a Croat mother in the Lika region of Croatia. The present Serbian Defence Minister, General Marko Negovanović, a former head of military intelligence, KOS, with one of the most effective networks in the whole conflict, is a Serb from Macedonia. The most hawkish member of the Serbian government, Budimir Košutić, advocated a crusade of retribution against Croats. As a child in Croatia, Košutić watched how his father was told to divide his children into two groups, one group would be shot, the other allowed to live. Mirko Jović, the head of the White Eagles, was a *došljak* in Vojvodina while Vojislav Šešelj, the leader of Serbia's Chetniks, was born in Eastern Hercegovina, one of the militant Serb regions in Yugoslavia.

Thus were the memories of the Ustasha–Partizan–Chetnik war revived after sinking in a distorted, collective sub-conscious for four decades. The war of 1991 ensured that the disease of hatred would survive to infect another generation. There is no sense attempting to apportion blame for the vile, murderous activities of the Serb and Croat extremists, for once the logic of conflict had passed the point of no return, the massacres were inevitable. Both sides must be condemned loudly for the excesses which at the time of writing are still being perpetrated and even encouraged by the highest authorities. Croatia's claim that it was committed to the most democratic European spirit was laughable immediately after the elections when Zagreb refused to take the fears of the Serb minority seriously. Even before the war began, the government was concerned to hush up nationalist-motivated crimes against its Serb population while when applying for recognition, its police and soldiers were involved in the slaughter of innocent Serbs in Gospić, Ogulin, Sisak, Karlovac, Daruvar, Virovitice, Zagreb and elsewhere. The victims were the so-called 'loyal' Serbs who had not crossed over to the JNA or the Krajina Serbs. These urban Serbs were among the greatest victims of the war, whose plight, however, is one of the least well known. Tens of thousands were hounded from their homes in the big cities either through direct intimidation, expulsion or through the pervasive climate of fear. The Croatian media, first and foremost HTV (Hrvatska Televizija), positively gloated over reports of massacred Croats while acting as eager accomplices in the cover-ups about crimes against Serbs. Apologists for the Croatian government argue tirelessly that such incidents have been exaggerated but that also any excesses were provoked by the relentless Serbian aggression and the much greater crimes perpetrated by the other side. Such arguments are morally redundant: if the Croatian government is to be accepted as a democratic government, it must ensure the safety and lives of its own citizens, all the more so if these are being threatened by legal representatives of the Croatian state. The tendency to justify atrocities by pointing to those committed by the opposing side will merely ensure that the pattern of reciprocal massacre remains unbroken. Ironically, the greatest victims of the respective nationalisms have been those Serbs and Croats who live under the administration of the other nation.

There are many well-documented massacres perpetrated by the Serbian forces during the conflict. The levelling of a whole town, street by street, house by house, makes Vukovar the most flawed jewel in this crown of shame. But how can one comprehend the evil insanity of the nationalist organization, *Dušan Silni* (Dušan the Mighty), who forced the Croat villagers in Lovas on the border between eastern Slavonia and Vojvodina to walk across a minefield?

How does one forgive the joint JNA–Chetnik operation in northern Kordun which began in early October? The bodies of dozens of Croat villagers were left putrefying in the open for a week before the local JNA commanders allowed the Croat Red Cross in to collect the corpses. JNA artillery bombed little boats containing frightened men, women and children fleeing across the Kupa from the notorious Chetnik units from Loznica and Valjevo in Central Serbia. What solace is left to the families of the twenty-four aged people in Vocin and Hum, two harmless villages in western Slavonia, who were slaughtered by the retreating Chetnik monsters, determined to leave a trail of scorched humanity in their wake?

One of the most revealing conversations I had during the war was with a Macedonian officer in the Yugoslav army who had deserted. His tank unit was based in the eastern Macedonian town of Štip:

On 17 September, we were told we were going to Pirot [a military garrison in south-east Serbia near the Bulgarian border]. But after seventeen hours we were disgorged on the front in Bobota near Osijek. We were then taken to the Laszlovo front [Laszlovo is a mixed Hungarian-Croat village south of Tenja and Bobota which was contested bitterly by both sides for the entire duration of the war]. I refused to go to the front and demanded to be released from my duties which was my legal right because we had been misinformed about our task. I was arrested and taken to Bobota where a field prison had been set up. Here I was screamed at, spat at, racially abused, they called me a Bulgarian and VMRO fascist and then they told me I was going to be killed. They did not actually touch me but they were on the verge of doing so when some colleagues from Štip, Serbs in the military police, intervened and prevented things from getting worse. They told me that I must either go to the front or they would have to leave me with the Chetniks in Bobota. They said they could do no more, so I returned to the front. We were under permanent attack there from the direction of Čepin [a village just south of Osijek on the main road into the city].

The army was badly equipped and totally unprepared for the type of war they were fighting. The Croat weaponry was invariably superior to ours. They had extraordinary German guns for their snipers which kept us almost permanently at bay. Both sides were constantly breaking the cease-fires which were a waste of time. However, there was a difference in motivation. Most of the JNA soldiers just wanted to go home alive, while the reservists who came mostly from Vojvodina, Hungarians and Serbs, rebelled in whole units, running away and mutinying. Croats were excused duty on the front line although I suspect this was because the commanders were afraid of treachery rather because of any respect they may have had for the Geneva Convention or anything like that.

I was there when one reserve unit arrived in the middle of the night. They had no idea where they were, they were forced to sleep in the wet and the cold open air. But worst of all, they had been sent to this bloody front *without weapons*!

There were a plethora of different uniforms on the Serb lines: Chetniks, who were kept at a distance from the JNA, and Arkanovci who were organized in special units to go into the villages when the defences had collapsed and clean up and take prisoners. There was tremendous tension between the JNA, the reservists, the non-Serbs in the JNA and the Serbs, the locals, the Arkanovci, and the Chetniks. For example, some Croats who stayed in Stara Tenja were killed by the Arkanovci provoking bitter protests from the local Serbs. But there was just as much tension on the Croat side between the Zengas (National Guard) and the MUP (special police), the latter being better paid, better organized and better fighters while the former were not only badly disciplined they were also on drugs and drinking a lot. If ever we took a Croat position, there was always evidence of much drug taking. Mutual slaughter occurred on both sides. In Karadžićevo, the Croats slaughtered a large group of aged Serbs, while in one incident in a village taken by the Serbs, the Chetniks threw a grenade into a bomb shelter where fifteen Croat civilians had taken refuge.

Another thing was that JNA soldiers informed the Croats. I was in Silaš when a mortar attack began at 15.00. The attack failed miserably as the tanks were in hidden positions. At 18.00 four grenades fell precisely on one hidden tank killing the three occupants inside. No other grenades fell. An attack like this could only have been carried out with inside information and a military investigation later established who had done this but I don't know what happened to him.

As an officer, I was given the chance to visit home one weekend at the end of October and I simply didn't return, so I am now classified as a deserter. The army may be preparing to move out of Macedonia but deserters here are still being picked up.

Serbs and Croats in eastern Slavonia can never live together because too much blood has been spilt and the Serbs will never let go of any of this territory. As far as I could work out, the Croats had provoked a lot of the nastiness in the first place but searching for the one who started it is a waste of time. Once it had started the massacres were unstoppable. It will never end whether they have a ceasefire, peace-keeping troops or whatever. This is not a war, this is extermination.

While working in the suffocating heat of a Belgrade summer, I was granted an interview with the President of Serbia, Slobodan Miloše-vić, who rarely deigned to speak to the foreign press. (Whereas Milošević made the mistake of not speaking enough to the foreign press, President Tuđman's error was the exact opposite: so frequently did he hold press conferences and interviews that he was forever shooting himself in the foot, leaving his long-suffering advisers to tend to the wound.) I was told of the interview half an hour before it was due to begin and after a terrible rush across Belgrade in the steaming heat to find a decent pair of trousers and a tie, I squeezed into an illegal parking space five minutes' walk from the President's office. Sweating and ruffled, I was then obliged to wait some forty-five minutes as the Great Man prepared to receive me. When introduced to him, I was immediately struck by how short he was, before my eyes were drawn to his extraordinary ears. When I introduced myself in Serbo-Croat, he drew back a little surprised, 'Oh, you speak Serbian?' Instead of commending me on learning this as most Serbs do, he asked: 'Why did you learn Serbian?' I explained to him that I had done some post-graduate study in Prague where I learned Czech and since acquainting myself with Yugoslavia, I had taught myself Serbo-Croat as an adjunct to my understanding of the country. A Serb nationalist would have immedi-ately warmed to a Serbian speaker – an autocrat like Milošević, however, felt uncomfortable with it.

The interview was conducted in English. He said nothing of any news value except that the Croatian government represented a resurrection of fascism. Unlike President Tuđman, he was not intimidated by a single question as each one was used as a platform to reiterate his main points: Croatia is guilty and has acted unconstitu-tionally, the positions of Serbia and Yugoslavia are absolutely correct and the only victims of this war are the Serbs. There was no more. The overall impression was much more effective than Tuđman's best effort. The most abiding feature, however, was the complete absence of anything resembling feeling or humanity in his attitude. Off the record at the end of the interview, I asked him whether Serbia still had any objections to Slovene independence (at this time the three-month moratorium on secession stipulated by the Brioni Accord was still in force and the official position of Yugoslavia and the JNA was that Slovenia must remain in the federation). 'Pah,' he sniffed, 'none whatsoever, the Slovenes can go whenever they like. There's nothing to stop them now.' Slovenia no longer held any special interest for Milošević. Instead he was interested in the tracts of fertile land, particularly in eastern Slavonia, populated in part by Croatia's rural Serbs.

In October while the sun was still warming the battlefields of Croatia, I decided to visit Novi Pazar, the capital of the Sandžak. This region which straddles southern Serbia and the north-eastern corner of Montenegro is named after an administrative unit of the Ottoman empire. Over 200,000 Slav Moslems live here, forming a bridge built unintentionally by the Turks between the Moslems of Bosnia-Hercegovina and the Albanian Moslems of Kosovo.

When you drive into Novi Pazar (the name means New Bazaar), you are funnelled into a narrow lane along which you have to fight with pigs and geese for space. On either side, an unbelievable number of shops are squeezed into a tiny space. They are mainly cafés and *ćevabdžinica*, sweet shops – selling everything from deli-cious fresh baklava to horrible stale Mars Bars – butchers, shoe shops and clothes shops. Most shop fronts have their wares dangling down from their awnings. The smells and sounds are uncompromis-ingly oriental, except that many young people have adopted western habits of dress and of just hanging loose. The narrow lane leads to a bridge after which the road broadens a little before a large car park surrounded by rather bland buildings. After the promise of the narrow lane, the centre of Novi Pazar is not just disappointing, it is depressing. As I emerged from my car talking English to my colleague, Laura Silber, from the *Financial Times*, a young Moslem turned to me and screamed, 'You. English. Wrong,' and spat on the ground with as much venom as he could muster. Just as the Serbs in Trpinja would not tolerate Germans, so the Moslems of Novi Pazar believed all British people were committed supporters of British policy in Yugoslavia. Germany was king among the Moslems here while the British were dirt.

A valuable object of serious study would be the hotels of Eastern Europe built under the communist regimes. In contrast to so many other buildings which are the same in Warsaw as they are in Tirana, East European architects were apparently given free rein when asked to design hotels. The goal, it seems, was to design the most outlandishly ugly structure while sticking to an essentially futurist concept. The results are staggering eye-sores which are none the less emphatically unique. The Hotel Vrbak in Novi Pazar is an exquisite specimen. Two large hexagons, each with its own bizarre atrium, have been joined together on two sides like a concrete Siamese twin. The exterior and interior follow the pattern of all other hotels: the colours are brown and depressing, complemented by the wilting plants which stand in shingle close to the reception area. Despite this, the colours are never drab enough to disguise the shoddy furniture, the broken lamps, the leaking pipes and the smell of urine in places you least expect it. The Vrbak is a prince among such hotels.

Madness is a permanent mood in post-communist Yugoslavia, but I am none the less dumbfounded when my old acquaintance, Slavko, walks into the hotel. Four years ago, I would have said friend, but over the past two years, Slavko has developed a bad case of virulent nationalism and an unswerving belief in Milošević. I duck to avoid him. Much as I would have liked to know what on earth Slavko was up to in Novi Pazar, I could not face listening to another of his Serbian sermons. Slavko is a first-class *muvator*, a wheeler-dealer without parallel. He buys and sells illegal factories, keeps his entire work-force happy and contributes much to the Serbian economy. But having got religion, he had begun to harangue me publicly for my critical position on Milošević and Serbian intentions in the Balkans in general. Despite his politics, however, Slavko's presence in Novi Pazar testifies to the town's ability to attract the low life of all nationalities. Slavko hates the Moslems almost as much as he hates the Albanians and the Croats – but he knows that the Moslems of Novi Pazar run the best money market in the whole of Yugoslavia. Apart from being a potential arena of war if the fighting between Moslems and Serbs in Bosnia runs out of control, more money changes hands daily in Novi Pazar than anywhere else in the country.

That night, Laura and I went to investigate the money market. The rates for hard currency were substantially more attractive than they were in Belgrade, Sarajevo or Zagrèb. The traditional money dealers in the big cities, especially in Belgrade, were Albanians from Kosovo, but here they were Moslems. We sat down in a café. It stank of human detritus, the beer was undrinkable and there was not a single sober or sane soul in the bar to talk to.

I was beginning to despair of the Novi Pazar population until the next day, I went to meet officials from the SDA (the Party of Democratic Action). This was the sister organization in Serbia of the larger SDA in Bosnia-Hercegovina. The Moslems of the Sand-žak had decided to organize their own referendum for political autonomy from Belgrade – they were as aggrieved, as distressed and as fearful of the future as the rest of Yugoslavia's nations. Their main leader, Suleiman Ugljanin, is unfairly regarded as something of a lunatic. The men who I spoke to in Novi Pazar were intelligent and measured in their political outlook. They had scrupulously gathered statistics detailing the discrimination which they suffered at the hands of the Serbs and were more careful to document their grievances than many other minorities. One could not help being sympathetic, but the overwhelming impression which Novi Pazar left on me was that it was not just Yugoslavia which was falling apart. Every region inside Yugoslavia had fallen prey to the political leprosy. The concept of statehood had gone haywire and although the right to self-determination is entirely legitimate, the nations of Yugoslavia were in danger of dicing themselves to such a degree that the Balkans as an economic and social region would find it very difficult to function.

While I was in Novi Pazar, the JNA was completing one of its most unforgiving attacks in Croatia: they were encircling the port of Dubrovnik from all sides, including from the sea. To prepare for their assault on Dubrovnik, they had ripped their way through several strips of coastal land which were effectively undefended. European Community monitors were attempting desperately to negotiate a ceasefire between the Croat defenders of Du-brovnik and their JNA attackers. At the same time, a pack of journalists was attempting fruitlessly to enter by ship from the north, while another pack sat in Herceg-Novi, where the last JNA headquarters on the Montenegrin coast before Croatia was stationed. After reaching Titograd (the capital of Montenegro whose old name, Podgorica, has since been restored) Laura and I decided to travel onwards to Herceg-Novi in the hope of being allowed into Dubrovnik.

The sky was a glorious blend of deep blue and dashing red as we set off from Titograd towards the Montenegrin coast. This road which crosses the marshland on the very northern tip of Lake Shkoder is one of the most beautiful drives imaginable. In contrast to the barren hinterland around Knin, the mountains which rise steeply from the western edge of the lake are adorned with a ravishing palate of matte red and green flora – a fitting preparation for the resplendent Dalmatian coast. Almost immediately after the peak has been reached, the road plunges down thousands of feet towards Petrovac whose lights twinkle cosily in the twilight. The drive north along the coast towards Herceg-Novi passes by a tight knot of exquisite little resorts – Sveti Stefan, Miločer and Budva – three little protrusions off the coast boasting a cluster of little white houses covered by light red tiles. They overlook pristine, sandy beaches and a rich blue sea. At night the air is warm and thick with the luscious smell of pine while crickets and other bugs click, rattle and purr all night. There is no need to eat lotus leaves to become trapped here.

Our reverie was terminally disturbed as we drove through Tivat towards the ferry which would take us across the bay of Kotor. Hundreds of Montenegrin reservists were returning from the Dubrovnik front in open-backed lorries waving Yugoslav flags, pictures of Montenegro's great nineteenth-century hero, Njegoš, and firing guns wildly into the air. These were part of the mob which had scorched the earth along the last tapering twenty kilometres of Croatia – Konavle.

The Serbian and Yugoslav authorities were determined to integrate the tiny republic of Montenegro in its military operation inside Croatia. They encountered little difficulty persuading the political leadership in Titograd to back their programme as President Momir Bulatović had invariably supported Slobodan Milošević's position during the discussions between the republican presidents during 1991 and 1992. Bulatović leads Montenegro's Communist

Party which, together with the opposition National Party, identifies itself with *srpstvo*, a concept which insists that Montenegrins are ethnically, linguistically and politically inextricably linked with Serbia. Roughly two-thirds of Montenegro's 500,000 strong population adheres to the idea of *srpstvo*, while a third is resolutely committed to the idea of *crnogorstvo* which insists that the two peoples have quite distinct historical and political traditions which cannot be reconciled. One of *srpstvo*'s most vociferous contemporary supporters is Branko Kostić who took control of the rump Yugoslav Presidency as it was abandoned first by the Slovene Janez Drnovšek, then by its Croat president, Stipe Mesić, and finally by the Macedonian Vasil Tupurkovski and the Bosnian, Bogić Bogićević. Kostić turned the Presidency into an entirely reliable instrument for Milošević and the JNA leadership to wield as and how they wished. He also helped to commit Montenegro's resources to the war in Croatia, although just as Serbia denied any participation in the war, so did Montenegro.

Despite this firm political bond, President Bulatović had also to consider the resistance to the war which surfaced very swiftly when thousands of Montenegrin reservists were mobilized. Many of these were sent up to the western and eastern Slavonian fronts and many died. Among Serbs from central Serbia, there is a widespread belief that the war in Croatia was not theirs and they had no reason to fight it. The rejection of the war aims was reflected in the massive incidence of desertion and call-up evasion. In Belgrade, when a mass mobilization of reservists was ordered, only 10 per cent of those liable responded. At the time, thousands of young men in Belgrade were sleeping in different flats and houses every night to avoid the call-up. The inability of the opposition to turn anti-war sentiment into a valuable political instrument did not mean that this sentiment just disappeared – Serbia found it very difficult to motivate young Serbs in the numbers needed for what was an exceptionally labour-intensive conflict.

When stories and rumours began circulating that hundreds of Montenegrin reservists were being killed by the day in the north of Croatia, resistance to the war developed even more swiftly in Montenegro than it had in Serbia. President Bulatović was aware that given the unpredictable behaviour of Montenegro's social psychology once it had been aroused from its usual state of catatonic indolence, he had to do something about this. Bulatović is in his late thirties and if he plays his cards right, he could remain an influential figure in Montenegrin politics for a long time to come. The Montenegrin leadership persuaded the JNA authorities to reduce the number of reservists being deployed in the north and instead agreed to allow them to be used to push the front through Konavle to Dubrovnik. This was a brilliant tactical switch – deeply cynical, but a master-stroke none the less. The Croat resistance in Konavle was virtually non-existent. The Montenegrin reservists were sent up both from Herceg-Novi and across from Trebinje in eastern Herce-govina, which lies twenty miles east of Dubrovnik as the land rises sharply. Most of these reservists were mobilized in Nikšić, a miser-able industrial wasteland in northern Montenegro, and fabled as one of the most primitive and violent towns in Yugoslavia. The Mon-tenegrin reservists sliced through Croatia's defences with the sharp-ness of newly-tempered steel. It was a pushover and the rewards were substantial.

Herceg-Novi is a pretty resort tucked inside the mouth of the bay of Kotor. Montenegro had enjoyed a bumper summer as all the Serbs who would otherwise have holidayed on Croatia's Dalmatian coast transferred their custom to Montenegro. But by now, Herceg-Novi was peopled only by reservists and a small band of journalists. None of the Yugoslav peoples has as close a relationship with guns as the Montenegrins, who share with their Albanian neighbours to the south a primitive and extensive clan system based around a few large, influential families. The Montenegrin coast has boomed since the internationalization of Yugoslavia's tourist industry, but the hinterland remains very poor, propping up a patriarchal and intoler-ant social system which has retained certain aspects of the region's violent traditions such as the blood revenge.

After some tenacious arguments with the JNA press officer in Herceg-Novi, Laura and I managed to join a group of other journalists who would travel by bus to the Croat resort of Cavtat and then on the Red Cross boat to Dubrovnik. This was only possible because a temporary cease-fire between the JNA and the National Guard had been negotiated under the auspices of the tireless European Community monitors.

About twenty-five journalists left Herceg-Novi at seven o'clock in the morning on a commandeered bus. The village, Igalo, where Tito owned a spectacular villa, is the final resort before the border. From Igalo the road rises and Croatia begins at the crown of this hill. From the minute we crossed into Croatia, the work of the Montenegrins became all too visible. They had plundered and burned every single house. Each was pock-marked with bullets or left with gaping holes from mortars and grenades. A sign directing visitors to the Konavoski Dvori, one of the finest restaurants in Croatia, lay twisted by the side of the road. The Konavoski Dvori, to which people would travel literally hundreds of miles for a meal, was obliterated. There were no contents left in any of the houses, everything had been taken by the marauding reservists. This is what had motivated the Montenegrins and led to such a dramatic turn-around in support for the war. Videos, televisions, furniture, jewellery and material goods of all other kinds flooded into Nikšić and Titograd where the going price for a brand new video recorder was between fifty and seventy-five German marks.

Each village was a shrine to the animal instincts of these young men. At Ćilipi airport, which services Dubrovnik, they broke into the Duty Free shop and as one of them explained, 'We began the party of a lifetime. It lasted two days and two nights, we had endless roasted lamb on a huge spit and all the whisky, vodka, gin and cognac we liked. It was wonderful.' Just past the airport, a road sign welcoming visitors to Dubrovnik was bent back and scraping the ground. Scrawled in English on the reverse side were the words, 'United Kingdom of Serbia'. From the back of a Zastava hatchback, an unshaven soldier was passing out immaculate four-colour posters of Njegoš. His colleagues were distributing them around any sign, tree or house-front they could find. This was now Njegoš's country – all evidence of human creativity having been pillaged and raped. It was a full week since Konavle had been taken by the army. None the less on my return, I watched how the reservists set fire to a beautiful monastery which is one of the most impressive buildings you see as you cross the border from Montenegro – this was sacrilege on a number of levels.

Arriving in occupied Cavtat compounded my depression and revulsion at what this army was doing. The local people in this wonderful resort were cowed and frightened, queuing up for bread and nervously anticipating their further treatment at the hands of the JNA and its reservists. Some were prepared to speak. They said that in Cavtat itself, the JNA leadership had ensured that the Montenegrins did not perpetrate the same excesses as they had done along the rest of Konavle. Shops had of course been stripped of most things of value, but for the most part houses and people remained untouched, except for the thorough search for suspected members of the National Guard and the Croat police. Food, however, was a serious problem for the people of Cavtat and the military did not seem exceptionally concerned to solve the problem. The people of Cavtat were cut off from the outside world: without telephone communications, with no possibility of sending letters. To this day, they remain under occupation.

Two gunships sailed into the harbour to be moored. The sailors looked quiet. They did not display the same mad, jubilant faces as the reservists. After a wait of only an hour, we were allowed to board the Red Cross boat which duly sailed from Cavtat towards Dubrovnik. The gunboats followed us, taking a wider circle and then surveying our progress. As we passed by the resorts of Plat, Mlini and Kupari, we could see the luxury hotels from which black smoke still billowed through enormous holes which used to be roofs. The artillery of the JNA had simply pounded these innocent holiday resorts out of existence.

The make-up of the army command in this region offers a partial explanation of the wantonness of the destruction. Throughout the conflict, the army was divided into several factions, each with its own agenda. They were bound by a single common interest, the need to preserve their privileges. The Yugoslav National Army was reputed to be the fourth most powerful in Europe which in a country with a population of merely 24 million gives some idea of its significance in political life. The breakup of Yugoslavia threatened the existence of the 70,000 career officers in the army, 70 per cent of whom were Serbs or Montenegrins. The need to preserve Yugoslavia was by no means based on purely material necessities. The beliefs and ideologies of many of the commanding officers had been forged in the heat of a most appalling civil war and Tito's Yugoslavia had provided these people with a comprehensible solution. It

emerged fairly early on in the conflict, however, that although
hostility to Tuđman and his government in Croatia was widespread,
among some officers this was motivated by a commitment to
Yugoslavism while among others it was driven by Serbian nationalism. The most prominent supporters of the latter were stationed in
Banja Luka (General Nikola Uzelac, later transferred), General
Ratko Mladić in Knin and Colonels Torbica and Tarbuk in Hercegovina. Military operations which were carried out by these people
were often beyond the control of their superiors. Their tactics
indicated that not only were they fighting to save Yugoslavia, they
intended to hand retribution to a government which they were
firmly convinced was Fascist.

The most blatant example of their fanaticism took place on
6 December 1991. It was reported that Cyrus Vance, the UN Special
Envoy to Yugoslavia, had reached an understanding with Slobodan
Milošević and the Defence Minister, General Veljko Kadijević, on a
peace agreement which would envisage a cease-fire followed by the
deployment of UN troops in the three crisis areas. On the same
day, the troops surrounding Dubrovnik, where a local cease-fire
agreement was theoretically in force, launched a merciless ten-hour
attack on all parts of the port, including the historic buildings of the
old town. This completely undermined the Vance agreement. Kadijević was forced to apologize and he called for an investigation to
find out who had ordered the attack – an implicit and humiliating
admission that the Defence Minister who was also a member of the
three-man Chief of Staff did not control all his forces. Cyrus Vance
had to return to New York sadly aware that while he might well be
making real headway with Kadijević, any agreement could depend
on the will of others.

The little ferry docked at the small harbour of the old town.
Gruz, the much larger harbour around the old town and inside the
bay, had been destroyed along with all its boats by artillery fire.
The last time I had visited Dubrovnik was on 23 December 1990.
I had just spent an exhausting week monitoring the collapse of
Albanian Stalinism and my colleague, Alison Smale, and I had
decided to drive straight back to Vienna without stopping, a
twenty-four hour haul. At four o'clock in the afternoon, we cruised
along the southern approach to Dubrovnik. Despite being two days

before Christmas, it was 18°C. A giant sun was slinking behind the Adriatic horizon. Its light bounced off the sea, showering the white stone of Dubrovnik's old town with a deep shade of yellow. We stopped off for a delicious meal and simply admired the town's celestial tranquillity. I had rarely felt more content.

How dreadful was the contrast the following year. I immediately took a stroll down Stradun, the long strip of exquisite marble-like stone from where the rest of the old town rises quickly on both sides. The first thing I noticed in the steep, narrow stairways of the old town was a considerable amount of rubble, indicating that despite JNA protestations to the contrary, grenades had indeed fallen on the old town. Many more would fall during later attacks but each stone chip testifies to the philistinism of the JNA. Many Yugoslavs were angered by the international concern expressed for the fate of Dubrovnik's buildings when so many human deaths were going unnoticed. One can sympathize with this anger but Dubrovnik functions as a powerful and instructive symbol which well demonstrates just how desensitized to human values the warriors of the Yugoslav war had become. The Croat defence forces bear a share of this responsibility. They were returning fire from gun and small artillery positions on the old town walls, goading the JNA into firing on them. They were cunningly exploiting international outrage for military purposes. When one photographer attempted to record the nests on the old town walls, his camera was confiscated by the Croat National Guard and the film destroyed.

Walking up the steep stairways, the stench grabbed the back of my throat and almost caused me to vomit. The people of Dubrovnik had been without electricity and water for almost a month, batteries were in desperately short supply, and the sewage system was beginning to suffer. The Republic of Dubrovnik, one of Europe's great trading points, had a long tradition of public hygiene, having introduced Europe's first garbage collection system at the beginning of the fifteenth century. Even then, heavy fines could be imposed on citizens who polluted the town. Dubrovnik's tradition of cleanliness was placed under severe strain by the privations which the JNA operation was imposing on them. The fire brigade was distributing four litres of water per person per day to everyone in

Dubrovnik, although as the siege continued, the amount was reduced. Food distribution was handled exceptionally well and the collective response to the entire crisis was a model of social organization. The greatest enemy facing all those I spoke to, aside from the fear they felt when under attack, was boredom.

Despite everything, nobody I spoke to had even considered giving up the defence of their town. This included a number of Serbs, relations of friends of mine in Belgrade. In contrast to almost all other communities in Croat-held territory, the Serbs in Dubrovnik were fully integrated in the defence of the city while complaining of no discrimination. Indeed they were even more determined that Dubrovnik should remain independent. The history of Dubrovnik is unique in Croatia: the town and the surrounding area have a quite distinct identity from the rest of the republic as the city enjoyed its own independent statehood for many centuries. They were as affected by the crisis in 1990 and 1991 as by all others, but they retained their separate identity although their sympathy for Zagreb's cause was greatly increased by the JNA operation. I left Dubrovnik after a short while, leaving some of my colleagues on the quayside. They were preparing for a unique, depressing but extraordinary experience during which they would suffer the same privations and bombardments as the townspeople. I had to continue my journey. On this occasion, I was bound for Mostar, capital of Hercegovina where the most courageous and ruthless of all Serbs and Croats were eyeing each other across the Neretva river with the most profound loathing.

5 AUGUST 1991–MAY 1992:

Bosnia-Hercegovina – Paradise of the Damned

Šamac is a shambles. Civilians in the half-Croat, half-Bosnian town which straddles the Sava look frightened. The fighting has not reached Šamac properly, although there has been the occasional exchange of artillery between the Croat National Guard and the Yugoslav People's Army (JNA). Across the river is Bosnia, a helpless staging post for the army's aggression against Croatia. In Slavonski Šamac on the Croatian side, they scuttle rather than walk, perhaps believing that by adopting an air of urgency they will ward off the day when Šamac comes under attack. In most areas of Croatia, one can almost touch the fear in towns but in small villages, even those near the fighting, you can still see many small children running around the streets. These children are one of the most baffling sights of the war. But in Šamac there are no children on show.

The bridge at Šamac is made of iron. The arches are supported by thick girders, giving it the appearance of a railway bridge. At least ten Croat National Guardsmen are patrolling the makeshift border because although in early August nobody had yet recognized Croatia's independence, Croats already considered Yugoslavia, including Bosnia, a foreign country (except, of course, those parts of Bosnia, namely western Hercegovina and Posavina, which they regard as integral parts of Croatia's lands). My passenger is a Serb from Osijek, Professor Gordana Ajduković, so our documents are studied with considerable care although the border guards are never anything other than polite. One lane of the bridge is blocked completely by three large articulated lorries and, in case there is any doubt, the Croats have hung boards all around the bridge warning that it is mined. The mines are easy to spot as we creep by the dusty Yugoslav lorries which according to the Croats are also filled with explosives.

To enter Bosanski Šamac is to return to reality from the sinister looking-glass world of Croatia. The inhabitants shop, relax and talk, apparently unaffected by the nervousness across the river. Bosanski Šamac is populated mainly by Croats and Serbs with a small Moslem community. Yet despite sharing a national mix, few people in Šamac and other parts of Bosnia during 1991 considered the war in Croatia to have any bearing on their life-style beyond the severe economic privations which it caused. Everything here was in order inasmuch as this is possible in a republic whose inhabitants are notorious for their indolence. The traffic flow on all roads was as one would expect despite a petrol shortage. My eyes soon adjusted to the absence of Croatia's improvised military vehicles, which added a bizarre touch to the republic during the war. These were transit vans which shuffled around the battle fronts like deranged armadillos following their curious refits of reinforced metal sheets through which gun barrels peeped. But in Bosnia they vanished, of course, and the only reminders of war were the occasional convoys of JNA vehicles taking excitable reservists northwards to their baptism of fire on the lush cornfields of Slavonia.

On this sunny day in July, the steep slopes surrounding the road south from Šamac to Sarajevo were covered with trees which were green but dry. Occasionally a cottage or slightly grander house would become visible high up a hill but most people live in large villages which are distinguished by their red roof tiles and cream-coloured brickwork. They could be Italian, they could be Czech – the only thing which might identify a Bosnian village as unique is the white minaret of the mosque which shoots up in the town centre in the form of a small rocket. The nose is invariably decorated with a number of loudspeakers. According to Bosnian Moslems, the muezzins of Yugoslavia started using PA systems to call the faithful to prayer before anyone else in the Islamic world.

The Slav Moslems of Bosnia are the only nation, certainly in Europe and possibly in the world, who are nominally identified by their religion and not their language or ethnicity. Most are Slavs (Croats and Serbs) or more accurately in Bosnia's case, Catholic or Orthodox Christians, who were converted during the five centuries of Ottoman rule in Bosnia, although doubtless there is a rich mix of Turkish, Albanian, Jewish and Egyptian blood as well, given the ethnic fluidity of Ottoman imperial structures. Before the collapse of the Porte's rule, the Moslems were identifiable as the land-owning aristocracy of Bosnia, that is, they were associated with class and religion rather than nationhood. For many centuries, Bosnia's rulers, local and regional, came from this class, so while other Balkan nations were busy creating and then nurturing a modern national identity in the nineteenth century, there was less impetus for the Bosnia Moslems to do this – they were already established as the privileged of the region. It was not until the inter-war period that the Moslems began to transcend their religious and class origins and instead to assume a national identity. Like all other minorities in the Kingdom of Serbs, Croats and Slovenes, they had to subordinate any sense of community they may have developed to the dominance of the three main southern Slav tribes.

The impact of the Second World War and the genocidal struggle between Serbs and Croats was felt most keenly in Bosnia. The majority of Moslems co-operated with the Croat Fascists, the Usta-shas, against the Serb-dominated Partizans. This was particularly marked in Hercegovina where the most primitive branches of the Serb and Croat tribes live, and in eastern and southern Bosnia. Each district in Bosnia has a monument listing the fighters who died fighting for Tito's Partizans in the National Liberation Struggle. During my visits to Bosnia, I would always visit the monument to see the relative number of Moslems and Serbs who died – in most regions four Serbs died for every Moslem. In some areas, like the north-western Moslem enclave of Cazin–Bihać, support for the Partizans was much stronger among the Moslems and this local co-operation yielded a very different relationship between Serbs and Moslems after the war.

Following the creation of Tito's Yugoslavia, the Moslems were originally granted the status of a minority. Because of the difficulty presented by a nationality identified by religion in a country commit-ted to principles of atheism, the communist leadership originally hoped that the Moslems of Bosnia-Hercegovina (BiH) would simply orient themselves naturally towards either Serb or Croat culture, leading eventually to their natural extinction.

However, as was so often the case in state socialist countries, the opposite occurred. It was during this period that the Moslems adopted all the characteristics of a modern nation. At the height of Yugoslavia's isolation after the break with the Cominform in June 1948, Tito decided to move large amounts of heavy industry from the peripheral regions of the country into mountainous Bosnia for security reasons. The poorly-educated Moslem artisan classes were rapidly transformed into a literate working class, while the ambitious educational programme of the Communist Party unwittingly encouraged the development of a Moslem intelligentsia, as it did an Albanian and Macedonian intelligentsia. In the 1960s, young Moslem graduates and professionals were able to articulate the needs and requirements of their community as a distinct entity within Yugoslavia for the first time. The student unrest which swept Europe in 1968 found a powerful resonance in Sarajevo, where for the first time young Moslems were able to force concessions from the Party which grudgingly admitted that their people fulfilled all the requirements of a Yugoslav nation. As latent nationalist tension between Serbs and Croats within the Yugoslav League of Communists emerged into the open, for the first time since the war, between 1966 and 1972, Moslem functionaries in the Bosnian League of Communists successfully applied pressure on the leadership in Belgrade to elevate the Moslems' status from national minority to constituent nation. This was finally achieved in 1971. They argued that, within Bosnia, the presence of the Moslems would dilute any actual or potential resentment felt between the republic's Serbs and Croats. Tito was convinced by this argument and the Moslems' elevation to nationhood was enshrined in the constitution of 1974. From then on, they were no longer referred to as 'moslems' with a small 'm', but as 'Moslems' (in Serbo-Croat Moslem is only written with a capital when it refers to nationhood).

In addition, the key concept of tri-national parity entered its mature phase. In every sphere of Bosnian life (with the critical exception of the JNA) the three communities were equally represented. The importance of this concept cannot be underestimated as its violation by the Moslems and Croats, as well as by the international community, is at the core of the Serbs' decision to fight. It implies that Bosnia's polity consists of 'three constituent nations' and that major constitutional changes may only be made if agreed to by all three sides. This reaches to the very heart of post-war

Yugoslavia, a state which, uniquely, was constructed on a dual concept of sovereignty: the sovereignty of the republics and the sovereignty of the nations. Independence, it follows, cannot be granted to a republic unless the nations of the republic also seek that independence.

It was at this time that Tito had wanted to find some form of political compensation to allay the fears of non-Serbs in Yugoslavia who were concerned that the crushing of the Croatian Spring in 1971 meant a revival of Serb domination in Yugoslavia. The verbose and baffling result was the 1974 constitution which makes *Das Kapital* seem like light reading. However, it included two very important new provisions. The first was the strengthening of local power in Serbia's two Socialist autonomous provinces, Kosovo and Vojvodina. The second was to enshrine the Moslems in Bosnia and the Sandžak as an official Yugoslav nation. Following this recognition of Moslem nationhood, it was argued that Serbs and Croats might gradually discard the popular belief that the Moslems remained at heart either Catholic or Orthodox Slavs. Although largely secular, the explicit religious origins of the Moslems' identity (they have no specific ethnic or linguistic criteria to differentiate themselves from Serbs or Croats of Bosnia, neither do they have a Belgrade or Zagreb to turn to for material, political or spiritual aid) have made the process of defining their nationhood exceptionally difficult. Not only do many Moslems incline towards certain aspects of either Serbian or Croatian culture, Serbs and Croats under the influence of war psychosis have now revived their dangerous belief that Moslems remain at heart Orthodox or Catholic Christians who will at some future point return to the fold, willingly or otherwise.

In the middle of a sloping field some fifty miles from Sarajevo lies a metal plaque honouring the geographical centre of Yugoslavia. There is a little café called simply The Centre of Yugoslavia whose owner as late as the winter of 1991 still insisted that he would not change the name. 'What else can I call it?' he asked rhetorically. 'The Centre of a Ghost State?' According to a study commissioned by the Bosnian Presidency in the spring of 1992, over 10 per cent of Sarajevo's population (56,473 people) still called themselves Yugoslavs even though their state had already landed in purgatory.

Throughout the history of the two Yugoslav states, people who lived in Bosnia-Hercegovina were known in the media and in colloquial language as *Bosanci* or *Hercegovci*. Over the past two years, the peasantry of Hercegovina (Serb or Croat) has vigorously reasserted its traditionally separate identity from Bosnian people. At the same time, however, Bosnia has been rapidly losing its identity. The word *Bosanci* dropped out of the vocabulary in Serbia and Croatia first as the nationalist agendas of the Croatian Democratic Union (HDZ) and the Serbian Socialist Party (SPS) began to speak of lands which were historically indivisible parts of Serbia or Croatia. Soon in Bosnia itself people stopped calling themselves Bosnians. Instead most became Bosnian Serbs, Bosnian Croats or Moslems. The Serbs and the Croats later dropped the auxiliary word Bosnian.

This process of differentiation was the initial step towards war in the republic. From the start of Yugoslavia's disintegration, those who understood the implications of this country's collapse were most concerned about the impact it could have on Bosnia. Until the presidents of Yugoslavia's six constituent republics began their fruitless discussions on a peaceful solution to the crisis, the situation in Kosovo was universally regarded as the greatest threat to peace and social stability in the Balkans. The revival of the conflict between Serbia and Croatia, in particular when this flared into war in June 1991 (disregarding Milošević's fatuous assertion that Serbia had nothing to do with the war in Croatia), brought Bosnia to the edge of the catastrophe. For a long time, this was by no means obvious and the majority of Bosnians remained committed to maintaining the peace (Hercegovina is a different case, as Serbs and Croats here regarded open hostilities as almost inevitable once fighting had begun in Croatia).

The decision by the European Community to recognize Slovenia and Croatia pushed Bosnia into the abyss. Once this had happened, the Bosnian government had only three roads along which it could travel and each led to war. It could have stayed in the rump Yugoslavia and been ruled over by Milošević and Serbia. It could have accepted the territorial division of Bosnia between Serbia and Croatia, as suggested by Tuđman and Milošević. Or it could have applied for recognition as an independent state. The Croats and

Moslems considered the first solution unacceptable; the Moslems and Yugoslavs, the second; and the Serbs, the third. This enforced choice could not have been presented at a worst time – Serbia and Croatia had been radicalized by the trauma of a war which neither side had yet won and neither side lost. This has hung over the UN peace-keeping operation in Croatia like a big, black cloud. It also meant that the Croats and Serbs could continue their fight by proxy in Bosnia-Hercegovina, as indeed they did. In addition, there had been an enormous build up of arms throughout the former Yugoslavia.

Bosnia's national mix ensures that it cannot be divided without war. At the same time, Bosnia has never existed, since the medieval kingdom, as an independent state. A sovereign Bosnia-Hercegovina would create severe economic problems for its inhabitants and the threat of conflict between the national communities would most likely be immanent. Nor, however, can Bosnia belong to either Croatia or Serbia – it can act as a bridge between the two but its relationship with both republics must be equal and agreed on by both sides. Bosnia has always survived by dint of a protective shield provided either by a Yugoslav state or the Austrian or Ottoman empires. Of all the entities making up the former Yugoslavia, Bosnia boasts the longest history as a definable state, kingdom or republic. None the less its internal stability was invariably guaranteed by an external power which mediated between the three communities (the sublime Porte, Vienna, the inter-war royal dictatorship or Titoism). On the one occasion that this broke down between 1941 and 1945, the results were horrifying: a nationalist, religious war whose violence surpassed that of all other wartime conflicts in the region.

For this reason, the Bosnian President Alija Izetbegović tried exceptionally hard to counter the bald secessionism of Tuđman on the one hand and the merciless unitarism of Milošević on the other. The Bosnian dilemma also gave a serious meaning to the idea of an 'asymmetrical federation' which was put forward by the Slovenes during initial discussions on constitutional change in 1990. The asymmetrical federation envisaged Yugoslavia as an entity with slightly more authority than the CIS. It also included the provision for republics to have closer structural ties with other parts of the federation to which they claimed a particular affinity – therefore the Serbs from Bosnian Krajina could develop special education or economic relations with Serbia proper, while the Croats of western Hercegovina and Posavina could enjoy a similar relationship with Zagreb.

Back in what were, for Bosnia, peaceful summer days, both Gordana and I were greatly relieved to be away from the nightmare of Osijek. She had been a committed Yugoslav who had joined the Croatian Socialist Party, a small organization comprising both Serbs and Croats. Gordana belonged to its small group of MPs in the Croatian *Sabor*. Small and dark, she gave the impression of being extremely frail, but she and her family bore much suffering over the next few months with dignity. This was before a JNA grenade which destroyed her flat in Osijek combined with the anti-Serb sentiment in the city to force her to leave eastern Slavonia for Sombor, a largely Hungarian town in Vojvodina. On this occasion, her escape from Osijek was only temporary. She had been invited to a conference of parliamentary parties from all the republics in what was or was not still Yugoslavia, depending on your nationality or political persuasion. The conference was the idea of the Democratic Party in Serbia. Parties from all six different legislatures had agreed to attend including Milošević's Socialist Party of Serbia and Tuđman's Croatian Democratic Union. The participants were due to stay at the Hotel Bosna in Ilidža, a suburb of Sarajevo known for its hotel and spa complex which had been created by the Bosnian League of Communists in honour of itself.

Dragoljub Mićunović, the leader of the Democratic Party from Serbia, was the conference host. He and his party had expended considerable effort bringing together so much mutual loathing around a single oval table in such a civilized manner. The intention of the participants was to achieve what the leaders of the six republics had failed to do so abysmally: to unearth the road to peace. Mićunović made this plain in a tactful and encouraging opening speech. He finished by saying that simultaneous translation of the proceedings into Slovene and Macedonian would be provided. This harmless remark was the signal for the remaining guests to inject a lethal dose of Balkan absurdity into the proceedings which would demolish any marginal hopes that the conference might have produced anything of value.

Neven Jurica, the leader of the Croatian Democratic Union delegation and an uncompromising Croat nationalist, raised his hand on a point of order. 'I was pleased to hear that Slovene and Macedonian translations will be provided but there are other languages as well to be translated. What about our Hungarian and Albanian colleagues?' A fair enough question to which Mićunović fairly replied, 'I wish we could provide them with translations but you must understand that this entire event is financed by the Democratic Party and our financial resources are limited. Those interpreters happen to be Democratic Party members who speak Slovene and Macedonian. Unfortunately we do not have any members who speak Albanian or Hungarian. If we did, we would provide them.' Brushing aside this reasonable explanation Jurica continued with his precise, icy logic, 'While we are on the subject of language, I would also like to request a simultaneous translation of the proceedings into Croatian.' Jurica's request, which would be akin to somebody from Glasgow requesting that a Londoner's speech be translated into Scottish English, provoked uproar and laughter. An avalanche of fists thumped the table, one delegate walked out in disgust never to return, the assembled observers had tears of laughter in their eyes but there was more to come as one of the delegates from Sarajevo stood up and screamed above the commotion in all seriousness, 'I demand a translation into Bosnian!' (The equivalent of Irish English.)

This farcical beginning was at the same time the nail in the conference's coffin. It was clear that the key participants in the conference, above all the HDZ and the SPS, had come committed only to their dialogue of the deaf. Before long Jurica had stated that there was no point in holding the conference unless all present offered an unequivocal denunciation of the Yugoslav People's Army and insisted on its immediate and permanent withdrawal from the territory of Croatia.

The SPS was represented by Radoman Božović, at the time Prime Minister of Vojvodina and later the Prime Minister of Serbia, after which he was put under house arrest in March 1993 on suspicion of being involved in a huge corruption racket. Božović was an extraordinary figure because of his uncanny resemblance to his lord and master, Slobodan Milošević. His hair, it is true, is black but with the same shaving brush projection as the Serbian President's. His haughty glaze and square set jaw – the same. The men are identical even down to the flappy ears. Most striking of all, however, is the same ability to bulldoze and destroy proceedings using a skilful combination of all the Balkan politicians' worst characteristics: deceit, corruption, obstruction and, if necessary, violence. As Jurica held out for an unrealistic and unhelpful denunciation of the JNA, Božović countered with a demand for the condemnation of the secessionist states, Croatia and Slovenia, and 'the fascist government in Zagreb'. Just like Bosnia itself, this conference was going nowhere.

Despite this, the seductive surroundings of the Hotel Bosna placed a considerable psychological distance between the war and Bosnia-Hercegovina. Indeed, it was still a long way off and not all political conditions for the war to begin had been met. Three of the most important, however, had been fulfilled.

The core of the Bosnian tragedy is to be found in the republic itself. By organizing parties along national lines, all three communities bear responsibility for the country's appalling fate. Driving across Bosnia in 1990 just prior to the elections afforded me a brief glimpse into the republic's miserable future. One village drowning in a sea of green crescents, which proclaimed the (Moslem) Party of Democratic Action (SDA), would give way to another, where the *šahovnica* (denoting the Croatian Democratic Union – Bosnia and Hercegovina, HDZ – BiH) was sovereign, or where every wall was covered with the four Cs and the acronym SDS (the Serbian Democratic Party). In some villages, the western half was green while the eastern half was red, white and blue (Serbian) while in many towns it was easy to identify the predominantly Croat, Serb or Moslem districts. Many doomed settlements were a jumble of all three. This deeply entangled demography would ensure that if terror and war were to break out in any region of Yugoslavia, the pressure on the three communities in Bosnia-Hercegovina to fight would be overwhelming. The war would be a continuation of the struggle between 1941 and 1945. Not so much in its political implications (as both the internal and external circumstances had changed considerably), but in terms of a revival of unresolved conflicts, prejudices and vendettas on a local level. It was certainly striking how the bestiality of the war (which springs the boundaries of moral comprehension) was one of the first aspects to reassert itself as the Serb offensive against eastern Bosnia resulted in several massacres of innocent Moslem and Croat civilians while in Posavina Croat forces are alleged to have behaved mercilessly against the Serb peasantry.

In order to restore the balance after 1945, Tito's tactic was to throw the hatred into history's deep freeze by enforcing communal life on the three communities using repression, and if necessary, violence. Tito believed that only drastic measures could erase the memory of hatred. As a consequence, until the late 1980s, if a Bosnian Serb were tried in Sarajevo for political crimes then surely, in a few weeks, there would be a trial of a Bosnian Croat and a Bosnian Moslem regardless of whether the latter two had been involved in any political activity or not. Similarly, if a Moslem fundamentalist were sentenced (as the President Alija Izetbegović was, following the publication of his theses on an Islamic state), then a Serb and Croat would soon hear the prison gates closing behind them. This was, of course, a despicable abuse of human rights but the theory assumed that a few juridical indiscretions were preferable to a fratricidal blood-bath. Tito's tactic was, of course, flawed because when the resentments were taken out of the historical deep freeze, the memory of hatred proved to be as fresh as ever after it thawed.

Bosnia could only have been saved if a political party which spanned the three communities had emerged as the most powerful after the collapse of communist power. The poverty of the pluralist system based on the three national parties was demonstrated by the structures which it spawned. In its eighteen-month-long existence, the Bosnian parliament failed to pass a single law – instead it issued a string of declarations and memoranda which were invariably contested by one of the three national groups. Another perversity was the refusal of the SDA leadership to break their formal government coalition with the SDS long after the war had begun and Sarajevo was being starved and bombed in what probably ranks as one of the greatest war crimes perpetrated by the JNA and Serb irregulars in the entire conflict. A spokesman for the SDA explained that if Izetbegović's party broke with the SDS, then Izetbegović and his fellow presidency members would lose their mandate. So the party had decided to sustain formally its partnership with an organization which had long since revealed itself to be a cowardly band of terrorists. Thus, although the impossibility of developing a pluralist system in Bosnia based along nationalist lines was self-evident long before war had broken out, all three communities continued to insist on its logic even while it was turning the entire region into pulp. The Moslems, of course, stood to derive least benefit from the nationalist political structure because, unlike the Croats and Serbs, they were guaranteed no material or strategic help from outside. As such, Alija Izetbegović and the Moslem leadership also bear a historical responsibility for the breakdown of the consensus between the three Bosnian communities, for they were the first to organize a political party, the SDA, along national-ist lines on 26 May 1990.

During the turbulent days of March 1991 in Belgrade, presidents Milošević and Tuđman had held the last of a series of bilateral meetings, on this occasion in Karađorđevo, a town in Vojvodina. Here they agreed firmly on the principle of the division of Bosnia. In his culpable naivety, President Tuđman believed that this would both prevent war in Croatia and in Bosnia as well as satisfying his obsession which demanded that Croatia must be united with western Hercegovina and Posavina in the north of Bosnia. For his part, President Milošević was merely keeping an important option open. His commitment to the division of BiH (which he later formally renounced) guaranteed Tuđman's agreement at the March meeting which enabled Milošević to return to Belgrade waving a Chamber-lainesque statement that was instrumental in quashing the last flicker of the opposition movement which had exploded on 9 March. In July, after the war in Croatia had already broken out, President Tuđman stated publicly that the solution to an all-out war in the crumbling Yugoslavia was the division of BiH between Croatia and Serbia. This meant that while Germany was busy lobbying on behalf of the Croatian leader for the recognition of Croatia, citing the dual principles of self-determination and inviolability of present borders, Tuđman was openly advocating that these lofty ideals be ignored in the case of BiH.

While Tuđman concentrated on his favourite pastime of shooting himself in the foot, Milošević was being kept informed of a different and suitably more sinister operation which involved real firearms. This was RAM, a plan whose name was never uncovered beyond its acronym. It has been alleged that the full extent of this programme was Milošević's concept of a core Yugoslavia dominated by Serbia. This envisaged the encouragement of secessionism in Slovenia combined with the slicing off of the peripheral, Serb-dominated areas of Croatia. It also, naturally, envisaged Bosnia-Hercegovina as an integral part of the core Yugoslavia. There is no proof as to whether such a comprehensive plan existed and given Milošević's immense skill as an unpredictable improviser it is unlikely that he would ever commit himself to a rigid strategy.

That within the project of RAM there was a place for Belgrade's strategy in Bosnia-Hercegovina, however, is beyond doubt thanks to testimony provided by the former Prime Minister, Ante Marković, which led to some thorough research by Belgrade-based journalists. Organized from the Serbian capital by the SPS MP Mihalj Kertes, a Serb whose name indicated the presence of Hungarian antecedents, at the heart of this programme lay the distribution of arms throughout the Serb communities of BiH. Kertes has the reputation of being exceptionally unpleasant. He preaches a political philosophy which is both racist and authoritarian, and partly explains his success as a politician in both the pre-communist era and after its demise. Throughout 1990, Kertes ordered the dispatch of hundreds of thousands of pieces of weaponry mainly to the two militant Serb regions of BiH, Bosanska Krajina in the north-west and eastern Hercegovina in the south-west. Some material was also dispatched to the third Bosnian region to declare itself a Serbian autonomous unit, Romanija, a poor mountainous area to the east of Sarajevo which is home to a strong mix of Serbs and Moslems.

Throughout 1991, Kertes's secret convoys of lorries bulging with guns and munitions ploughed their furrow with a diligence not usually associated with Serbs. Eastern Hercegovina and Bosanska Krajina were especially privileged recipients of this booty as they were both to play a critical logistical role during the war with

Croatia. The Dubrovnik operations of the JNA were organized from Trebinje and Nevesinje, the eastern Hercegovinian capital, while Banja Luka, the capital of Bosanska Krajina, was the JNA headquarters for the western Slavonian front. Later on, however, the significance of RAM became clear for internal developments in Bosnia as well – when war broke out, not only did the Serbs enjoy the formidable support of the JNA, their outrageous paramilitaries were also exceptionally well armed. In August, when his humiliation was reaching its peak, the federal Prime Minister, Ante Marković, revealed the existence of RAM and leaked a tape conversation between President Milošević and General Nikola Uzelac, who ran the Banja Luka corps of the JNA with his own particular touch of evil. During this conversation, Milošević ordered Uzelac to release weapons to the leader of the SDS, Radovan Karadžić. As ever, this particularly damning truth did nothing to dent Milošević's reputation as the king of the Balkan teflons.

The JNA's complicity in RAM and later in the military operation in BiH was not simply dictated by its predominantly Serbian composition. After the break with Stalin in June 1948, Tito developed a programme which saw the removal of most military industries and installations to the mountainous heartland, BiH, and away from Yugoslavia's exposed periphery. Over 60 per cent of Yugoslavia's military industries were based in Bosnia (and over 60 per cent of these were situated in Croat or Moslem regions). Without Bosnia, the JNA had no means of sustaining its bloated officer corps, and Milošević had made it clear to the military leadership that Serbia had no intention of offering it security. As early as September 1991, President Izetbegović urged Lord Carrington's conference on Yugoslavia to pay immediate attention to the question of the JNA in BiH. With considerable foresight, Izetbegović proposed that the European Community open a fund which could finance the pensions of Bosnian officers and provide for the gradual dismantling of the JNA in Bosnia and the local military industries. Preoccupied by the war in Croatia, neither the conference nor anyone else heeded Izetbegović's entreaties and, faced with the option of losing their material base in an independent BiH or guaranteeing their survival with Serbian support, the officers of the JNA in Bosnia refused to pledge loyalty to the new state when asked (although Izetbegović did begin serious discussions with an apparently open-minded leadership on the issue before the recognition issue polarized positions).

The handling of the recognition issue by the European Community and by Germany was especially crass in its neglect of the significance of the JNA's position in Bosnia-Hercegovina. Even a cursory study would have concluded that the JNA would under no circumstances allow the departure of the bulk of BiH from Yugoslavia. The encouragement given to the Bosnian Moslems and Croats by the international community in January 1992 was bound to provoke the JNA into mobilizing its forces in Bosnia.

The final factor driving Bosnia to war was the recognition issue itself, as we shall see later.

The hills around Velika Kladuša are more reminiscent of Sussex than the forbidding rocks of the nearby Dinaric mountains. This peaceful, largely Moslem town in north-west Bosnia right on the border with Croatia has a special place in Yugoslavia's evolution as the home of Agrokomerc, the largest food distribution company in the entire country, which was considered one of the most successful enterprises in Yugoslavia. Its director, Fikret Abdić, is a Moslem businessman and politician whose care for his political constituency, the peoples of the Cazin and Bihać region, is only matched by his predilection for corruption. In 1988, it emerged that Agrokomerc had effectively been printing money for itself by abusing on a grand scale the bank bond system, peculiar to Yugoslavia, whose financial institutions were dangerously mixed up structurally with the enterprises to which they lent capital. The entire economy of north-western Bosnia was threatened with collapse but Abdić succeeded ultimately in saving the company by some remarkable political brokering.

Abdić was partly helped by the exceptionally good relations between Serbs and Moslems in the Bihać–Cazin region. This is a Moslem enclave surrounded by territory in Croatia and Bosnia which is largely inhabited by Serbs. During the Second World War, these Moslems worked much more closely with the Serbs in the struggle against fascist Croatia than was the caae elsewhere in Bosnia. In addition, the rural dwellers of Cazin, Moslem, Serb and

Croat, joined together in the spring of 1954 to launch the only peasant rebellion recorded in the history of post-war Eastern Europe. It lasted but a few days and was repressed with unrivalled brutality by the communist authorities. It goes unnoticed in almost all histories of Eastern Europe but for the local population it remains a significant experience which has tightened the bond linking the national groups.

In August 1991, the area had been recently cut off from communications with Zagreb and the sense of isolation among people was growing. Bihać played a critical role during the war in Croatia as it was home to one of the most sophisticated military airports in Europe. The airport was located underground and was used as the launching pad for MiG air strikes against both Slovenia and Croatia. Military personnel were forever trundling in and out of the town. In addition, the local SDA leadership had begun a purge of Serb officials who controlled many state enterprises. This was the normal practice throughout BiH. The dominant party in the region would undertake a purge of the administration although it was never as severe as the HDZ purge of Serbs in Croatia.

Despite this growing political tension in Bihać, ordinary people remained impervious to the game of chauvinist brinkmanship. At the local library, I was introduced to a young English teacher named Nada, a Serb who had been blessed with the strikingly beautiful bright-green eyes whose high incidence among all three national groups in BiH scotches the impassioned theories of racial purity. Nada was almost shocked by my inquiries concerning the relations between local Serbs, Croats and Moslems. 'Of course,' she said, 'we are aware of what is going on in Croatia but I have never been interested in the nationality of my colleagues and friends. And I am not going to start now.' She was backed up by a fellow teacher, Fatima, who was a Moslem. 'I simply cannot imagine there ever being problems with Serbs here,' she said. In fact, because of its peculiar history and because Serbs did not harbour territorial claims against Moslems, Bihać–Cazin had so far escaped the war in Bosnia even though barricades were thrown up throughout the town soon after heavy fighting erupted in neighbouring Bosanska Krupa. Fikret Abdić personally succeeded in persuading both the Moslems and Serbs of Bihać to remove their barricades. In May 1992, the JNA evacuated Bihać's underground airport but blew it up before they left – $50 million worth of high technology which the Croats or Moslems would now be denied. At the end of that month, fighting broke out in Bihać, killing off its cherished innocence.

The atmosphere in Sarajevo was even more positive than in Bihać–Cazin. Here, in October 1991, everybody assured me that there would be no war in Bosnia. President Izetbegović, the devout Moslem with the pacific blue eyes and avuncular smile, insisted that people's awareness of the potential for violence in BiH automatically precluded the possibility. One of the main criticisms of President Izetbegović, levelled usually by Serbs, but by Croats as well, is that he wants to create a fundamentalist Islamic state in Bosnia-Hercegovina. The argument is based largely on a text he wrote in the early 1970s which outlines the structures of an Islamic state. (It is important to realize that if we were to judge the six presidents of the former Yugoslav republics by their characters of twenty years ago, then Slovenia would have a Stalinist as head of state; Croatia, a raving anti-Semite; Serbia a blood-thirsty Bolshevik; Montenegro an adolescent; and Macedonia another Stalinist. While little has changed in Croatia and Serbia, the other presidents have moved on. None more so than President Izetbegović, who does have fundamentalists in his party but who has always stressed the pluralist intentions of his Presidency.) Together with President Gligorov of Macedonia, Izetbegović argued passionately during the political negotiations of 1990 for a gradual transformation of Yugoslavia into a confederal union. The Gligorov–Izetbegović plan was the only solution to the Yugoslav crisis which might have ended peacefully. It was scuppered, of course, by Milošević in the first instance, and never received the support it deserved from presidents Kučan and Tuđman. President Izetbegović suffers from regular attacks of naivety but he is consistently well-intentioned, humane and has discarded any youthful fundamentalism that he may once have felt. This does not, however, excuse Izetbegović the error of having encouraged the formation of a democracy based not on political or economic interests but on national groups – the death of Bosnia.

The Serbs in Sarajevo were even less fortunate with their leadership. Before entering politics, Radovan Karadžić had been the resident psychiatrist with Sarajevo's football team. His scruffy hair-style casts a scrappy shadow over his unmemorable features, but these were compensated for by the histrionics he engineered whenever talking about the Moslem threat to Serbs. Particularly after the outbreak of war in Croatia, Bosnia's Serbs were genuinely concerned about their physical safety if BiH were to be detached from Yugoslavia thus cutting their umbilical cord with the Serbian motherland. The SDS leadership argued, not entirely unreasonably, that Serbs had fought two world wars on the winning side in order to ensure the security which a constitutional connection with Serbia would guarantee. But what the SDS leadership refused to do was to take into account the aspirations of anyone else living in Bosnia. For a while, it seemed as though Karadžić's slightly more moderate deputy, Professor Nikola Koljević, might have held sway. Koljević held the chair at the English department at Sarajevo University and was invariably wheeled out to speak to foreign journalists as he does have an excellent command of English. On some important issues, Koljević spoke out against Karadžić's stated position but he never had the political nous to depose his superior. Koljević confessed that he was frightened by the development of politics in Bosnia. He described how towards the beginning of 1992, when he travelled to Banja Luka to speak at a political meeting there, Milan Babić, the king of Krajina, had sent four 'gorillas', as Koljević described them, to assassinate him. At the time, Milošević was pressurizing Babić into accepting the UN peace plan brokered by Cyrus Vance. The Serbian President had enlisted the support of Karadžić and Koljević among others to aid him, so the Krajina leadership regarded Koljević as a traitor. Koljević explained how he had narrowly escaped injury. Unconsciously he was also testifying to the fact that the closer the Serbs or any national group come to grasping the holy grail of national unity, the more divided and bitter they become among themselves. Although scared and doubting the wisdom of SDS policy, at crucial moments, Koljević lamely capitulated and, together with Karadžić, he scuttled from Sarajevo in April 1992 like a rat before lending his dubious authority to the criminal siege of Bosnia's capital. Neither Karadžić nor Koljević had the final say in Serbian-controlled BiH as this was the preserve of a nationalist intellectual, the historian Milorad Ekmečić. This was the only man among the Serbs who was accorded as much respect as his confidant and co-conspirator, Dobrica Ćosić.

None of these people could ever be described as representing the Serbs in Sarajevo and other towns like Tuzla. For the urban population, Karadžić, Koljević, Ekmečić, Ćosić and Milošević were thugs who were simply making their lives difficult. They were by no means enamoured of the incompetence and insensitivity of large parts of the SDA leadership, but they were embarrassed by the SDS who, until the war broke out, were regarded as buffoons. After the war started, they were regarded as cowardly criminals. This vast social gap between Sarajlije (people from Sarajevo) and the Serb peasants developed into an unbridgeable ravine when the latter imposed their siege on the former, Serbs, Croats and Moslems alike.

The Croats have a similar problem. In Sarajevo and in western and northern Bosnia, the Croats are content with their identity as Bosnian Croats. In western Hercegovina, however, they are, as one Croat fighter explained, 'the most radical Croats. We are, if you like, more Croat than the Croats.' A trip across the arid, desolate terrain of western Hercegovina illuminates the character of the area. After evacuating Sarajevo during the worst fighting there, I had to travel along the most isolated mountain tracks in western Hercegovina to arrive safely in the Croat port of Split. Deep into the mountains, one of our vehicles suffered a puncture. We were several thousand feet above sea level, the sun was scorching and the white rock was covered by the parched green of hardy shrubs. To our right an awkwardly thin wedge of rock shot up almost inexplicably out of a ravine. As I surveyed the peak of this wedge, I noticed the glint of a gun barrel catching the sun. Like lizards, two villagers (although where the village was was beyond me) were glued to the rock but none the less able to train their guns instinctively on anything that moved. Mars must be more hospitable than western Hercegovina and it is hard to imagine anybody wanting to conquer it (even the Serbs admit freely that 'western Hercegovina is Croatian and will never be anything else'). None the less, whenever we stopped, it was but minutes before Croatian soldiers arrived almost unnoticed to check on our activities.

President Tuđman's declaration after war broke out in Bosnia that no Croatian Army units were operating on the territory of BiH was one of the baldest lies of the war because western Hercegovina was riddled with units of the Croatian Army (*Hrvatska*

Vojska). In Posušje, a small district town which is a few miles from the border with Croatia, most traders refuse to accept Yugoslav dinars (which was theoretically still the legal currency there), taking only the new Croatian currency – this was an exceptionally rare example of Balkan traders cutting off their noses to spite their faces. Posušje has been swamped by the Croatian Army. The extraordinary conversion of an Opel Rekord drives by. The passenger and boot section have been simply amputated and replaced by a flat-bed truck section on which is mounted an anti-aircraft gun. A young Croat soldier with a callous smile swings the gun menacingly. All the Croatian Army soldiers sport short, smartly-styled hair, sunglasses, fatigues and an automatic weapon of some description or other. Every other car has a foreign registration because as soon as fighting broke out in Hercegovina, the western Hercegovnians came streaming back from the diaspora – these people are absolutely committed. On 10 April, the anniversary of the Croatian fascist state, the NDH, Andrej Gustinčić, my friend and colleague from Reuters, awoke in a small valley in western Hercegovina with guns and artillery audible a few miles away. On the hillside, he was confronted by three huge letters written in burning tires: NDH. As one western Hercegovinan put it, 'Only three things grow here: snakes, stones and Ustashas.'

Despite these weird creatures which festered in Bosnia's social undergrowth, the people of Sarajevo, or the *raja*, as urban Bosnians are called, were still blissfully optimistic that they would be spared war. Kemal Kurspahić, the jovial editor-in-chief of Bosnia's daily *Oslobođenje*, almost convinced me with the help of three glasses of *rakija* in his office that popular wisdom was by no means taken in by the games and manipulation of the three national parties. Senada Kreso, a dear friend who worked for Sarajevo television, would take me round the cafés and bars insisting that there were no Serbs, Croats and Moslems here only Sarajlije, as they are known in Serbo-Croat. It was difficult to disagree – while war was raging in Croatia and economic life being savaged in Serbia, Sarajevo's social life continued to be the envy of hedonists from around Europe. Sarajevo, where East and West not only tolerated but thrived off each other's cultural influence, was for me one of Europe's greatest achievements. Until the day when violence could no longer be resisted, Sarajevo laughed off the threat to peace. Humorous graffiti proliferated throughout the city. 'Tito – come back!' appealed one street artist while below another had reproduced Tito's distinctive signature and added, 'You've got to be kidding!' But in a certain sense the refusal to believe that war could come to Sarajevo was also partly responsible for the catastrophe – there was an element of Nero's fiddle-playing about it, although it is hard to know what anyone could have done about a process already well advanced. Sarajevo's optimism was best explained by Gavrilo Grahovac, a remarkable Sarajevo Serb who is the director of Svjetlost, the most successful Serbo-Croat publishing company. When I confronted him with the noose closing around Bosnia's throat, he said: 'But then, you see, Misha, that's when the slaughter begins. And what you are doing with your logic is you are leaving me with no hope. And you cannot take away my hope.'

The late afternoon sun of October casts shadows which stretch and blacken many parts of Mostar. I enter Hercegovina's beautiful capital from the south-west passing the military airport and the barracks which house the Montenegrin and Serb reservists whose presence has unsettled this multi-ethnic town. Mostar is famous above all for its Ottoman architecture symbolized by the old footbridge which arches high over the Neretva river. When I visited Mostar in October 1991 when sporadic shooting between reservists and townspeople was already an everyday occurrence, the autumn shadows seemed already to have handed down the sentence reading 'Vukovar' on this precious town. A walk across the bridge along the bazaar which was usually heaving with tourists was an uncanny, chilling experience. The shops were open displaying their souvenirs, leatherware and wooden carvings, but the traders sat listlessly, not reacting to unexpected pedestrians who wandered by every quarter of an hour. Nobody was buying, nobody was selling – the town had already died.

In the local hotel, I spoke to a Swedish military intelligence officer who had been seconded to the European Community Monitoring Mission in Bosnia. Throughout the wars in Slovenia, Croatia and BiH, the monitors were comforting but strange figures. They emerged from their white vehicles, dressed all in white and projecting a clinical, even dreamlike, quality. It was as though they were emissaries from outer space who had been sent to save the human race from itself. Almost all monitors were military intelligence officers, a fact which created some resentment among the JNA and even among the Croat military. Never in the history of warfare have so many foreign intelligence officers been permitted to wander around freely gathering information. None the less, I am convinced that their mere presence helped save lives in Croatia and BiH and they took considerable personal risks. Five monitors have so far died, four when their helicopter was brought down by a Yugoslav air force jet and one who was killed on duty near Mostar.

My Swedish monitor in Mostar was extremely helpful and we discussed the various troop movements in the region. We were able to establish that both Croat and Serb forces were preparing to dig in around the front defined by the Neretva river and that there had been particularly busy activity among the JNA reservists around Stolac, a town with an overwhelming majority of Moslems and Croats but claimed by the Serbs as being on their side of the Neretva river. Politicians around Europe may have been hoping that a negotiated settlement to the Bosnian conundrum was still possible, but in Hercegovina the auld enemies were flexing their muscles in anticipation of war.

Hercegovina is divided by the river Neretva, whose mouth is in Croatian territory but which soon enters Hercegovina. The Serbs consider the Neretva the dividing line between Serb and Croat territory. The Croats however claim that many of the communities on the eastern side of the bank are Croatian and so must come under their jurisdiction. Towns like Čapljina which straddle the Neretva have sustained some of the worst destruction and, at the time of writing, it is hard to imagine how life in Čapljina can ever be restored. This war between the Serbs and Croats is but one of three wars which broke out in BiH. The straightforward struggle between Serbs and Croats intersects with the second war in Mostar. This is a war of territorial acquisition initiated by Bosnian Serbs and the JNA at the expense of the Moslems. The Croats claim all of Mostar for themselves while the Serbs say that the town on the right side of the Neretva is theirs. Nobody asks the Moslems, however, who are the largest national group in the city. Indeed, the

Croats in this region are also involved in an act of territorial acquisition. Their forces are controlled by the so-called Croatian Defence Council (HVO) which receives its instructions not from the Bosnian authorities but from Zagreb – in certain instances, the Croats have deliberately obstructed the work of the legally constituted Bosnian Territorial Defence.

After the war began in April, a monstrous JNA commander from Serbia, Miodrag Perušić, surrounded Mostar and began destroying the town systematically. This sandy-haired madman in his late forties probably wins first prize in the keenly contested 'Most Bloodthirsty General' stakes of the Yugoslav wars. In the first month of the Bosnian war, Mostar received the worst battering of all and like Sarajevo was subjected to the dual JNA tactic of intimidation through bombardment and hunger in order to hurry its surrender. Mostar became the Vukovar of Bosnia-Hercegovina with the only difference being that throughout the siege of Vukovar, Croat forces were able to supply the town with food and ammunition every night across the cornfields from Vinkovci. In Mostar and Sarajevo, no food, no medicine and no ammunition made it in and nobody made it out.

During the Second World War, the Serb, Croat and Moslem population of Mostar was famous for resisting the temptation of mutual loathing which gripped the rest of western and eastern Hercegovina and the Neretva valley. Mostar Croats saved Serbs, Serbs protected Moslems and communal life revived in Mostar faster than almost anywhere else in BiH after the war. However, Mostar's military airport and its strategic position doomed the town in 1992. Zdravko Grebo, a professor of law at Sarajevo University and a former politician, made several visits to Mostar during the run-up to the war. Perhaps it was because he came from Mostar and could see how the struggle was developing there that Zdravko had some unique insights into what was happening in his country. Of all the hundreds of new people I have met in the former Yugoslavia since 1990, Zdravko was among the most far-sighted and illuminating people whom I befriended. In his forties and a veteran of the student protests of Sarajevo 1968, Zdravko untangles the apparently unfathomable conundrum of Bosnia-Hercegovina. Long before war had visited this condemned land, Zdravko had outlined the road to disaster which had been mapped out in advance by the proposed division of the republic.

Yet Zdravko is not merely a strong, clear thinker. He is a Bosnian who oozes humour and culture. His parents were Moslems from Mostar but he had been brought up in Belgrade and he continued to call himself a Yugoslav, even after he openly admitted that Yugoslavia no longer existed. 'What else can I call myself?' he mused, 'I can hardly start calling myself a Moslem or a Serb after all these years.' Bosnia (and Sarajevo especially) had the highest percentage of people who designated themselves Yugoslavs in the national census. When Yugoslavia was submerged in the blood of its own people, these Yugoslavs and the identity to which they still clung, were washed away into a river of poisoned history – yet another group of innocent victims among the millions.

On a Saturday morning in early May 1992, after the siege of Sarajevo had begun, Zdravko and I take a stroll downtown. It is only in the morning that one can risk going out as most of the snipers in the hills have not really begun their work yet. They are probably sleeping off their hangovers. Zdravko takes me on a guided tour of destruction wrought upon Baš-Čaršija, the Turkish old town in the centre. Although the people of Sarajevo are being subjected to the most dreadful terror, they retain a determination to lead their lives normally wherever possible. They go to cafés, they buy newspapers (the staff of *Oslobođenje* and *Večernje Novine* worked heroically to ensure a paper came out every day) and they stand and talk despite being exposed to the guns and cannons of the JNA and Serb irregulars surrounding them. The Bosnian Territorials and the Moslem paramilitaries, the Green Berets, have, of course, recruited from the criminal classes and the lumpen proletariat and they have already injected their own brand of corruption into Sarajevo's enforced war economy. There are many reports of Moslem paramilitary units taking the law into their own hands and a few documented cases of retribution against innocent Serbs, but the problem appears to be less widespread than it was in Croatia. The people of Sarajevo accept the corruption associated with the war economy as inevitable.

As Zdravko and I walk down the street appropriately named JNA street, every second passer-by comes up to embrace him. A humble Moslem shop-owner grabs his arm. 'Professor, tell me, you are a very wise man. Does the international community know what is happening in Sarajevo or is it because of ignorance that they do not send us military help?' Next we bump into Sidran, the man who wrote the screenplay for the film *When Father was Away on Business* the Cannes Prize-winner directed by the Sarajevo film-maker, Emir Kusturica. Sidran is very short and plump and the epitome of Sarajevo life – he spends weeks locked up in a room writing furiously before hitting town for three days and nights drinking solidly and never sleeping. He and Zdravko start talking, others arrive and the conversation broadens. As it was in Dubrovnik, one of the greatest enemies of the Sarajlije is boredom. The presence of people like Grebo and Sidran cheers everyone immensely – they are true tribunes of the people who never sink into populism.

Bosnia-Hercegovina casts a spell on all who live there or who were privileged in the past to acquaint themselves with the republic. Sentimentalism plays little part in this – it is through the middle of Bosnia that East meets West; Islam meets Christianity; the Catholic eyes the Orthodox across the Neretva, the line of the Great Schism; Bosnia divided the great empires of Vienna and Constantinople; Bosnia was perhaps the only true reflection of Yugoslavia. It is both the paradigm of peaceful, communal life in the Balkans and its darkest antithesis. Nowhere else does the local culture resonate with so many sounds which have defined European consciousness in such a fundamental way. The physical majesty of Bosnia-Hercegovina unwittingly reflects this. Above all history springs from the four rivers, the Una, the Sava, the Drina and the Neretva which, with the exception of the latter, outline what appear the almost natural borders of this artificial and yet eminently durable political unit. Above the rivers, the mountains, stark in Hercegovina and across the Romanija pass, covered in luscious green in the north and the east. Each town appears to boast either a man-made object or a natural phenomenon of exceptional value: the fourteenth century Turkish stone bridge over the Drina in Višegrad, the steep waterfalls in the middle of Jajce whose gush can be heard all around town, the blue mirror lakes at Bileća and Jablanica.

And, of course, there is Sarajevo itself. Built along a valley in central Bosnia, Sarajevo stretches like a long, spindly finger along several miles. The Ottoman architecture dominates particularly in the Old Town, although the Habsburgs were not idle during the four decades of rule from Vienna, putting their sub-Wagnerian stamp on municipal buildings like the post office, to emphasize their commitment to social progress. Tito's planners dumped a number of socialist realist buildings in the centre of town but strangely they do not seem to jar as much as they do in other East European cities. The most relaxing part of town is Baš-Čaršija with its bazaar and its unrivalled čevapčići and burek. Sarajevo used to boast the finest, most sophisticated cuisine in Yugoslavia before the JNA decided to starve the city out.

The death sentence for Bosnia-Hercegovina was passed in the middle of December 1991 when Germany announced that it would recognize Slovenia and Croatia unconditionally on 15 January 1992. So distressed was Alija Izetbegović by this news that he travelled to Bonn in a vain effort to persuade Kohl and Genscher not to go ahead with the move. Izetbegović understood full well that recognition would strip Bosnia of the constitutional protection it still enjoyed from the territorial claims of the two regional imperia, Serbia and Croatia.

Izetbegović was not the only one who recognized the danger for Bosnia implicit in a premature recognition of Croatia. In one of the most strongly worded documents issued during his period in office as Secretary-General of the UN, Perez de Cuellar wrote to Genscher urging Bonn to reconsider its decision to recognize Croatia as this would provoke 'the most terrible war in BiH'. This request was dismissed by Genscher who was celearly determined to go ahead in recognizing Croatia regardless of the cost to Bosnia. The German government's public intention to recognize unconditionally also undermined the mechanism agreed on by the European Council of Ministers to grant recognition only to those republics who fulfilled certain criteria. This work was entrusted to the Commission headed by Robert Badinter, the chairman of France's constitutional court, which was attached to the Hague Conference on Yugoslavia. It published its findings the day before the German-led recognition. Badinter stated that of the republics requesting independence, only

Slovenia and Macedonia had satisfied his commission. Croatia failed on two crucial points: firstly, Zagreb was not in control of all of its territory, and secondly, it had not provided sufficient guarantees for the protection of its minorities, most notably the urban Serbs who still lived in territory under Croatian control.

The German decision to recognize Croatia undermined the deliberations of the Badinter commission. But immediately after the German government had persuaded and cajoled the members of the European Community to ignore the commission's findings and recognize Croatia and not Macedonia, the EC then reverted (in the case of Bosnia, although not in the case of Macedonia) to the Badinter principles. If the Bosnian government held a referendum, the EC told Izetbegović, and a simple democratic majority assented to independence, then it would be granted. Together the Moslems and Croats could muster that majority although it was a flagrant breach of the principle of securing agreement of the 'three constituent nations'.

Not only did the German decision seal the fate of Bosnia-Hercegovina, it made a mockery of the consensual foreign policy which the European Community was striving to build on its way towards economic and political integration.

Once Croatia and Slovenia had been granted international recognition, Izetbegović was faced with an impossible choice. Either he would remain in a Yugoslavia dominated by Milošević and Belgrade which would have been simply unacceptable to all Moslems and Croats in BiH, or he could accelerate moves towards independence by holding the referendum stipulated by Badinter, thus hastening the onset of war. Izetbegović was thus forced by German-led EC policy into the same mistake that Tuđman had made voluntarily: he embarked upon secession from Yugoslavia without securing prior agreement from the Serbs.

At this point, Izetbegović entered his own kingdom of fantasy, announcing the referendum and preparation for independence. He repeatedly stressed that the danger of war in Bosnia-Hercegovina was now over, just at the time when it had never been more unavoidable.

Despite predictions that conflict in Bosnia would follow the outbreak of war in Croatia by a matter of weeks, a balance of fear arose in the multi-national republic which contributed amazingly to the development of a temporary immunity against war. All appeared frightened by the dimension of violence promised by the struggle in Bosnia, including the Serbs who were preparing most actively for it. During this stay of execution which lasted nine months, BiH enjoyed a last spell in its legendary performance as the star of Yugoslavia – a now seemingly unreal place where the celebration of a joint Bosnian history appeared decisive over the narrow national options offered by the three party leaderships.

But despite holding out courageously for nine months, the end of peace in Bosnia began on the weekend of 1 March, the day which Izetbegović's government had set for the referendum. The democracy of the plebiscite had been used in Slovenia and Croatia in order to justify their departure from Yugoslavia. In Slovenia, it was democratic enough because there it was almost exclusively Slovenes who voted. In Croatia, although an overwhelming majority voted for independence, the referendum's legitimacy was in doubt because Croats voted to take with them a large number of Serbs from Yugoslavia who, as we later discovered, were not overjoyed about leaving. In Bosnia, the Serbs had already held a plebiscite of their own, four months prior to this. Needless to say, this vote carefully organized by the SDS produced a result of which Stalin would have been proud. The SDS MPs had already walked out of the parliament in Sarajevo and formed their own rival Serbian parliament in Bosnia-Hercegovina and so, although all three parties maintained the absurd fiction of a three-way coalition cabinet, government had already broken down long before the referendum at the beginning of March. The process of recognition clearly brought the denouement forward but BiH had already created its own crisis which showed no signs of being solved peacefully.

But whatever their tactics, the Serbs insisted on the maintenance of Bosnia's central political mechanism of constitutional parity which is both just and reasonable. The international community sanctioned the disintegration of the Yugoslav federation without paying any heed to this system which had guaranteed peace, albeit an uneasy one, between the country's various peoples over a forty-year period. It could perhaps have been replaced with something new, but nobody did. By ignoring this, the Bosnian Serbs, who make up a third of the republic and who had fought bitterly during the Second World War to be constitutionally attached to Serbia proper, were being denied their statehood. They promised they would fight, and the international community and the rest of Bosnia should have taken them more seriously.

Plebiscite democracy does not boast a successful history in the Balkans and Central Europe. Despite the blind optimism of the Bosnian Moslems and Croats, not to mention the blithe ignorance of the international community, nothing indicated that this plebiscite circus would have a positive outcome. The Serb plebiscite was justified by the SDS within the framework of the three constituent nations although its procedural legality was dubious. The March referendum was also a pointless exercise as the Serbs had announced they would not recognize its result, and certainly, it was a clear violation of the principle of three constituent nations in which Bosnia's policy was still clearly rooted.

Given the unmistakable warnings that the Serbs had given about their hostility to independence, the triumphalism which accompanied the referendum seemed misplaced, to say the least. The two ballots merely exposed with greater clarity than ever the poverty of trying to run a democracy along nationalist lines.

On the day of the referendum, barricades were thrown up by Serb militants around various parts of Sarajevo. In a demonstration of the courage which Sarajlije would show much more of later on, the people took to the streets, defying the automatic weapons and marching up to the barricades. Some were even dismantled despite the presence of armed Serbs. The following day, President Izetbegović defied the danger of the streets and took a huge procession of people around Sarajevo. The barricades were gradually removed and the President, slightly intoxicated by this display of people power, celebrated what the demonstrators believed to be their victory over the terrorists.

In fact, by now President Izetbegović had committed a number of serious errors. On 18 March in Lisbon, he agreed to a proposal advanced by the Serbs which the Croats also accepted. This required Bosnia to be split into three national regions, the cantonization of the republic. This is when the so-called 'map game' began which involved the three delegations sitting in Lisbon and bargaining over towns and districts in Bosnia. The Serbs demanded 65 per cent of BiH's territory while the Croats wanted 35 per cent. This left the Moslems (who made up 44 per cent of the population) precisely nothing. Zdravko Grebo remarked to me later on that the Croats and Serbs agreed on one formula which left the Moslems with 5 per cent of the republic's territory. 'They want to create a Moslem reservation, like the ones in North America for Indians, only with much less land. The only industry which the Moslems will then have is tourism – people will come and pay to see the only indigenous Moslems in Europe.'

Although Grebo is correct that the Serbs and Croats would ideally have liked to carve the state up between them, the maps gave the Moslems roughly the same amount of territory that they were granted under the Vance-Owen plan which Izetbegović was to sign a year later on 24 March 1993. The only difference was that if Izetbegović had agreed a year earlier there would probably have been no war. For after returning to Sarajevo, Izetbegović promptly announced that the Lisbon maps were unacceptable and that he would instead go ahead with the drive towards full independence.

This is when the war began. Contrary to popular belief, fighting did not begin on 5 April in anticipation of Bosnia's recognition by the European Community and the United States. Along the Neretva river in Hercegovina and in the north in the Croat-dominated town of Bosanski Brod, heavy battles broke out in the week beginning 22 March. In the blighted town of Brod, over forty people were killed during that first week. Hercegovina and Posavina are of considerable strategic importance, the latter especially because it is along this region that the Serbian corridor connecting Serbia proper to the Serb stronghold of Banja Luka runs. Once the referendum had been held, the Serbs and Croats of Bosnia knew that the fighting was imminent so it was no surprise that they began to fight in these peripheral, but crucial areas.

This was part of the first Bosnian war, that is the battle for territory between Serbs and Croats. However, on this occasion the Croats were assisted by new Moslem paramilitary formations – the Dragons of Bosnia, the Patriotic League and the Green Berets whose fatigues bore the official arms of Bosnia, six fleurs-de-lis on a blue background with a white stripe running though it, another icon thrown into the battle of symbols. Some Moslem fighters had sewn on their uniforms the words *Allah-u-akbar* (God is Great). Thousands of refugees fled Bosanski Brod. The Croats and Moslems left for Slavonski Brod over the Sava, although this Croat half of the town was badly bombed by Yugoslav air force jets during the fighting. Serb refugees scurried towards Serbia, as confused and terrified as the Croats and Moslems. The refugee problem caused by the fighting in Croatia had placed an enormous burden on the economies of both Serbia and Croatia. The appalling fate of over one and a half a million people displaced during the Bosnian war, however, was more than the limited and battered resources of Croatia, in particular, could cope with. The refugees finally brought home to other parts of the continent that there were European dimensions to the wars in Yugoslavia.

After Bosanski Brod, the Serbs, who until this point still enjoyed some sympathy among part of the international community, launched an offensive which would leave them isolated in the world except for the tentative support of Russia and Romania and the unequivocal backing of Belgrade's Balkan ally, Greece. This must not detract from complex origins of the Bosnian conflict for which the Serbs are not solely responsible. This in turn cannot excuse the barbaric behaviour of the Serb paramilitary organizations who committed crime after crime against civilians.

The Serbs stormed the urban centres of eastern and then southern Bosnia. Bijeljina, some ten miles from the Serbian border in the north-east of Bosnia, was the first to fall to a pattern which involved the army eliminating the Territorial Defence before a pack of Arkanovci (Arkan's men) were sent in to 'cleanse the territory' (*rasčistiti teren*) just as they had done in eastern Slavonia. The crimes began – the Arkanovci started killing Moslems (men and women) in cold blood, apparently revelling in their demonic work. Zvornik, an industrial town on the Drina, was the next to follow. Here the Arkanovci discovered the local correspondent of *Oslobođenje* and threw him out of the window of the high-rise building where he lived.

Bratunac, Srebrenica, Višegrad and Foča all followed suit quickly although in Višegrad the army's path was stopped by the extraordinary Murad Šabanović, a desperate Moslem fighter, who took control of the hydro-electric dam on the Drina above Višegrad and threatened to blow the installation sky high, a move which would have had incalculable consequences for the entire region. Dramatic negotiations over the air waves of Radio Sarajevo included Šabanović telling the chief of the JNA in Bosnia, General Milutin Kukanjac, to go fuck himself. The Vice-President of Bosnia, Ejup Ganić, until this point one of the most impressive politicians in Bosnia, began his steady descent into madness on this day, when he started wailing on air. The army stormed Šabanović's position after he had partially opened one of the sluice gates allowing a relatively harmless tidal wave down the river. When the army took control of the dam, they discovered that Šabanović had not planted explosives on the dam after all. This is one of the great mysteries of the war – how an acknowledged pyromaniac, which Šabanović was, had failed to lay his hands on explosives when the country was replete with weaponry.

The Serbs left a terrible trail of blood and destruction in their wake as they closed the noose around Sarajevo's neck. Soon after Foča was taken by the Serbs, Andrej Gustinčić of Reuters succeeded in entering the town after a hair-raising journey through the barricades:

Gangs of gun-toting Serbs rule Foča, turning the once quiet Bosnian town into a nightmare landscape of shattered streets and burning houses. The motley assortment of fierce-looking bearded men carry Kalashnikovs and bandoliers or have handguns tucked into their belts. Some are members of paramilitary groups from Serbia, self-proclaimed crusaders against Islam and defenders of the Serbian nation, others are wild-eyed local men, hostile towards strangers and happy to have driven out their Moslem neighbours. No one seems to be in command and ill-disciplined and bad-tempered gunmen stop and detain people at will.

The Moslems, who made up half of the town's population of 10,000 people, have fled or are in jail. Many of their houses have been destroyed or are in flames. Black smoke billows from two houses which belonged to Moslem residents. Entire streets have been destroyed, restaurants reduced to cinders and twisted metal, apartment blocks charred, the hospital hit by mortar fire. The Serbs say that despite the damage, only seven or eight of their own men and about twenty Moslems were killed in the fighting

169

which began on 8 April. They say the Moslems began it. A feverish distrust of all that is not Serbian and a conviction that they have narrowly escaped genocide at the hand of Islamic fundamentalists has gripped Foča's Serbs.

'Do you see that field?' asks a Serbian woman, pointing to a sloping meadow by the Drina river. 'The jihad (Moslem Holy War) was supposed to begin there. Foča was going to be the new Mecca. There were lists of Serbs who were marked for death,' the woman says, repeating a belief held by townspeople and gunmen. 'My two sons were down on the list to be slaughtered like pigs. I was listed under rape.' None of them have seen the lists but this does not prevent anyone from believing in them unquestioningly.

The gunmen say that about 100 of them belong to the Serbian Guard, an ultra-nationalist paramilitary group based in Belgrade, while a further 150 came as volunteers from Serbia. They all share a sense of righteousness, a distrust of Europe which they say has betrayed them by sympathizing with the Moslems, and a determination that Foča must be a Serbian town. Among them is Milorad Todović, a bearded office worker from Belgrade. 'You want war, I'll give you war,' he said. 'A bullet for you, a bullet for me and may the stronger man win.' A native of Foča, he said he returned when he heard stories about the lists and says soon Europe will have to join Serbia in the battle against Islam. 'Imagine, there were infants on that list.'

Would Moslems be allowed to return?

'Those who have not sinned can come back,' he said. 'Ethnic minorities have always lived happily in Serbian states. They lived better than Serbs because we let them take advantage of us. Serbs are good people.'

Two houses burned in the town, even though there is no longer any fighting there. A member of the Serbian guard explains that it is the Moslems who set them on fire to prevent Serbs from moving in. But the only remaining Moslems appeared to be some 300 men in the town jail. Guards say the prisoners are extremists who took part in the fighting. But the prisoners claim they were rounded up in their homes and workplaces after the fighting began, beaten and brought to the prison where they have spent the last two weeks.

'No one knows how it started,' said Esad Soro, thirty-seven, a truck driver. 'We were brought here from our homes. None of us offered resistance. I didn't leave my house before that. I didn't dare.'

The aim of this offensive – the second war launched in Bosnia-Hercegovina – was territorial acquisition. Karadžić was determined to gain 65 per cent of Bosnia's territory to found his state (the

Serbian Republic of Bosnia-Hercegovina) which was an international pariah even before it was properly constituted. The territory formed a huge crescent running along the four rivers from Bosanska Krupa in the north-west through Doboj in the centre, to Bijeljina in the north-east. From there it stretched south along the Drina towards Višegrad before bending westwards through Foča towards eastern Hercegovina.

When fighting broke out around Sarajevo in earnest on the weekend of 4 and 5 April 1992, the third Bosnian war had begun. Its outbreak was intentionally timed by the Serb forces, under the direction of Karadžić and the JNA, still led at the time by General Kukanjac, to coincide with the international recognition that independent Bosnia-Hercegovina was to be granted the following Monday. The first war involved Serbs and Croats; the second was between Serbs and Moslems; the third war, although as cruel as the other two, pitted Serb irregulars, largely culled from the surrounding peasantry together with JNA and its awesome arsenal of heavy artillery against the sophisticated, urban dwellers of Sarajevo and the other major towns, notably Tuzla and Bihać. The battle for Sarajevo was launched by Karadžić doubtless for strategic reasons, but if successful it would also signal a victory for the primitive and irrational over the civilized and the rational. The case of the Serbs has often been misrepresented and their genuine fears and concerns dismissed when they should not have been. But the behaviour of Karadžić, the Arkanovci and other paramilitary groups, and the JNA in Bosnia-Hercegovina destroyed their reputation abroad. No injustice had been perpetrated against the Serbs of Bosnia or of Serbia to justify this rape of Bosnia-Hercegovina.

From the beginning of the conflict in Croatia, one question above most others has exercised minds inside and outside the country: what causes this depth of hatred which has provoked atrocities and slaughter on such a wide scale over such a short period of time? In retrospect, it seems clear that the wars of the Second World War did not end with Tito. The conflict inside Yugoslavia between 1941 and 1945 assumed such bloody proportions that, were it ever to revive, it was always likely to be merciless. Even for those like myself who have observed not merely the war itself but the dense web of political intrigue which led to it, the extent or nature of the violence is beyond any framework of moral comprehension. Obviously, the conflict has been caused by complex historical and political forces. But the hatred has a slightly different origin. To a large degree, the wars of the Yugoslav succession have been nationalist in character. They are not ethnic conflicts, as the media would often have it, as most of those doing the killing are of the same ethnos. Indeed what is striking about Bosnia-Hercegovina, in particular, is just how closely related are the Serbs, the Croats and the Moslems. Religion is the crucial factor dividing these people, although this is not a confessional conflict. For centuries, these people have been asked to choose between competing empires and ideologies, which have invariably been defined by religion.

On occasions, great earthquakes have erupted along this powerful historical fault line. It is then that the Bosnians have been enlisted in the service of this or that great power. The Bosnian Serbs, Croats and Moslems have been adorned with many different cultural uniforms over the centuries by which they identify one another as the enemy when conflict breaks out. Despite this, underneath the dress they can see themselves reflected – it is the awful recognition that these primitive beasts on the other side of the barricade are their brothers which has led to the violence assuming such ghastly proportions in Bosnia. The only way that fighters can deal with this realization is to exterminate the opposite community. How else does one explain the tradition of facial mutilation in this region? How else can we account for the high incidence of women and children being killed in cold blood? The Orthodox, the Catholics or the Moslems can only claim victory when the heretics have been wiped out or expelled from their homes. Ceasefires brokered by the United Nations may come and go in Bosnia-Hercegovina, the fighters on all three sides will almost certainly ignore them. The Serbs will continue until they control 65 per cent of Bosnian territory; Croat guns will not rest until western Hercegovina and Posavina have become integrated into Croatia; and despite the best attempts by the Serbs to exterminate them and the Croats to disenfranchise them politically, the Moslems will mount a guerrilla campaign against which the struggles in Northern Ireland and the Basque country will pale into insignificance. Historically, the only way to keep these people apart once the fighting begins has been for an outside power to intervene and offer its protection to all citizens, in particular, from imperial urges of Croatia and Serbia. History will judge whether the international community is able to rise to the mighty challenge posed by war in Bosnia-Hercegovina.

I had not been in Sarajevo for almost three months when I left Belgrade in early May for the Bosnian capital. After several days of sunshine, the day was overcast as I left in a tired Sarajevo-built Volkswagen Golf which had been passed down from hack to hack returning to Belgrade from the war zone. I was the fourth journalist to take possession of it. The windscreen had amazingly not been hit by bullets or shrapnel which was a fate that a majority of the journalists' cars suffered. We stopped for a brief cup of coffee close to the Serbian–Bosnian border, only twenty-five miles or so from Bijeljina. Before the coffee arrived, a sleek column of UN vehicles shot by, their flags fluttering in the wind. We all leaped up and jumped in our cars to follow what we thought would be our best protection against the dreaded wildmen of the Serbian barricades. The journey through most of Bosnia presented no problems. We stopped in Tuzla for lunch, going so far as to fraternize with the UN personnel who come from Sweden and Argentina. Since the fighting broke out, Tuzla has been hailed as the 'oasis of peace'. What a sad city of hope this is. It is true that in Tuzla, the Reformist Forces won in the general election, making it the only region in Bosnia where there was a supranational political leadership. Yet even though it rejoiced defiantly in its multi-national composition, Tuzla was surely doomed when I passed through it. I skipped over to a shopping centre to gauge local sentiment. Everybody's response was the same – they were grateful that they had been spared the violence until now, but they assumed it would not be long before they were the next to feel the force.

Until fifteen miles outside of Sarajevo, the journey was smooth. At the first sign of trouble, the UN (who at this time could still pass through roadblocks with ease) dumped its journalist posse and left us to deal with the suspicious Serbs. As one of my colleagues was detained briefly, I took a short walk with a local Serb policeman to discuss the situation with him. He confirmed the countless observations which I had made when talking to local fighters of all nationalities – he was not a man of evil. On the contrary, he explained how he found it very difficult to shoot at the other side of his village, because he knew everybody who lived there. But the war had somehow arrived and he had to defend his home. The man was confused and upset by the events but he now perceived the Green Berets and the Ustashas to be a real threat to his family. 'We cannot let them form an Islamic state here,' he said with genuine passion. 'Are you sure they want to?' I asked him. 'Of course they want to. I don't understand why you people outside don't realize that we are fighting for Europe against a foreign religion.' There was nothing disingenuous about this simple man. His only mistake was to believe the nonsense that his local community had learned from Serbian television and the local branch of the SDS. He, too, is a victim.

On this occasion, the Serbs are more helpful than usual in guiding us to our destination: Ilidža and the Hotel Bosna. I drive up to the leafy grounds of the hotel complex where just a few months earlier, I had watched the irrationalists from the leadership of Serbia and Croatia exchange insults. Both Božović and Jurica were doubtless comfortable, surrounded by the trappings of power in Belgrade and Zagreb. But the Hotel Bosna is forced to stay and witness the obscene results of nationalist intransigence.

Ilidža lies about two miles west from the city limits of the Bosnian capital. There is a small Moslem majority in the little spa suburb but it is controlled by Serbian forces. It is on the front line and lying low in the valley is extremely exposed to attack from the Territorial Defence (TO). The embryonic Bosnian army has no opportunity to dislodge the murderous artillery and snipers which control the hills to the north, south and east of Sarajevo. But inasmuch as the Serbs have an Achilles heel, Ilidža is it. If the TO can break through here, it has the opportunity of linking up with fighters in the town of Visoko where it has supplies of ammunition.

On my first afternoon in Ilidža, I decide to drive into Sarajevo. It is a beautiful hot afternoon but I listen with unbending concentration to my friend Tony Smith from the Associated Press. 'Once you get past the Territorials' barricade, you just put your foot down. The danger spots are close to the UN headquarters which is the old post office engineering building, by the television station and then later around the Hotel Bristol (that's sniper alley) and around the Holiday Inn. Whatever you do, don't go beside the river where the main post office is, as that is where you are most exposed.' With weather-beaten faces and flak jackets strapped around our T-shirts, we get into our cars and I follow Tony's Toyota which has been hit by a grenade at the back. When we reach the city limits, our feet hit the floor and we shoot off down the main Sarajevo road at eighty-five miles an hour, dodging burnt out buses and huge concrete slabs which the TO has erected as barricades on the way. Never have I witnessed such an eerie scene. Broad daylight in a capital city and there is not a soul on the streets. Newspaper skips in the wind. This is not Sarajevo – this is the Twilight Zone, and it is real.

I spend the next few days racing in and out of Sarajevo. No food is allowed through the barricades. Most of the city's telephones do not work. It is an unfathomably surreal experience. I see the television station, the front of which has been obliterated by electronically-guided missiles. I see people queuing listlessly for bread. The Serb forces confiscate any food-aid destined for Sarajevo. One day I go to the airport to see the UN take delivery of twelve tonnes of food. The UN arrives but the food is already gone. Doubtless it is already cheering the stomachs of the snipers and artillery units up on the hills. Back in Sarajevo, I smell the stench of rotting flesh while visiting the hospital and mortuary. The doctors, nurses and aid workers can no longer cope with the number of deaths and injuries they are having to deal with. Everyone I see looks tired and underfed. Many men have given up shaving, com-pounding their drawn features. There is, of course, no escape from their fate and one or two people admit to me quietly that they are expecting to die in the next few weeks. Despite the crushing depression, people still try and lead a normal life. During one delightful beer I share with Gavrilo Grahovac, I listen to the sing-song academic theories of Professor Muhammed Filipović explaining quite cheerfully why the entire city of Sarajevo is now facing death. Sleeping in Ilidža, I am safe for the moment but I decide to spend one night with Zdravko who lives with his parents in the centre of town right next door to the headquarters of the TO. Sitting on the balcony talking as dusk turns to night, I notice how quickly I have become used to the thunderous crashing of artillery and the deadly crackle of automatic gunfire. As we get slowly drunk on some *Hercegovačka loza* (local spirit) which I brought in from Ilidža, the sense that life is coming to an end becomes overwhelming. The drink both generates the feeling and dampens its effect – Sarajevo comes to an end, why bother living? Grebo explains the anger in the city about the incompetence of the Presidency which has assumed all power. There is no war cabinet and no proper defence of the city. Indeed, when I ask Bosnia's Defence Minister, Jerko Doko, what his strategy for the defence of Sarajevo is, he replied: 'Actually I come from Mostar and I've only been here for a year, so I don't know the city very well.' Perhaps it is fortunate that Doko has no control over the city's defences. That is in the hands of the fighters on the ground.

The Presidency building, which has taken quite a few direct hits, becomes more Kafkaesque by the day. It is surrounded by members of the Territorial Defence who are alternately exceptionally surly and obsequiously pleasant. Although the Territorial Defence is extremely poorly equipped, some of its leaders are experienced professional soldiers. Although bereft of any political leadership, it has afforded spirited resistance to the Serbs' heavy artillery. All Sarajlije say the same – the Serbs can destroy the city and they can occupy New Sarajevo but they will never take the old town. Unlike Vukovar, you cannot send tanks into the narrow alleys of central Sarajevo – the town is ideally suited to defensive urban warfare. Everyone in Sarajevo is prepared to join in that fight when the Serb forces enter the town.

Back in the Presidency, I am taken to see the Vice-President, Ejup Ganić. Before, one of the most accomplished politicians in Sarajevo, Ganić now spends much of these interviews asking me what he should do. This was when I realized how political power was withering inside the cocoon which the Presidency had spun around itself. While Ganić was interrogating foreign journalists about his next policy move, Alija Izetbegović was locked away in his office. Ever since he was released after being taken hostage by the JNA, Izetbegović had lived the life of a recluse. The abduction of the President was a bizarre highlight of Bosnian history. On returning from talks in Lisbon, the army spirited Izetbegović away to the barracks at Lukavica close to the airport. That evening, negotiations were held, via the good offices of Radio and Television Sarajevo, between the army leadership, Ejup Ganić and the redoubtable Colm Doyle, an Irish army officer popular with everybody, who was in Sarajevo as Lord Carrington's personal envoy. This became a gripping piece of improvised theatre with a number of twists and turns in the plot, not the least of which was Vice-President Ganić's apparent readiness to decide the fate of his President without consulting him. Twenty-four hours later, the President was taken from Lukavica to the headquarters of the JNA in the centre of town which was surrounded by members of the Territorial Defence. Finally, Colm Doyle secured Izetbegović's release by guaranteeing General Kukanjac and his men safe passage out of Sarajevo with UN protection. Two hundred yards after the convoy had left the barracks, Izetbegović was taken to the Presidency but on the initiative of its commander, a unit of the Territorial Defence stormed the army convoy and killed four soldiers including two colonels.

The incident was a disaster for the UN and a disaster for the people of Sarejevo as it gave General Kukanjac, who escaped the attack on the convoy, a green light to smash the city. On returning to the Presidency building, President Izetbegović refused to shake hands with Ganić, whom he accused of being ready to sacrifice the President's life. Life in the Presidency became pretty gloomy after that. With Ganić suffering from creeping dementia and Izetbegović sulking or contemplating in his office, the man who took over the running of what remained of Bosnia was Stjepan Kljuić, a bearded, quiet Croat who had in the past lost battles against his colleagues in Zagreb and Mostar who favoured secession for Bosnia's Croats. But, as the only senior member of the Presidency who still appeared to be functioning normally, he simply assumed power. None of these people had a constitutional mandate – parliament had been dissolved illegally before it had agreed to grant the Presidency emergency powers. The government still existed but like Jerko Doko, the cabinet wielded no authority. Its members were window-dressing, fashioned to give the impression of legality where none existed.

I am dreaming, not for the first time, of the war. I am walking down the streets of Sarajevo. Grenades and mortars are exploding in close proximity but I sense no danger to myself. It is bright and sunny, other people are out on the streets. Every so often a sniper's bullet detaches somebody's head from their shoulders. This is a clinical affair – there is no blood, no gunge, there is a ping and then a head falls off. All the time the mortars are getting louder and louder and falling ever closer to me. Although I am still convinced of my invincibility, I none the less feel the urgent need to run and hide. The bangs and explosions are getting louder and closer. I awake and immediately sit bolt upright. All my senses are bulging and straining in an attempt to process the stimuli they are picking up. It takes less than a second. It is five o'clock in the morning and around me every conceivable form of artillery is being fired. On this occasion, however, it is not just outgoing artillery, it is incoming as well – Ilidža is under attack from the Territorial Defence and I am in the middle.

I get downstairs and there is an atmosphere of controlled chaos among the other journalists. A mortar has landed in the BBC TV's edit suite – equipment has been damaged but mercifully, the room was empty at the time. Moslem snipers are close to the hotel and the Serb defenders are looking tired, nervous and under considerable pressure. Bullets streak in through windows at the back of the hotel and the roof of the building takes another couple of direct hits. Later on, the shelling of the Hotel Bosna is stopped after an appeal to TO fighters from the Presidency to prevent any injury to foreign journalists. None the less we are pinned in the hotel for nineteen hours while the battle rages around us. It is odd, but there I never feel frightened, probably because I have too much work to do (I had always assumed that in such a situation, I would be immobile with fear).

The Serb response to the attack on Ilidža was predictably merciless. I talk to people in Sarajevo by phone. Zlatko Dizdarević at *Oslobođenje* tells me that the shelling has never been worse. The hotel where UN personnel are staying has been hit and several of their vehicles are on fire. Down town the heavy artillery is pummelling Baš-Čaršija again, the Presidency is under fire and so for the umpteenth time is the television and radio building. During the fighting I eavesdrop on the phone conversation of a JNA commander. 'Is that the Territorial Defence?' he asks. 'Well, get me

Vehbija Karić immediately. Tell him it's Vinko Elez on the phone.' This is when my ears pricked up. Here was a JNA officer wanting to talk to the deputy head of the TO. Before Karić made it to the phone, Elez muttered: 'I'll blow his bloody Baš-Čaršija sky high if he doesn't listen.'

'Karić, is that you? . . . Now listen, I don't care about what's going on around us at the moment. We had an agreement that when we received prisoners back, they would be in good condition. We are taking good care of all your people and you know it. Several of my men were returned today and they all bore the marks of some bad beatings . . . And listen, I want you to put a stop to what the Green Berets are up to near Vogošća – we have reliable reports that Serb women and children are being taken off . . . Now just listen. You get your people in order and do it now, or else we are all going to contribute to the greatest genocide in the history of mankind. Have you got that? . . . Good, well get going.' I then spoke to this commander who was clearly an honourable officer. There was a body of officers in JNA who tried to adhere to the Geneva Convention. This was an impossible task but I received the strong impression that this commander was trying to minimize the bloodshed in this disastrous situation.

The BBC orders all its personnel out of Sarajevo as soon as it is possible to leave. This is a great relief to many of us. In this situation, it is impossible to take the decision oneself to leave. As a journalist, one feels morally bound to stay, however great the danger. If the news organization orders its people out, they are freed from much of the guilt which leaving induces. Even despite this order, many of us feel depressed about leaving. The next morning at six o'clock, a convoy of some thirty-five shattered journalists pulls out of the Hotel Bosna. A few stay on – one of them, a friendly young Catalan journalist, Jordi Puyol, was killed three days later.

'I would never run from here before the war ends,' Zdravko adds when discussing those Sarajlije who could afford to leave before the going got tough, 'but the minute it finishes, I'm going. There's nothing left for me now.' Zdravko won't go because of his parents. But this is a warning for the future, if the man who personifies all that is vibrant and exciting about Bosnia-Hercegovina and Sarajevo has indicated he wants nothing more to do with the place. We have all failed Sarajevo: the European Community, the Croats, the journalists, the Serbs, President Izetbegović, the United Nations, Karadžić, Balkan traditions, Milošević, Titoism, Tuđman, the three churches, the Americans. I could add to the list endlessly.

6 JUNE 1992–JUNE 1993:

Beyond Hades

'We had to decide: do we make a run for it or do we sit it out? The shelling had got very loud and seemed to be coming from all sides of the village although we agreed that it was weaker to the north, towards Doboj. The problem about heading for Doboj is that we had already heard that the most terrible things had happened there. One family decided finally to try to go south towards Maglaj. We watched them leave – the mother carrying a baby and two children who were ten and twelve. The mother was the first to fall with the baby, then the ten-year-old boy and, as the girl tried to grab the baby from her mother's arms, she too was hit. So we stayed. When they came, they separated us into three groups: women, men and older men. I spent six weeks in Trnopolje and was fed bread, but I wasn't beaten. We heard some screams now and then but it didn't seem as bad as the things that I'd heard about in other camps. And now I am here in Zagreb. Where my daughter and granddaughter are, I don't know. Where my sons and grandsons are, I don't know. But I know in my blood, they are dead.'

'When they arrived, I recognized one who was a local boy. He was in the same class as my son at school. I was with my neighbour and her fourteen-year-old boy in my kitchen. She grabbed him to protect him. They hit me with a gun, so I lay on the floor and watched how they pulled them apart and forced a gun into my neighbour's hand and made her stick the barrel of the gun down her son's throat. I screamed, 'No, no, please,' and the local Višegrad boy hit me so I lost consciousness. When I came to, I was lying in a small pool of my own blood. My flat had been ransacked and completely destroyed. I do not know what happened to my neighbour.'

'It was late at night and I was told not to go out but I had to see if my friends were all right. On the outskirts, I ran into a Croat patrol. They took me back to a house in the next village and first they beat me, then they raped me. I think there were about five of them. I was locked in for, it must have been, several hours, and then some more came back and I was raped again. Then there was a big battle and after two days, our fighters rescued me and I was evacuated to Belgrade.'

As vile as it was, the war in Croatia did not prepare us for the gruesome quagmire into which Bosnia-Hercegovina (BiH) was to sink. By the time the fighting in BiH began in the middle of March 1992, journalists had already exhausted their vocabulary of pejoratives to describe the revolting behaviour of Balkan warriors. But, whereas the scribes had worn down their tools, the victims in Bosnia were condemned to experience a yet more ghoulish fate than the peoples of Croatia – the Balkan war unchained.

The three stories above were told to me by a Croat refugee in Zagreb, a Moslem refugee in Sarajevo and a Serb refugee in Belgrade. Anyone who has visited Bosnia during the war could fill an encyclopedia with similar and worse. The atrocities in BiH have been so numerous and widespread that such tales now appear mundane. The entire region has been roasted alive on an open fire.

Bosnia-Hercegovina does not exist any longer. The history of Europe's shortest-lived state in modern times seems to be coming to an end as the aim of Croats and Serbs to divide the territory between their two regional imperia approaches realization. However, this is not necessarily the end of the war, which still has a richly textured future. As I write in June 1993, the fighting has entered a new phase of its bizarre logic. Croats and Moslems, who for many months maintained the remarkable fiction of a military alliance posited on two incompatible war aims, have engaged in an orgy of mutual slaughter. It has become a free-for-all. The Zagreb-based Moslem sociologist, Alija Hodžić, has described it as being 'like the thirty years war where you are never sure who your enemy is. And where your worst enemy can become overnight your closest friend, provided he is an enemy of your most immediate enemy.'

Over 100,000 people have been killed and probably many more. Nearly half of Bosnia's 4.2 million people have been displaced. Many thousands of women have been raped. Whole cities razed to the ground, not to mention the countless villages which have disappeared from the map. All this is the result of but a limited Serbo-Croat war. The large-scale Serbo-Croat conflict which would swallow the civilian populations of Zagreb and Belgrade has not happened yet, although it still might. So far the struggle has been fought in the eastern and southern extremities of Croatia and the entire territory of BiH. It has been the tale of how the two largest peoples in the former Yugoslavia have attempted to define the contours of their new, free and deeply democratic nation states by force, with the hapless Bosnian Moslems trapped between these two sets of flesh-ripping teeth.

This does not exonerate Bosnia's Moslem leaders of a share of the responsibility. They coaxed their people into a war for which they were criminally unprepared, and at times have both consciously and unconsciously allowed the mass slaughter of their own in the hope of receiving weapons from the West so that they might fulfil their political agenda. Neither does this essential political framework define the relative responsibility of the armies and volunteers for the degree and extent of the atrocities committed in Bosnia. That is a separate issue. Our understanding of the war in BiH has, regrettably, been clouded by the level of suffering and the tendency of many witnesses to confuse the moral questions raised by the conflict with the political issues which caused it.

As such, it has become commonplace to assume that Serbia, driven by irrational blood-lust, is now determined to start a war in the southern Serbian province of Kosovo, 90 per cent of whose population is Albanian. This is a fundamental and dangerous misapprehension of the nature of the conflict in the former Yugoslavia. At the heart of the wars lies the struggle for territorial acquisition and not blood-lust. The Serbian authorities are in absolute control of Kosovo and therefore have no motivation for provoking an armed conflict there. They have happily disenfranchised the Albanians both politically and economically without jeopardizing their stragetic interests. With both an active war in Bosnia and a frozen war in Croatia on their hands, the Serb leadership is most unlikely to risk opening a third front (as a war in Kosovo would surely mean a full-scale Balkan war) when there is nothing to be gained.

Yet a broad perception has developed outside the Balkans that these are wars fuelled by 'ancient hatreds', as the British Prime Minister, John Major, has characterized them. In addition, the theory that the perpetration of atrocities is a central war aim (of the Serbs, in particular) has gained wide currency. This represents a failure of historical understanding which has led to a frequently crass interpretation on the part of the international players involved in the current drama. It has often been encouraged by the local authors to further their political ends, and together, this has ensured that, on the whole, the nebulous blob, which parades under the epithet 'the international community', has contributed to a worsening of the crisis. In order to comprehend the atrocities, we must understand the politics and not the other way round.

After the referendum in Bosnia-Hercegovina which took place on 29 February and 1 March 1992, relations between the Croats and Moslems on the one hand, and the Serbs and the JNA on the other, began to deteriorate in the northern Bosnian town of Bosanski Brod. For some weeks prior to this, the JNA had consolidated its positions around Brod in order to shell its twin city, Slavonski Brod, on the Croatian side of the Sava river. Brod is one of the most important towns in Posavina, the predominantly Croat-populated strip of territory on the south side of the Sava.

During the summer and autumn of 1991, the rural Serb population of eastern Bosnia and eastern Hercegovina were busy forming their Serbian autonomous regions (SAO) in violation of the Bosnian and Yugoslav constitutions. In response, the Croats also created two illegal *Zajednice*, or communities, of Hrvatska Posavina (HZP) and Herceg-Bosna (the latter representing the Croats in western Hercegovina and central Bosnia). The HZ Posavina separates two predominantly Serb areas, north-eastern Bosnia and Bosanska Krajina, the most militant Serb community with its capital in Banja Luka.

The infamous northern corridor of the Serbs, needed to link these two regions, must run through a large part of the HZ Posavina. It is around the area of Brod that this link is most tightly squeezed, measuring less than a mile across in parts. There were other reasons why fighting broke out here first. Brod itself was over 50 per cent Croat, but a large number of the surrounding villages to the east were exclusively Serb. The town was also critical for both sides as the Croats could supply weapons and men across the Sava at this point. Finally, there is a large oil refinery in the town, the presence of which doubtless played a role in both sides' strategic thinking. Like several such neuralgic areas in the Bosnian war, no side has ever enjoyed full control of the territory and although the Serbs established the contours of their corridor early on in the war, this communication link has been frequently closed as a result of Croat incursions on the territory.

The tenuous access of the Banja Luka Serbs to their brethren to the east informs their militant approach. It is no coincidence that their hard-line views are shared by the other most far-flung limb of the Serb nation in BiH, the eastern Hercegovinians. Their long-term existence, too, depends on the successful establishment of a logistical corridor which would bond them with eastern Bosnia across the Serb headquarters in Pale, the beautiful ski resort, fifteen miles south-east of Sarajevo.

But first things first. Before embarking on the major push to define their corridors, the Serbs had to install themselves as absolute masters of eastern Bosnia, the area which lies west across the river Drina from Serbia. The economic and military life of the Bosnian Serbs could only function unhindered if they had free and immediate access to Serbia proper. Four of these districts, running north to south – Zvornik, Bratunac, Srebrenica and Višegrad, had an inconveniently large Moslem population. Moslems formed an absolute majority in all of them, the greatest density being 73 per cent in Srebrenica. To the north of Zvornik, in the Bijeljina district, the Serbs accounted for 59 per cent of the population but there was a large Moslem minority.

Bijeljina was the first town to be hit by the Serbian militia in early April before the European Community and the United States recognized an independent Bosnia on 7 April. The assault was led by Arkan – Željko Ražnjatović. But although Arkan and his Tigers provided the vanguard, most of the fighters were irregular locals who had formed the Serbian National Guard of Semberija and Majevice. The JNA did not participate in the fighting, indeed, the local barracks was opened for civilian refugees, both Moslem and Serb, who were fleeing the conflict. The battle for Bijeljina lasted two crisp days and did not, in contrast to some of the more lurid newspaper reports, result in the widespread destruction of the town.

On 4 April, after the fighting had died down, Arkan held talks with Fikret Abdić, the Moslem leader from the Bihać district who was representing the Bosnian Presidency. Also present were

Karadžić's third-in-command, Biljana Plavšić, and leaders of the JNA in Bosnia. Abdić and Arkan issued a joint statement over the local radio appealing to citizens not to worry and to return to the streets. There were few reported cases of any atrocities or killings of Moslem civilians.

Less fortunate were the Moslem inhabitants of Zvornik. This grimy yellow industrial town is the most important link joining Serbia and Bosnia before the Drina widens to the south. A large number of Serbs who fought here have travelled from a few miles up the road in the Chetnik stronghold of Loznica in Serbia where the fascist leader, Vojislav Šešelj, commands much influence. The rape of Zvornik saw the first serious atrocities committed against civilians. Zvornik also propelled the second surge of refugees after Brod, many retreating south and west to other Moslem communities yet to be visited by violence, and many crossing the bridge to Mali Zvornik in Serbia. Serbia has taken in many thousands of Moslem refugees from Bosnia during the war although they have rarely received the same sort of welcome as the Serb refugees. None the less, it is important to note that Serbian society has suffered as much as Croatian society under the strain of refugees from the wars in Croatia and Bosnia, although neither has been so comprehensively ruined as Bosnia itself.

There is some evidence to suggest that in general, during the first months of the Bosnian war, the units commanded by Arkan accorded a degree of respect towards the Moslems in the region, whereas others, including Šešelj's people, considered the campaign to be an open-ended licence to butcher. This did not, of course, prevent terror from spreading among local Moslem populations when rumours proliferated that Arkan was visiting their region.

But the contrast between Bijeljina and Zvornik revealed something of greater significance than the stylistic differences separating Serbia's two most notorious militia leaders. Instead, it concerns the issue of 'cleansing'. In the first instance, this policy of the systematic expulsion or liquidation of a minority population invariably occurs once a political struggle has escalated into an armed struggle. It is by no means a novel practice. When war begins in the Balkans, the local civilian population of the defeated nation immediately assumes a strategic threat to the victorious fighters. Bijeljina was from the outset firmly in the hands of the Serbs, while the Moslems or Bosnian government forces had no possibility of returning the military strike. This was not the case in Zvornik. Here there was a Moslem majority which had too be erased, as well as Moslem forces which still posed a serious threat to the Serbs to the west and south.

Initially, 'cleansing' is a military tactic which is mistaken for the central war aim because it is executed in such a horrifying fashion. Of course, as the war continues, dragging in most areas of the republic, the hostility between the nationalities reaches fever pitch. The idea of including a minority population in the conquered territory becomes less acceptable as the doctrine of 'national purity' strengthens.

This explains the paradox of how the Moslem population in eastern Hercegovina was not subject to mass atrocities and expulsion until a year after the war began. Of course, they suffered the most appalling discrimination – their houses were blown up, they were forced to observe the most rigorous curfews, individuals were murdered and beaten up – but they were not expelled or massacred *en masse*.

Arriving at Doxato we found it like a town of the dead, everything burned and devastated, and such an odour of blood and decomposed bodies as I never hope to encounter again. Indeed, five minutes before we entered the town, while driving through the plain, the stench was insupportable. In this plain were heaps of corpses thinly covered with sand, where the survivors had tried, for sanitary reasons, to cover up their dead, but they were all too few to do so thoroughly, and for all practical purposes the bodies were unburied. Practically all of the Greek portion of the town was burned, and one saw everywhere in the streets charred remains of what had been human bodies.

The Turkish quarter was, with a few exceptions, unburned. According to the accounts of the survivors, it was there that the greater part of the massacres took place. I saw many rooms where the floors were soaked with blood, and rugs, mats, and cushions were covered with blood and human remains. I was informed of one courtyard that the house and environs were the property of a Turk, who, on hearing of the possibility of a massacre, had sent round to the Greeks of Doxato to offer a sanctuary to their women and children, and that after upwards of 120 were assembled there, he and several of his compatriots, under the direction of a Bulgarian officer, had butchered them all!

Were it not for the slightly archaic prose, this testimony by a British officer visiting the aftermath of the massacre of Greeks in Doxato during the Second Balkan War of 1913 could have been printed in any newspaper around the world from a reporter who had visited a razed village in Bosnia-Hercegovina, although on this occasion, the Greeks would almost certainly have been Bosnian Moslems. There are countless similar examples from all other Balkan conflicts which have broken out since the first half of the nineteenth century. The most intense experience of this kind prior to 1991 was, of course, the multi-faceted fratricide in Croatia, Bosnia, Serbia and Montenegro during the Second World War.

The previous Balkan wars should have served as a warning to Europe as to the patterns of violence if an armed conflict were to break out in Bosnia-Hercegovina in particular. If history was not a disciplined enough teacher, then the events in Croatia during the ten months before the outbreak of war in BiH should have rendered the implications of war in Bosnia crystal clear. The tactics of the Serbian Democratic Party (SDS) in Bosnia until March 1992 were frequently those of an overweening bully, but their demand for a political solution which guaranteed the rights that they had fought for in two world wars was mistakenly ignored. One thing that should not have been ignored was the Serbs' systematic preparation for the armed conflict in the event of an irrevocable breakdown of political consensus. So dreadful are the consequences of a war in Bosnia, that it is behoven unto European politicians and diplomats to do all they can to stop it from happening. Instead, they encouraged it by their actions. This is why Germany bears a heavy moral responsibility for its actions.

The reasons for the German recognition of Croatia are hard to fathom. Serbian claims early on in the war that the Germans were using Croatia as the vanguard with which to establish the Fourth Reich were plain ridiculous. In the heat of war, the more subtle theory advanced by some Serbs that the Germans were pushing for an outlet to the Adriatic sounded more plausible but on examination, it, too, is a weak example of conspiratorial nonsense. Until the issue of Croatian recognition leaped up the political agenda in Bonn, the German government had taken a much more far-sighted view of events in Eastern Europe and the former Soviet Union than their allies in the United Kingdom and the United States. Leaving aside the disastrous speed at which Chancellor Kohl forced unification with East Germany for reasons of short-term political gain, Germany was the only Western country to contribute to the stablization of the Soviet Union by spending over $60 billion within the framework of the withdrawal of the Red Army from East Germany. By dint of its proximity to Eastern Europe, Germany was much more concerned about a potential destabilization of Eastern Europe due to economic collapse after 1989. It was also aware of the area's economic potential if the regional decline could be reversed. This is reflected in the relatively high sums invested by Germany in some East European countries after the revolutions. It soon became clear, however, that German and, to an extent, Austrian commercial interests in Eastern Europe were focused on a narrow band of regions: western Poland, the Czech Republic and Hungary. Slovakia was excluded from this privileged group. Slovenia and Croatia were definitely in. It is no coincidence that this select band of countries has deep economic, cultural and confessional ties with Germany. As such, it is both natural and understandable that Germany would want to re-establish those ties after 1989. Such a policy is welcome, until Germany stumbles across the delicate relationship between Serbs and Croats. Then its benign influence, wittingly or not, turns malign.

Economic co-operation with Slovenia and Croatia was limited by dint of the uncertain situation inside the former Yugoslavia. None the less, when the newly elected Slovene and Croat governments moved towards a policy of secession from the Yugoslav federation in 1990, they quickly received German support for their efforts. This increased noticeably after the outbreak of war in June 1991, and Germany became the main advocate of recognition within the European Community. The Vatican and Germany's Catholic hierarchy (especially in Bavaria and the Rheinland) applied considerable pressure on the Bonn government to recognize the two republics. Austria's Foreign Minister was also a vocal advocate of recognition persuading all of his Austrian People's Party and a large section of the Austrian Socialist Party (excluding Chancellor Franz Vranitzky, however) to join his campaign.

The central argument in favour of recognition was that such a move would end the war in Croatia because to withhold it, would give the JNA the green light to continue its aggression. In a response, dated 13 December 1991, to the letter of Perez de Cuellar, the UN Secretary General, urging that the European Community refrain from premature recognition, the German Foreign Minister, Hans-Dietrich Genscher, spelled it out:

According to the European Community and the monitors, the Serb leadership together with the JNA bear the chief responsibility for violating the ceasefire in Croatia and the Hague Conference has been stagnant for many weeks.

The refusal of recognition of those republics which desire their independence would necessarily lead to a further escalation of the use of violence by the JNA since they would regard this as a confirmation of their policy of aggression. I would like to point out that according to the Treaty of Helsinki and the Paris Charter, the borders in Europe are inviolable and cannot be changed by force. Therefore, the EC has demanded that the internal and external borders of Yugoslavia be respected.[1]

Recognition came, although it did not bring peace with it. Indeed, as soon as it was announced that Germany would recognize Croatia and Slovenia unilaterally, there was an upsurge in fighting. The cease-fire between the Serbs and Croats was negotiated within the framework of the Vance plan for Croatia which effected the deployment of a peace-keeping force in the Serb-controlled regions of Croatia. Leaving aside the constitutional issue of Croatia seceding without reaching a prior agreement with its Serb minority, recogni-

---

1. Nach den Feststellungen der EG und der Monitoren trägt die serbische Führung zusammen mit der jugoslawischen Volksarmee die Hauptverantwortung dafür, daß in Kroatien die Waffenruhe nicht eingehalten wird und die Haager Jugoslawien-Konferenz bereits seit mehreren Wochen stagniert.

Die Verweigerung der Anerkennung jener Republiken, die ihre Unabhängigkeit wünschen, müßte zu weiterer Eskalation der Gewaltanwendung durch die Volksarmee führen, weil sie darin eine Bestätigung ihrer Eroberungspolitik sehen würde. Ich darf darauf hinweisen, daß für Europa nach der Schlußakte von Helsinki and der Charta von Paris gilt, daß die Grenzen unverletzlich sind und nicht mit Gewalt geändert werden dürfen. Die EG hat deshalb die Respektierung der inneren und äußeren Grenzen Jugoslawiens gefordert.

tion has done nothing to stop the JNA policy of aggression, as perceived by Genscher. Croatia to this day does not control a third of its territory. So recognition failed in its central aim.

There is a second issue. Genscher referred to those republics which 'desire their independence'. Macedonia desired independence and yet when the great day of recognition, 15 January, arrived, Germany passed it over under pressure from the Greeks, even though Macedonia had fulfilled all the requirements which the EC has laid out for recognition. Athens agreed to recognize Croatia provided Germany did not recognize Macedonia. Therefore the German government acted not out of principle but out of self-interest.

That self-interest is explained by a combination of several factors. Germany's political weight in Europe has increased significantly since unification. It is now, without question, the *primus inter pares* of the European Community, if not its unchallenged leader. For the past three years, the policies of the Bundesbank and the German government (although not always synchronized) have had a decisive impact on the economies of most other European states. German political clout has been gained at the expense of British and French diplomatic power which has waned steadily since 1989. This is most clearly reflected by the increased attention which both the Bush and the Clinton administrations have paid to Bonn, and by the diminishing influence of London and Paris in Washington.

It appears that for Hans-Dietrich Genscher, the recognition of Croatia outside of a comprehensive solution to the Yugoslav crisis became the litmus test of German diplomatic muscle after 1989. The Bush Administration resolutely opposed such a move, while several members of the European Community also argued against it. So strong was the *Aussenamt*'s (foreign ministry) commitment to Zagreb that Bonn was prepared to break asunder the principle of a common European foreign policy if any of the other eleven members refused to recognize. In several member states there was a vigorous tussle inside government. According to one senior Foreign Office official, the British government had still not decided two days before the official recognition date, 15 January, whether to accept the German position or not. There were two lines of thinking inside the FO. The first, centred on the Embassy in Belgrade, argued flatly against recognition. The second, known as the Brussels lobby, maintained that because Germany had afforded Britain so many concessions at Maastricht then it would be churlish to oppose Germany's main foreign policy concern of the early 1990s, particularly as Britain's interst in Yugoslavia was limited.

The issue was thus decided within the framework of some rather Machiavellian horse-trading. Bonn went full steam ahead with its policy despite the opposition of the United States, the United Nations, the Hague Conference on Yugoslavia and indeed the presidents of Bosnia-Hercegovina and Macedonia, Izetbegović and Gligorov.

If Bosnia-Hercegovina had not existed, the impact of the decision would have been limited. The UN peace-keeping regime which was established soon after the end of January 1992 in the Serbian-held Krajina was the product of a negotiating process which Cyrus Vance had begun the previous November. But Bosnia did exist. At issue is how much Genscher and Kohl, who also bears responsibility, understood that Croatian recognition would virtually guarantee war in Bosnia-Hercegovina. It also depends on whether Germany had fully understood Zagreb's position towards an independent Bosnia.

Until large-scale fighting broke out between Moslem and Croat units in March and April 1993, Croatia's policy towards Bosnia-Hercegovina had been ambivalent and skilful. The Bosnian Croats supported the cantonization of Bosnia as envisaged by the Lisbon agreement of 18 March, 1992, as whole-heartedly as Radovan Karadžić. When Alija Izetbegović reneged on this commitment, the Croats switched to supporting full-blown independence of BiH, at the same time shelving their demands for a new constitutional order until the dust had settled following Bosnian recognition. Zagreb was among the first states to exchange diplomatic recognition with Sarajevo.

It was perfectly natural, given the rush for secession from Yugoslavia, that Zagreb should be concerned about the Croat community in Bosnia which made up some 18 per cent of the population. The Croats of western Hercegovina, in particular, were implacably opposed to BiH remaining inside a rump Yugoslavia dominated by Belgrade, and fears for their safety and economic status were probably quite justified. At the same time, Zagreb could only realize its aim of establishing close ties with the Croats of Bosnia if the republic were to detach itself from Yugoslavia. It was clearly much easier for the Croatian government to consolidate its influence over the compact Croat territories of an independent BiH, just as it would have been easier for Milošević to have his way in the republic if it had remained part of Yugoslavia. Thus it was that the Bosnian Croats and Serbs, pursuing, if not identical then very similar political aims, began to wage war on different sides.

Alija Izetbegović's war aim was the restoration of a unitary state with a relatively centralized government in Sarajevo. This was always incompatible with the war aims of the Croats, but neither side could realize their aims without first establishing Bosnia's independence from Yugoslavia. Thus it was that the Bosnian Croats and Moslems found themselves fighting on the same side, despite their mutually exclusive war aims.

Bosnian fears about Croatia's dual policy were aroused a month after the outbreak of war when Karadžić met, in the south Austrian city of Graz, with Mate Boban (the head of the HDZ – BiH from western Hercegovina) who had ousted, with Tuđman's blessing, the more moderate Croat, Stjepan Kljuić. They agreed in principle on a division of Bosnia which would give the Croats 20 per cent of the territory, the Serbs 65 per cent of the territory and the Moslems 15 per cent. In response, Kemal Kurspahić, the editor of *Oslobodenje*, replied with a bitter attack on Tuđman entitled '*Danke, Njofra*'[2] an ironic reference to the ghastly song '*Danke, Deutschland*' which swamped radio and television output in Croatia after the country's diplomatic recognition:

Your obsession with the idea of the division of Bosnia-Hercegovina is not, of course, new. We heard about it at the time you were still bouyed up by the euphoria of your election victory with your talk of 'Croatia in her historical borders', and variations on the theme 'what shall we do about Bosnia', and we know full well about your secret and public agreements on the subject with Milošević and his local satellites [in Bosnia].

2. The word 'Njofra' is Tuđman's first name, Franjo, in the popular slang, *šatrovački*, which inverts the syllables of a word.

From the very start, you shared with your most hated enemy, . . . whose desire to create a 'Greater Serbia' caused so much misery to thousands of people in Croatia, this love for Bosnia-Hercegovina. A Bosnia carved up by the two of you.

On your own admission, you both discussed it in Karađorđevo.[3] Then in your official residence, the Banski Dvori, you considered the practical aspects of the divided spheres of interests with the quisling twins, Koljević and Boras,[4] belonging to that fascinating species of humans who rip apart the state on whose presidency they sit . . . And finally, following your latest outburst about the division as the 'best' solution, these two [Karadžić and Boban] shamefully agreed in Graz on the division of BiH according to their principle: 65 per cent to the Serbs; 20 per cent to the Croats; and 15 per cent to the Moslems – at the very time when Karadžić's forces are mercilessly pummelling the Croatian regions of this republic! I recall just one of their difficulties – should Mostar be half Croat and half Serb, or simply all Croat despite the fact that Moslems make up the relative majority in the city!

The Graz Accord failed because Karadžić and Boban were not able to define who should control Mostar, as Kurspahić pointed out, and also because of disputes over some areas in Posavina. None the less, discussions on various levels continued throughout the following year between the Croats and the Serbs although of course the two militias continued to battle it out with vigour. Almost immediately after the Graz Accord, the first conflict between Bosnian government forces and the HVO (the Croatian Defence Council – the army of the Bosnian Croats) was recorded in a small village, Kopaonik, just north of Busovača, in central Bosnia. The retreating JNA left a munitions dump here (which according to sources in Sarajevo was intended as a present to the HVO). The Moslem and Croat militias then engaged in a shoot-out, which the Croats won,

3. In March 1991 before war broke out in Slovenia and Croatia, Milošević and Tuđman held talks in one of Tito's opulent retreats in the Vojvodina town, Karađorđevo. Here, they concluded that the most effective way to avoid war in Yugoslavia was to divide Bosnia between Croatia and Serbia.

4. Nikola Koljević was Karadžić's deputy and a member of the Presidency of Bosnia-Hercegovina before the Serbian Democratic Party vacated their seats. Franjo Boras represented the HDZ–BiH on the same body.

to see who could control the arsenal. Busovača, ignored by the world's media at the time, was an early rehearsal for the conflicts that would explode less than a year later between Croats and Moslems.

The Bosnian government considered the alliance with the HVO necessary not only for military purposes, but also because Croatia had accepted tens of thousands of Moslem refugees on their territory. In addition, the economic activity of the beleaguered Bosnian state was absolutely dependent on the good will of the HVO and Croatia. Most important of all, the illegal weapon supplies which the Bosnian army needed so desperately, all came through Croatian-held territory.

Croatia's position was complicated by an internal political struggle. President Tuđman's vision was the establishment of a Lesser Croatia, that is Croatia proper together with the compact Croat territories of BiH. The model for this was the so-called Cvetković-Maček *Sporazum* (Agreement) of 1939. In the hope of salvaging royal Yugoslavia, the Serbian Prime Minister, Dragiša Cvetković, conceded extensive automony to the Croat leader, Vlatko Maček, which led to the creation of the Croatian Banovina, an area which roughly corresponds to Tito's Republic of Croatia combined with the territories allotted to the Bosnian Croats under the Vance–Owen peace plan.

Tuđman's most vociferous opponent was Dobroslav Paraga, the leader of the fascist Croatian Party of Rights (HSP) and its military wing the HOS. Paraga demanded *Hrvatska do Drine* (Croatia to the river Drina), i.e. it should include all of Bosnia-Hercegovina up to its river border with Serbia. However, in the context of the current war, the HSP explained that they wished for a confederation of Croatia and BiH. Under no circumstances would they tolerate the division of Bosnia between Serbia and Croatia.

In June and August 1992, relations between HOS and the HVO in Hercegovina and Mostar began to deteriorate rapidly. Large numbers of HVO fighters began to defect to the ranks of HOS. In Hercegovina and particularly around the Mostar area, some 30 to 40 per cent of HOS's fighters were Moslems who were suspicious of the HVO's aims and sympathetic to the HOS rhetoric of a united, sovereign Bosnia. President Tuđman decided to intervene personally in the affair, attempting to reduce the influence of HOS which he saw as a serious threat to his Bosnian project.

The commander of the HOS forces in western Hercegovina, Blaž Kraljević, was born in the town of Ljubuški in western Hercegovina. In the early 1960s, he took his huge frame, pot belly and clipped beard and moustache to Australia where he worked as a small-time businessman. He returned to Croatia at the outbreak of war in 1991, bringing with him that familiar twang of antipodean English spoken with a Croatian accent. Despite having no previous military experience, he quickly generated tremendous loyalty among his HOS fighters who, although poorly armed, played an important role during the first few months of the war in Hercegovina. A month after the Graz Accord had been signed by Karadžić and Boban, Kraljević's forces pushed into eastern Hercegovina and occupied Trebinje for a few hours. This provoked the wrath of Boban who had promised Karadžić that Croat forces had no interests in eastern Hercegovina.

At his headquarters in Ljubuški (like most fighters in the Yugoslav war, his birthplace held a profound attraction for Kraljević), the HOS leader sat next to a poster showing a Croatian family with two children against the silhouette of a house. The image was ringed by the maxim 'Man Builds the Home – Home Builds the Man'. His approach to life's more complex philosophical questions was quite similar to that of the Bosnian Serb commander, Ratko Mladić, although, as a character, Kraljević was considerably more likeable. Underneath the maxim was the slogan *Za Dom Spremni* – Ready for the Homeland, which was coined by the brutally Fascist regime of Ante Pavelić, the leader of the war-time Independent State of Croatia. Early in August 1992, Kraljević gave a fascinating interview to the Zagreb news magazine, *Danas*, which had not yet been consumed by Tuđman's propaganda machine:

Many people are asking what is the point of having two Croatian armies, HOS and the HVO, in this region. What are the differences?

Mate Boban has ideas which are different from HOS's and I consider his policy hostile towards Bosnia-Hercegovina. Above all, this relates to the question of Bosnia's division. In contrast to the HVO, we protect all citizens of BiH from the aggressor, Croats in particular, of course, and we try to play fair without ulterior motives. We simply want to liberate and protect Bosnia from the Chetniks.

How strong is HOS at the moment and how many fighters do you have?

HOS is slowly losing the battle for heavy weapons. Boban has enough heavy weaponry but he keeps them under the tight control of the HVO so we don't have access to them. Everything we have, we either bought or we confiscated from the aggressor, the JNA. If we had the sort of weapons which the HVO has got, all fighters would have joined HOS by now. We estimate that we already have a larger force [in terms of men] than the HVO because their strength lies only in heavy weaponry. For obvious reasons, though, I can't tell you exactly how many men we have. The fact is, however, that every day we get new men joining up and every day more are coming from the HVO over to us.

What are the reasons for the skirmishes between HOS and the HVO which have become more frequent recently?

We liberate certain territories and then the HVO comes to hold the line which is, of course, much easier. We were the first ones to enter Stolac and Čapljina ... and later the media all claimed that it was the HVO ... We don't care whether someone is in HOS or not but it is a question of morale. But I would like to ignore politics until after the war has finished and then the politicians can get on with whatever they want. However, Tuđman and Croatia have everything under their control here and some very strange things have been happening. We could make a lot of progress because the Serbs are on the run. But someone for some strange reasons is always preventing us from doing so and we would like to end this war as fast as possible.

What strange things have been happening?

Look at Stolac, Mostar, Neum ... They have not been completely liberated and so the question arises: why hasn't this been done? Why don't we go on? Because we could. So, every day people are dying from some damned shell of the long-distance artillery of the Chetniks because we didn't finish the job properly. Whose interest is that in? These are the murky political games I was talking of. If we had control of the heavy artillery, we could liberate Bosnia-Hercegovina without difficulty. But these weapons are under Boban's control and his policies do not favour BiH. If Mate Boban's policy doesn't change and quickly, and by quickly I mean this week or next, we will denounce him as an aggressor. We won't have any choice and this would not be good as we do not want to fight either with Croats or Moslems.

Tomorrow you have a meeting in Mostar with the HVO commanders. What will you be discussing?

How do you know about that meeting?

Journalists do not reveal their sources. But can you tell us whether it is in connection with the recent order which came from the Chief of Staff of the HVO which prevents HOS and Bosnian Army forces from entering and leaving Mostar, and that your people should be disarmed and arrested?

I am going to Mostar to try and calm the situation because we don't want to start shooting with the HVO. We have given the order to our commanders on the ground to co-operate with the HVO. Their order to arrest members of our units is the best proof of their bad policies. They are trying to divide us which is bad because our aim should be the same – the liberation of Bosnia-Hercegovina.

Kraljević suggested that the Croats and Moslems in BiH were on the verge of adding a new fratricidal twist to the Bosnian conflict. But a few days after this interview was made, Blaž Kraljević and a dozen of his HOS comrades were ambushed as they were returning from Mostar in Croat-held territory. His car, which had the unmistakable registration number, HOS 001, was stopped by the military police of the HVO, after which a special unit of about thirty men (some rumours say they had come from Croatia to do the job) sprayed the HOS convoy with bullets from an anti-aircraft machine gun. Nine HOS members were killed including Kraljević. Some Croatian dailies reported it as a 'tragic mistake', but all evidences point to it being murder, carried out by the HVO with or without Tuđman's knowledge. The importance of Kraljević's death equals that of the gunning down of Josip Reichl-Kir in Tenja. Kraljević and HOS proved not only to be too autonomous as a military force, the political implications of what they were doing threatened Tuđman and Boban who by this time were apparently committed to the division of Bosnia-Hercegovina.

Defenders of the HVO and Tuđman respond by saying that at the same time, an agreement had been signed in Split between the HDZ–BiH and the Party of Democratic Action (SDA), Izetbegović's party. This agreement included a provision for the HVO to come definitively under the unified command of what was then called the OS BiH (Armed Forces of BiH which was later renamed the *Armija BiH*). The HVO order which Kraljević refers to concerning the disarming of Bosnian troops and HOS as well as the ban on them leaving and entering Mostar could hardly, however, be considered in the spirit of that agreement.

It is perfectly true that Croatian troops did much if not a majority of the fighting against the Bosnian Serb army in Bosnia and the HVO frequently accused the Bosnian government forces of not pulling their weight in some of the strategic battles. Yet this does not cancel out the essential paradox of the Croat-Moslem alliance. In certain respects, Izetbegović has nobody to blame but himself for the alliance's decay which accelerated so quickly from March 1993. He had very little choice, of course, because the Bosnian government forces would have been obliterated in a short time had they decided to confront both the Serb and Croat forces. None the less, he entered into a war which he had no chance of winning.

While the conflict between the HVO and HOS was maturing, there were curiously ominous developments afoot within the ranks of the Bosnian Serb fighting machine. On 27 April, in a predictably pompous ceremony, the federal assembly in Belgrade proclaimed the constitution of the 'third Yugoslavia' which had shrunken dramatically compared with its two predecessors. This time, it merely consisted of Serbia and Montenegro. As a consequence, the name 'Yugoslavia' was distinctly disingenuous as a third of the new state's population were not Slavs and besides the Montenegrins (more than half of whom consider themselves Serbs) and a smattering of Slovaks, Ruthenes and Bulgarians, there were only Serbs in this southern Slav federation. Beyond the undoubted need to establish a workable administration in Serbia and Montenegro after the recognition of Croatia, Slovenia and Bosnia-Hercegovina by the European Community, President Milošević's central aim in creating the new state was to recognize *de facto* the loss of the Bosnian and Croatian territories. This was primarily engineered for external consumption. He had always maintained that Serbia was not involved in the Croatian war and he would now use this back-door recognition of Bosnia to claim the same about the war on that territory. From now on, so Milošević's thinking went, Serbia could not be accused of promoting the Bosnian Serb war effort because the Bosnian Serbs were involved in a civil war in a neighbouring state.

The creation of the rump Yugoslavia was followed up a few days later when the country's Presidency ordered the withdrawal of all JNA bases in Bosnia-Hercegovina and any non-Bosnian citizens serving in it. The JNA, it seemed, was not interested in getting involved although this still left between 40,000 and 60,000 Bosnian Serbs with their hands on the bulk of JNA equipment remaining inside the territory. The next few weeks witnessed a painful negotiated withdrawal by JNA units from barracks throughout the territory. The Bosnian government was determined not to allow the equipment to leave the bases in territory they controlled. Not only did they reason that the bulk of this equipment had been paid for by their citizens, but also, they suspected with equal justification that should they let the guns and ammunition go, it would only be a matter of days before they would be turned on them. The Bosnian Serbs were similarly determined not to allow any of the arms to leave territory which they controlled. Even before the order had come from Belgrade, Vojo Kuprešanin, the chairman of the assembly in Banja Luka, warned infamously that army personnel were free to leave the autonomous region of Bosanska Krajina (as the Serbs still called the area at the time) but that 'not one bullet would be allowed out with them'. The situation was both dangerous and confusing as in many towns JNA troops were stationed in areas under bombardment by the Serbs although the latter naturally avoided targeting such bases.

The matter was eased somewhat by the presence in Sarajevo of the EC Monitors and the United Nations Protection Force (UNPROFOR) who had situated their headquarters in the Bosnian capital when deploying troops in Croatia, partly in the hope that this might ward off war in BiH which in retrospect, of course, looks naive in the extreme. Despite some extremely tense stand-offs, the army eventually pulled much of its equipment out, destroying anything of value that it was forced to leave. It also remained in control of Sarajevo airport for three months after the war broke out, thus greatly increasing the psychological pressure on Sarajevo's inhabitants, besieged as they were by the cowardly Serb backwoodsmen stationed around the hills and with no access to food supplies from outside the city.

Until the middle of May, the JNA inside Bosnia was in a state of confusion. On 9 May, however, the Yugoslav Presidency announced that the commander of the Knin corps, General Ratko Mladić, would be 'assuming the command of the army in Bosnia for a period of nine days'. Why the Yugoslav Presidency was in a position to name the temporary commander of the Bosnian Serb army ten days after they had explicitly renounced any connection with it remains a mystery. The appointment of General Mladić was a less than encouraging deployment for Bosnia's Moslems, Croats and town dwellers. He came initially for a ten-day sojourn and stayed for the whole war, rivalling, if not exceeding, Dr Karadžić in political importance among the Bosnian Serbs. Away from the conference rooms and on the battlefield, Mladić continues to distinguish himself as the most ruthless exterminator of the war.

Mladić was quick to instil discipline and purpose into the Serb forces fighting in Bosnia. One of the effects of this appears to have been the stepping up of atrocities on the one hand and the establishment of prisoner-of-war camps on the other. In mid-May, the most terrible rumours began to filter into Sarajevo about the crimes committed against the Moslem civilian populations in towns like Višegrad in the east, and Doboj and Prijedor to the north.

According to UN reports, the Serbs, who had a fairly straightforward strategy and the arms with which to execute it, were the most frequent violators of the endless cease-fire agreements which Lord Carrington, the chairman of the Yugoslav Peace Conference, negotiated. Members of the Bosnian government, however, were quick to understand that most of the world viewed them as absolutely innocent victims. Throughout the war, they have used this perception to undertake offensive actions and then portray themselves as victims. The majority of UNPROFOR members and aid workers who have died during this conflict have been the victims of Moslem units and, to a lesser extent, Croat ones. While suffering from a catastrophic disadvantage in terms of the amount of weapons at their disposal, they have been the consummate victors of the propaganda war waged around the world. In the summer of 1992, an Italian aid plane was shot down on its way to Sarajevo. The following day, newspapers from Washington to Tokyo reported that the Serbs had perpetrated this heinous act (the news agencies Associated Press and Reuters form the most consistently honourable exception to the slap-dash reporting of this war). When the official UN investigation finally came out, it concluded that the plane was almost certainly downed by Croat or Bosnian government troops. By then, of course, so many other things had happened that the results of the investigation received scant attention in the press.

In the first phase of the war, the world media focused most of their attention on the plight of the besieged capital, Sarajevo. There was no special reason why the Bosnian Serb leadership channelled so much of its military effort into the siege. While it was in their interests to cut communication links with the Bosnian government strongholds to the north and west, the gratuitous destruction of Sarajevo itself was merely an expression of hatred.

Nenad Kecmanović served for a short time after the war had erupted on the Bosnian Presidency. In August of 1992, he travelled to Belgrade with the approval of President Izetbegović to hold talks with Slobodan Milošević although he never returned to Bosnia. *En route*, he stopped off at the Serb headquarters in Pale when I spent a boozy evening with him and Nikola Koljević, Karadžić's deputy. Kecmanović was in a state of depression and anger as the Bosnian Serb news agency, SRNA, had blown his cover and reported erroneously that he had fled Sarajevo for his safety, having arrived in Pale 'in a very poor physical condition' (which implied he had been beaten up by Moslems). During the course of the evening, he cheered up a little and said to Koljević: 'You know, you are all too personally involved with Sarajevo and I think that is why you spend so much time on it.' 'Yes,' Koljević nodded his head sagely as is appropriate for the leading Serbo-Croat translator of Shakespeare. He then added absent-mindedly as an afterthought, 'Of course with everybody worrying about Sarajevo, it means that they don't pay much attention to what's going on elsewhere.'

In early August, however, the world did begin to learn about the bestial things that had been happening in eastern and northern Bosnia. This was largely due to some particularly courageous reporting on the part of journalists like Ed Vulliamy and Maggie O'Kane of the London *Guardian* and Roy Gutmann from New York *Newsday* (not to mention yet again the unsung heroes from the wire services). Probably the single most important news report was filed by the British Independent Television News journalist, Penny Marshall, who visited the prisoner-of-war camp at Omarska together with Vulliamy.

According to the Bosnian government, during the first four months of war, the Bosnian Serb authorities had established fifty-seven camps inside BiH in which 147,000 people were being held. The majority of these were Moslems, but in addition there were a large number of Croats as well as some 'disloyal' Serbs who had attempted to defend the local Moslem and Croat populations. These figures are almost certainly exaggerated as the government in Sarajevo had no access to reliable information about the camps. In some cases, they also referred to refugee camps in Serbia (to which the International Red Cross had access) as 'concentration camps'. In the case of the most notorious camp, Omarska, in the district of Prijedor, the number of detainees amounted to between 3,000 and 5,000 according to figures released by international humanitarian agencies. The Bosnian government insisted that the number was 11,000.

This is not to belittle the unspeakable suffering of the detainees, it merely serves to illustrate how difficult it is to ascertain the truth in this country. Intellectuals from Serbia and Croatia still debate violently the number of Serbs killed by the Ustashas at the Jasenovac concentration camp during the Second World War. Serbs argue it is between 700,000 and one million, while the Croats claim it is only a few thousand. The debate is not usually informed by the sifting of evidence scientifically but by rumour, hearsay and their historical parent – popular myth. It is absolutely inevitable that when the war subsides in Bosnia, a furious discussion will rage as to the numbers killed by all sides, the numbers massacred, the numbers raped, the numbers 'cleansed', and the numbers detained and tortured. We shall never know the exact figures but that will not stop an endless flow of literature making spurious claims with complete conviction. One or two scholars will approach the truth but it will be very hard to know which ones.

The evidence of the mass slaughter of defenceless Moslem and to a lesser extent Croat civilians by Chetnik irregulars is overwhelming. The worst excesses took place in eastern Bosnia, notably in the Zvornik and Bratunac regions; in some areas surrounding Sarajevo; in villages close to the eastern Posavina town of Brčko; and in the Prijedor region which borders onto the district of Banja Luka in the Serb stronghold of Bosanska Krajina. A single testimony will suffice to create an image of what these people had to endure. The reader merely has to multiply the experience by tens of thousands. Ekrem Avdić was a 38-year-old worker from Bratunac:

On Sunday, 10 May 1992, there was shooting from all directions around Bratunac. Our Serb neighbours had occupied half of the town. Reinforcements arrived from Milica and Ljubije. They were masked and sporting the Chetnik cockade. They asked if I had a weapon. I gave them my pistol and my licence. Then Čerković said that we all had to go to the sports ground to make statements. There were already about 6,000 to 7,000 civilians. They told us that we would all be transferred into empty Serb houses in Bratunac. At about six o'clock in the evening, they ordered us to empty our pockets and put everything to one side. A group of five or six collected all our money and put it into travel bags. They separated the men between fifteen and fifty years old and the women, children and older men. Miroslav Deronjić, the head of the local Serbian Democratic Party, walked through the prisoners. Mustafa Mujkanović asked him what would happen to us. 'Don't ask me anything. Nothing's going to happen to you. You're all going to be exchanged as prisoners.' The women and children were taken somewhere in lorries, while we were taken to the elementary school 'Vuk Karadžić'. There we saw about twenty people who had been badly beaten up. Some of them were dead. They had died from injuries sustained during the beating. They had been so disfigured by the beating that we were unable to recognize all of them. I did recognize the brothers, Nedžib and Hasim Husić, then Hasan Ibrahimović and Ibrahim Karamujić. They had thrown the beaten and the dead into one part of the room. They shoved about 500 to 600 of us inside. Those who couldn't fit in were shot dead with automatic weapons. Then the 'Vukovar Chetniks' arrived: a certain Banc, Mrki, Makedonac, Zoka Makedonac – about ten of them. They began to beat us with iron coshes, axe and hoe handles, and the butts of their guns. They went through us in order. We all surged towards a corner of the room and as a result nine were suffocated to death. They continued beating us all night. They brought drinks for themselves, spraying one another with beer and drinking. They beat the baker, Fejzo Raskalj, ceaselessly. They killed him on Tuesday, 12 May and then they brought his brother to show him how they had killed Fejzo and how they would kill him in the same way. I know that among the guards were my neighbours, Bubo Živanović and Nikola, a waiter. They cursed our Turkish Moslem mothers and Alija [Izetbegović]. On Monday, 11 May, they started to call our names which they had on some lists. They picked out Izet Ahmić, the head of the MBO [Muslimanska Bošnjačka Organizacija – the Moslem Bosniak Organization], Safet Delić and Hasan Ibrahimović. They beat the three of them, forcing them to carry the dead into the back of an estate car [station wagon] and to clean the floor of blood. New prisoners were being brought in the whole time. On Wednesday, they killed Izet and Hasan. Safet saved himself by hiding in the crowd. They brought in Medo Delić, my colleague, and his two sons. The younger son suffered from epilepsy. The 'Vukovarci' started to hit them immediately, saying 'What have you been doing until now, you Ustashas?' Medo begged them not to hit his younger son because of his illness. Bane immediately shot the younger son in the head and said, 'He's not going to be ill anymore!' Then he killed the older son and Medo. During the three nights that we were in the room, they killed several hundred people. Those who had been beaten up were taken out, thrown into a skip and burnt alive. They then placed the skip under our window. The bodies were transported by van and lorry and then thrown into the Drina. The survivors were bound together in tens and around 120 or 130 were slung into a lorry. The Serbian Militia from Bratunac then drove us to Pale. The local Serbs in Pale screamed, 'Give us the Ustashas so we can slaughter them!' Then for the first time they made a list of us. Altogether there were only 430 of us left. We were taken into some gym where we spent three days. Then they bound us again and took us in lorries to Visoko. We were forced to sing Serbian songs and the locals and militiamen threw empty bottles and stones at us. There were 399 of us left when we arrived in Visoko. They exchanged us civilians for Chetnik fighters.

Predictably, the history of the Second World War combined with the influence of more recent events to play an important role in defining which population centres were exposed to the more vile practices of the volunteers. Tension between Moslems and Serbs had been running high in Bratunac since well before the war broke

out in Bosnia-Hercegovina. In August 1991, when the war was still
raging in Croatia and while Bosnia was enjoying its last months of
peace, two young Moslem men were shot dead on a motorcycle as
they sped away from a roadblock at the entrance to a Serb village
just north-west of Bratunac. The Serb population during the Second
World War had been influenced by the Chetnik tradition emanating
from the nearby town of Loznica to the north while few Moslems
joined the local Partizan movement. So the Moslems were suspected,
not without justification, of having sympathized with the Ustashas
during the Second World War. The use of the word 'Ustasha' by the
'Vukovarci' in the above testimony implies a dual insult. First, it
accuses the Moslems of being fascists and secondly, by referring to a
specifically Croat movement, it is a denial of the Moslems' confession and nationality.

Probably the most complex and depressing tale concerns those
blighted men who ended up in Omarska (although most who made
it as far as the camp survived the war, unlike many hundreds from
the Prijedor and Kozara region whence they came). During the
summer of 1942, 60,000 Serbs, the bulk of whom were civilians,
had been hemmed in on the mountain of Kozara by German and
Ustasha forces. From the three towns of Prijedor, Banja Luka and
Bosanska Gradiška, the Germans (in whose ranks as a junior intelligence officer was Kurt Waldheim) then launched an all-out attack
on the Partizans, killing many thousands in the process. The remain-
der, including over 10,000 children, were then carted off to the
nearby Ustasha concentration camp, Jasenovac, where many were
slaughtered. Like the Kninska Krajina, this region, Bosanska Krajina,
has produced some of the most insecure, and hence militant, Serbs
of all. The memory of the Kozara massacre plays a central part in
this people's social psychology.

But before the Serb class of '92 vented their historical wrath on
innocent Moslems and Croats, who can hardly be blamed for the
sins of their parents, the peculiar political development in Prijedor,
in particular, added to the Serb lust for vengeance. For some
unknown reason, the former federal Prime Minister, Ante Marković, had decided to hold the founding conference of his Reformist
Forces Party in Prijedor before the 1990 elections in BiH. The
population of the Prijedor region was 44 per cent Moslem and 42

per cent Serb, while 8 per cent considered themselves Yugoslavs. Marković's campaign in the Prijedor region split the Serb vote, as many in the town itself voted for the Reformist Forces. As a consequence, Izetbegović's Party, the SDA, secured a relative majority which made Prijedor the only district in the Bosanska Krajina which was not under the control of Karadžić's Serbian Democratic Party. This created a problem for the local SDS leaders as they found it impossible to co-opt Prijedor into their SAO (Serbian Autonomous District) of Bosanska Krajina, the pride of Serb militancy. During the war in western Slavonija in the summer and autumn of 1991, General Nikola Uzelac, commander of the Banja Luka corps, mobilized the local population in order to take part in the fighting in Croatia, to the north. Not unnaturally, the Moslems refused to respond to the mobilization and in Prijedor, the SDA-dominated government refused to co-operate with the issuing of the call-up papers.

Although the war did not break out in the Prijedor region for two months, most locals expected it to erupt at any moment from 7 April onwards. They also feared it would be exceptionally brutal. The worst atrocity occurred in the large village of Kozarac which is a compact Moslem community. The Moslems surrendered without a struggle but the Serb forces destroyed the village completely, perpetrating a massacre of hundreds of civilians in the process. Kozarac (which is distinct from the Kozara mountain although only fifteen miles away) was infamous during the Second World War as its Moslem population were considered hardline Ustashas. Five hundred Serbs were murdered here in a single bout of mass killing.

The desire for a perverse settling of the historical account was extremely strong here. Moslems were thrown out of their houses and forced to sign papers handing all their property and worldly goods over to the Serbs. The men who escaped death were sent to Omarska and Manjača camps where they were beaten, some were tortured, some shot, although most suffered largely through insanitary conditions and chronic starvation which resulted in the dramatic television pictures which ITN spread round the world like wildfire.

Once the cat was out of the bag, the Serbs were keen to disband many of the camps as quickly as possible. Many of the larger ones were in the Bosanska Krajina region. At that time, the Serbs were still forging their corridor across Moslem and Croat territories. Supplies to Banja Luka, the regional capital, were sporadic and poor and the inmates of the camps were a serious burden. The International Red Cross (ICRC) and the United Nations High Commission for Refugees (UNHCR) were instrumental in securing the safety of these people and evacuating them to Croatia and other parts of an unwilling Europe. Some Bosnian government authorities accused the international agencies of thereby aiding the cleansing of these areas. It was sometimes very hard not to get the impression that the government was prepared to sacrifice its own people for its own political principles.

Moslem and Croat women from many parts of Bosnia were herded into schools and warehouses and raped repeatedly. The European Community commission which investigated the allegations of mass rape estimated that 20,000 Moslem and Croat women had suffered at the hands of Serbs, although like most other claims, they do not present any sources for this statistic. The figure may be much more, it may be much less. There is also strong evidence suggesting that several hundred Serb women were raped, notably in the Posavina region, by Croats and some evidence of systematic rape of Serb women by Moslems in villages close to Sarajevo. Again, a single testimony, recorded by Jeri Laber for the *New York Review of Books*, is sufficient to depict this ordeal:

'We were rich, on both sides of the family ... We had an apartment in Doboj and a family house in Grabska which we inherited ... The war began the night of May 1st ... They occupied Doboj and began taking over the Moslems' homes. We went to Grabska, the only completely Moslem village in the region; ten days later they began to shell us there. We sent our son away with my sister's family, but I decided to stay with my husband; we were founders of the SDA. How could I face my fellow Moslems if I left?'

Early in May, Fatima told me, she was separated from her husband by Serbian troops and taken to a high school building where she was held for twenty-eight days in a dark gymnasium packed with what she estimates to have been a thousand women. She was forced to sit for almost the entire time with her knees pulled up to her chest and her head down; she never spoke to anyone or dared to look around. At night she was raped in a classroom, sometimes by as many as ten men. There were occasional respites of two or three days when the Serbian paramilitaries went off to fight, leaving the women under guard of local Serbs. 'The worst was when they lost and came back angry and drunk. They would beat us hard; they had no sense of their own strength ... I was raped with a gun by one of those men, along with another woman and her daughter, while the others watched. Some of them spat on us; they did so many ugly things to us ... There was no passion in this, it was done only to destroy us ... if they couldn't rape me, they would urinate on me.' Fatima started to cry: 'They kept pigs, they came down from the mountains, they stank ... and now they are treating us this way!'

Most of the women were kept in these camps for several weeks before being exchanged as prisoners. Those able to bear children were almost all impregnated and many contracted sexually transmitted diseases. As soon as news of the mass rapes emerged, outsiders developed the theory that the rapes were the war aim of the Serbs. This is arrant nonsense. Just as Balkan wars have recorded countless massacres similar to those in Croatia and Bosnia, so have Balkan women always been subject to rape on a comparable scale during these conflicts. The testimony of those rapists who have been caught (the most notorious of whom was Borislav Herak, a Serb who had committed the most appalling bestial acts against Moslems), suggests that militia commanders used the act of rape in order to reinforce the psychology of violence associated with the war, and in many areas it appears as though participating in the rapes was expected of soldiers.

Of course, the rapists of all sides knew that these acts would humiliate their victims, although the facile perception of some Western commentators that this represented an especial insult to the Moslems because of their confession merely pandered to the idea that the Bosnian Moslems are raving fundamentalists, while somehow Serb and Croat communities can cope with the humiliation more rationally. The effect on these women's lives will be devastating but they will not be ostracized from their own community.

It is, of course, a humiliation within the context of a nationalist war of this type as the rapist intends propagating his blood line. However, the blighted offspring of the rape camps will in all probability be adopted or grow up in orphanages, assimilating the confession or nationality of the host family or local community. They are unlikely to assume the identity of their fathers. As the above testimony indicates, there is also an element of the rural revenge in the rape programme as well.

Of the three sides in the war, the Croats appeared to have followed the most closely the Geneva Convention in their treatment of prisoners of war, although since the outbreak of widespread fighting between Croats and Moslems, their standards have begun to slip. Moslem authorities kept Serb civilians and captured fighters in some extremely bad conditions and, on occasions, prevented international agencies from inspecting the internment camps.

The camps were the straw which broke the camel's back in Europe and the United States. Impatience with perceived Serb aggression in Bosnia-Hercegovina had already galvanized the United Nations Security Council to impose sanctions against Serbia and Montenegro on 1 June, 1992. The case of Yugoslavia demonstrated how complex the New World Order had become within three years of its proclamation by President Bush.

The pressure for some form of action to stop the fighting in BiH was growing among the international public, not just in the West but in Islamic countries as well. One of the turning points was the shelling of a bread queue in Sarajevo in the middle of May. The resulting carnage was recorded on possibly the most nauseating television footage of the war. In London at the time, I observed how entire news rooms stopped what they were doing and stared in deep shock at the pictures coming over the satellite feed. This sort of thing had been going on for well over a month but this war has confirmed that the influence of print or radio journalism is negligible when compared with the impact that a few minutes of video can have. The Serb forces around Sarajevo denied more vigorously than usual that they were responsible for the outrage. Instead, they insisted that Bosnian government forces had slaughtered their own people precisely in order to generate the effect which the incident provoked around the world. Already 'The Bread Queue Affair' has developed into a bone of contention between the makers of the Serb and Moslem mythology of war. I imagine that about ten people know the truth of the matter and they are unlikely to tell the story. Or if they did, who would believe them?

By now, however, the rather unwieldy procedure of the Security Council in New York was operating at an unusually high speed. In the resolution of 31 May which defined the sanctions against the new Yugoslavia, the Security Council referred back to its resolution of 18 May. In this it had demanded that the 'neighbours of Bosnia and Hercegovina undertake immediate steps with the aim of ending all outside interference and of recognizing the territorial integrity of Bosnia and Hercegovina'. In the resolution itself, it *'condemned* the failure of the authorities of the Federal Republic of Yugoslavia including the JNA' for not implementing the previous resolution. It *'demanded* that all elements of the Croatian Army still present in Bosnia-Hercegovina' be withdrawn with immediate effect. In diplomatic terms, the semantic difference is significant. The Serbs were to be punished, the Croats to receive a slap on the wrist. President Tuđman did go some way towards fulfilling the UN resolution of 18 May. Under diplomatic pressure, he eventually ordered a pull-out of Croatian Army troops fighting around Derventa and Brod, a move which led to a dramatic advance of the Serbs in the Posavina area. However, a tide of Croatian Army troops ebbed and flowed in western Hercegovina from their bases in Dalmatia over the whole year while the HVO received weapons, oil, food and other supplies from Croatia. The Croats were not involved in the whole-scale slaughter which the Serb forces indulged in. But that is not the point – they were in violation of the UN resolution and, were the Security Council being consistent, should also have had sanctions imposed on them. This was the first serious example of the international community reacting emotively to the level of atrocities committed by the Serbs, instead of responding to the underlying political causes of the war.

On the whole, sanctions have proved a waste of time until now. They have had no perceptible impact on the ability of the Bosnian Serbs to wage war; they have strengthened Milošević's political position, further weakened the Serbian opposition and made life miserable for those Serbs who are not responsible for the carnage; they have enabled many decidedly undesirable characters who do bear responsibility for the war and its unseemly prosecution in

Serbia, Montenegro and elsewhere to make large sums of money; and they continue to have grave consequences for the economies of Hungary, Romania, Bulgaria, Macedonia and Greece, five countries who should be receiving economic and financial support and not being penalized for Yugoslavia's violations of the UN Security Council resolutions. But Milošević has undoubtedly accrued even more political capital because of the different treatment of Croatia by the international community. In fact, neither Croatia nor Serbia should have sanctions imposed on them. The decision to apply a sanctions regime was an expression of indignation by the international community born of its own inability to respond to the crisis in Bosnia.

The international community has an enormous responsibility in the crisis region. Even if it were to act out of self-interest alone, it would have to recognize the danger which the war in the former Yugoslavia poses. What began as a struggle between changing and emerging political élites has increasingly taken on a nationalist and, still worse, confessional character. This has been reflected in the support given Catholic Croatia and Slovenia during 1991 by their brethren in the Vatican, Austria and Germany; the close dialogue between the three capitals of Orthodoxy, Moscow, Belgrade and Athens, during the crisis and, more worryingly, in the instrumenting of the Yugoslav crisis by Russian nationalists; and the solidarity with the Bosnian Moslems expressed by Turkey, Iran, Saudi Arabia and Pakistan. Three mighty confessional axes are forming in the Balkans and extending outwards to the west, the east and the south. It is in the most fundamental interests of the European Community and the United States, not to mention the blighted peoples of Eastern Europe and the former Soviet Union, to prevent these axes from becoming involved in an armed conflict of any sort.

But the responsibility for Bosnia-Hercegovina is more specific. By encouraging Croatian and Bosnian independence from Yugoslavia before a comprehensive settlement had been reached, the European Community and the United Nations unwittingly elevated themselves to the position of Bosnia's 'fourth constituent nation'. In the absence of outside intervention (which should take the form of diplomacy and peace-keeping, and not the form of arms supplies) Bosnia will be ravaged as a state and will become a permanent threat to peace in the Balkans. To an extent, the UN and the EC have recognized their position as the 'fourth constituent nation' by dint of the UNPROFOR operation and the efforts of the International Conference on the former Yugoslavia based in Geneva and co-chaired by Cyrus Vance and Lord David Owen. Unfortunately, the crisis in Yugoslavia has over the past two years accentuated the different interests which the 'Great Powers' have in the region. It has proved enormously difficult to find a consensual policy which might bind the very different approaches to Yugoslavia on the part of the United States, the European Community, Russia and Turkey – even with the EC, serious differences of opinion arise frequently. This is due to a number of reasons, although I would cite the growth of the confessional axes mentioned above, and the new competitive relationship between Europe, the US and Japan after 1989 as the two most influential. As long as the disparate members making up the 'International Community' continue to squabble about what should be done, the plight of Bosnia is likely to be exceptionally grave.

The efforts of Lord Carrington to establish a lasting cease-fire and bring the political leaderships back to the Lisbon table had failed by July 1992. The European Community monitors pulled out of Sarajevo in May because the situation was adjudged to be too dangerous, while the Bosnian capital's small band of UNPROFOR troops, whose mandate was to regulate the peace-keeping operation in Croatia, needed a new mandate badly. The British Prime Minister, John Major, offered to host an international conference on the former Yugoslavia to which the three sides in Bosnia would be invited along with the heads of the six republics of the former Yugoslavia, the prime minister and president of the rump Yugoslavia, the United Nations, the governments of the European Community, United States and Russia. The Kosovo Albanians, the Sandžak Moslems and other such groups were to be accorded observer status.

Following the proclamation of the rump Yugoslavia in April, the new federal parliament had elected Dobrica Ćosić, a.k.a. father of the nation, to become the young state's first president. In addition, they had co-opted as prime minister, at Milošević's instigation, Milan Panić. As a member of Yugoslavia's international cycling team, Panić had exploited a competition abroad to flee Tito's Yugoslavia in 1955. He made his way to America where, without a penny to his name, he built up a large and successful chemical conglomerate. Through this, he built up close connections with one of Belgrade's most powerful companies, Galenika, Yugoslavia's large pharmaceutical firm. Both Ćosić and Milošević were content with the choice, the former because he assumed this would aid contacts with the Americans (Panić was an American citizen) and the latter because he thought Panić would be easy to manipulate. Neither proved correct in their assessment, although Milošević was able to dispense with Panić once he had tired of his rather fresh approach to Yugoslav politics. After so many years in the States, he spoke neither English nor Serbo-Croat fluently. But Panić was a bouncy, active figure who took his new job very seriously and employed a weighty team of Serb and American advisers. It soon became clear that he was not content to act as a stooge for anybody and it is worth recording that he was the only politician with real authority in Serbia to stand up and publicly denounce the Bosnian Serb army and volunteers for their disgraceful atrocities in Bosnia-Hercegovina.

In the run up to the London Conference, fundamental policy differences began to emerge between Milošević and Panić, while Ćosić, keeping his cards quite close to his chest, assumed the middle ground between the two. Panić had correctly identified the central problem in Yugoslavia to be the conflict between Serbs and Croats. He was thus keen to come to an agreement with Zagreb which would involve Croatia asserting its sovereignty over the Krajina. He was also explicitly committed to Bosnian sovereignty, underpinned by a new constitutional order which would safeguard the rights of the 'three constituent nations'. The self-confidence of both Panić and Ćosić grew with their new authority. Milošević appeared to regard this as a threat and, as always when challenged by moderates, his support for the Krajina Serbs and for the Bosnian Serbs hardened. The differences between Milošević on the one hand, and Ćosić and Panić on the other, spilled into the public arena during the London Conference when the latter two insisted on talks with the Croatian President, Franjo Tuđman, and a negotiated settlement of the Yugoslav crisis which would recognize the independence of the former republics. Milošević stormed out of a plenary session in a fit of genuine anger and muttered darkly about the Serbian nation being sold out (which he often uses as shorthand to mean that he has suffered a tactical defeat). Milošević's ire was born of the fact that he had allowed his hold on domestic power in Serbia to slip to the extent that he was no longer the only politician defining policy in the international arena. Many observers, including myself, were fool enough to believe that Ćosić and Panić were capable of delivering a mortal blow to the Serbian President's political life. Instead while the Yugoslav President and Prime Minister exhausted themselves by jetting around Europe attempting to find a peaceful settlement within the framework of the Geneva Conference, Milošević was plotting their downfall. This he had executed with his usual efficiency within four months of the London Conference.

The London Conference opened with the dramatic announcement that Lord Carrington was stepping down as the European Community's mediator on Yugoslavia. Carrington had built his reputation as the man who negotiated the peaceful transfer of power from white to majority rule in Zimbabwe-Rhodesia. It is a measure of the extreme complexity of the Yugoslav situation that he retired hurt and defeated from the Balkan mess. He was disliked intensely by the Croats (who were convinced that he had family connections with Serbs) and had clashed sharply with Hans-Dietrich Genscher over the recognition issue. However, his influence did at times reduce the intensity of the armed conflict and the Hague Conference on Yugoslavia which he chaired did cover some important political ground before its *raison d'être* was entirely undermined by the European Community policy of selective recognition. According to one source at the London Conference, Lord Carrington resigned on the insistence of Dr Boutros Boutros-Ghali, the UN Secretary General, who reacted furiously when Carrington said the UN would send more peace-keeping troops to monitor a cease-fire in Bosnia. Boutros-Ghali argued, not unreasonably, that Carrington as the EC envoy had no authority to call for UN troop deployment. When invited by John Major to co-host the London Conference on Yugoslavia, Dr Boutros-Ghali said he would only do so if Carrington left.

Carrington's resignation paved the way for the appointment of

Lord David Owen, the former British Foreign Secretary and founder of the ill-starred Social Democratic Party, who joined Cyrus Vance as co-chairman of the standing conference based in Geneva, which was brought to life by the talks in London. By late August, when the conference was held, the Bosnian government had begun to press its demand for the lifting of the UN arms embargo on the Bosnian government which had been imposed on all former Yugoslav republics the previous September. The London Conference was explicit in its rejection of these demands, preferring instead to concentrate its efforts on the Geneva Conference, which the London meeting conjured into life, and the expansion of peace-keeping operations in BiH. The Serbs had ceded control of Sarajevo airport to the United Nations in mid-June and a substantial amount of humanitarian aid was now being delivered to besieged areas although some Moslem areas in eastern Bosnia, notably Goražde, Žepa and Srebrenica, sometimes went for months without receiving any outside aid.

At the London Conference, the international community reiterated its commitment to Bosnian sovereignty and its refusal to accept any territorial gain by force. A general cease-fire was also proclaimed. The Bosnian government was clearly disappointed by the result because it had been hoping for some tough action against the Bosnian Serbs and Serbia itself. It was also here that Alija Izetbegović finally had to give up his idea of a 'Citizens' Bosnia', and accept that some division of power in Bosnia-Hercegovina was now inevitable. At one point, his delegation was on the verge of walking out in protest. John Major intervened and warned Izetbegović that if it did so, the Bosnian government would be left to the mercy of the Serbs. The feelings of most Moslems and those Croats and Serbs who supported the Bosnian government were summed up by Gordana Knežević, a senior journalist on *Oslobođenje*, who said in a BBC interview at the end of the conference that her 'thoughts were now with the people of Sarajevo. Because I know that this evening there will be no cease-fire there and that again they will suffer bombardment and destruction'. She was proved correct.

The Bosnian Serbs were unhappy, as was Milošević, because the conference supported Bosnian sovereignty. The Croats were pleased with the outcome because the proceedings had done nothing to damage their long-term interests, while the readiness of Panić and Ćosić to negotiate a solution to the problem of the Krajina gave them real cause to hope that their own frozen war might still be solved without bloodshed. The US, the EC, Russia and the United Nations seemed satisfied with the event although one senior Foreign Office official was right to warn that the whole agreement 'rested on the sands of Milan Panić's promises'. In practice, the London Conference had taken very few decisions. It had placed most responsibility for finding a solution to the Bosnian crisis on the mechanism which it inaugurated, the standing Geneva Conference.

Meanwhile the war continued and living conditions deteriorated steadily for those living in the besieged enclaves despite the sterling efforts of the ICRC and the UNHCR. Territories under the control of either the Serbs or Croats were able to develop a relatively primitive but functioning war economy because both were connected with their mother country. To a limited extent, the Bosnian Serbs and Croats paid their way, selling agricultural produce, in particular, to finance the fighting. Oil and ammunition, of course, the two most essential items, were moved into Bosnia from its western and eastern neighbours in large quantities and the sanctions of Montenegro and Serbia had virtually no impact on the supplies to the Bosnian Serbs. In the outlying areas under the control of Serbs, especially the Banja Luka region before the corridor was established, life for the civilian population was pitiful. In the Serb-held territories of Croatia, in particular Kordun and Banija, living conditions bordered on the catastrophic. One United Nations observer travelling the region reported that the supply of basic foodstuffs had virtually dried, that a box of matches cost $1 and that disease and malnutrition were beginning to spread, especially among young mothers and children. Once the corridor was established then conditions improved somewhat for the Krajina Serbs as well as the Bosnian Serbs.

The enclaves controlled by the Bosnian government were less fortunate still, because communication between the various areas was virtually impossible and so no overall economic infrastructure could be established. The government in Sarajevo proved especially inept at controlling the unbridled black market which soon fell under the influence of the criminal fraternity. The defence of

Sarajevo, particularly in the embattled outlying areas like Dobrinje in the west of the city, was largely dependent on Bosnians who before the war had run the underground in Sarajevo, Frankfurt-am-Main and, to a lesser extent, Zürich and Stockholm. Many of those operating abroad returned to Sarajevo to form volunteer militia groups at the onset of war, financing their weapon and food supplies by controlling the black market. In the eyes of ordinary Sarajevans, their role was paradoxical. They were rightly regarded as heroes, risking their lives every day by battling against a much better equipped force. But they also had little time for the romantic ideals of the local population, the intelligentsia in particular. In the absence of any coherent authority, they also inaugurated press-gangs which would lift people off the street and force them to fight or dig trenches on the front line. The most vulnerable group was the Sarajevo Serbs, of whom some 80,000 chose not to fight with their brothers and sisters on the hills with whom they had little or nothing in common. The most notorious Moslem paramilitary leader was Juka Prazina who instilled considerable fear in the local communities where his men operated. None the less, in Sarajevo itself, there were very few nationally motivated murders but there were many incidents recorded of Serbs (and even Moslems and Croats) having their flats requisitioned and their property confiscated for no other reason than the militias prized them. By the end of 1992, the government recognized that the situation was getting out of hand and they implemented a reorganization of both the military and the police force. The paramilitary organizations were forced to submit to the command of the Armija BiH, while the local police was given increased powers to prevent the abuse of military power. A new Interior Minister, Jusuf Prašina, was appointed. Prašina was a professional policeman who was determined not to allow Sarajevo to collapse into anarchy and, according to local citizens, he achieved considerable success. Juka broke with the Bosnian authorities because of his criminal activities and his terrorizing of the local population. In response, he rebelled with a large number of men and joined the HVO, although at the time there were no open hostilities between the HVO and the Armija BiH. However, when the battle for Mostar flared in April 1993, Juka led his men against his Moslem compatriots on behalf of the Croats.

Nobody was able to stabilize the economy, of course. The coupons which the Bosnian government introduced in the early autumn were useful for buying local newspapers and some essentials like bread. But in order to augument the hand-outs from the UNHCR, people needed hard currency, and the German mark soon became the main form of payment in many areas of the republic not under Serbian or Croatian control. The Croatian dinar was dominant in western Hercegovina and some other Croat areas, while the Serbs had issued their own currency, the dinar of the Serbian Republic which was interchangeable with the dinar of the Republic of the Serbian Krajina from the neighbouring UNPAs. The price of goods in Sarajevo, Tuzla and other Bosnian government regions soon began to rocket. At the time of writing, a litre of petrol costs DM12 (£5, $8) while an egg costs DM4 (£1.50, $2.50). The average monthly wage in Sarajevo lies between DM2 and DM5, which puts the cost of eggs into a yet harsher perspective.

Just a few miles west of Sarajevo in Croat-controlled areas, the prices of goods were on average about 75 per cent less than in the capital itself. As a result, a large smuggling operation flowered. The problem was that in order to reach these areas, the pathetic inhabitants of Sarajevo had to cross territory which lay under the watchful guns of Karadžić's Serbian forces. People would scurry across this territory at night and many were shot dead or wounded. The Moslem militias began to resent the profiteering of the Croats and in the early part of 1993, shoot-outs between Moslem and Croat units broke out, prefacing the much wider war between the two communities which was launched with a vengeance later in the spring.

In the summer and autumn of 1992, water and electricity supplies were constantly being cut in Sarajevo, either through a lack of oil supplies or because the Serb forces deliberately refused to allow the repair of pumping stations. The United Nations worked extremely hard to maintain the utilities but were not always successful. The resilience of the civilian populations in the besieged enclaves proved quite remarkable. Over the summer, they succeeded in preventing epidemics but, as they all knew, the real survival test was the winter. In order to keep themselves warm, the inhabitants cut down most of the trees in Sarajevo, Tuzla, Bihać, Goražde, Žepa,

Srebrenica and elsewhere. After the tree wood was exhausted, books were the next to go. Whole personal libraries were sacrificed in an effort to stave off the bitter cold of the Bosnian winter. By scrumpling up the pages of books, moistening them and then letting them dry, people discovered that the paper was transformed into very effective slow-burning brickettes. Most people made an inventory of their books and began by burning the works of Marx, Lenin and Tito before graduating on to textbooks and cheap novels. Chekov, Shakespeare, Goethe and other masters were usually left until last and brought out for special occasions. Despite the hardships, people hung on to the normal patterns of their lives wherever possible. Theatre workers in Sarajevo mounted some impressive performances, including a full-scale production of the musical *Hair*. The newspapers, *Oslobođenje* and *Večernje Novine*, were printed every day of the war without interruption despite chronic shortages of raw materials and extremely dangerous working conditions. One enterprising man who wished to satisfy his daughter's obsession with tennis produced independent Bosnia's first ever glossy sports magazine in April 1993. The war was not without its humorous moments either. In April 1992 as fighting raged in and around Sarajevo, one of China's first private tour operators travelled to the Bosnian capital by mistake with a group of tourists from Peking having negotiated his way through endless roadblocks. 'Nobody told me there was a war going on here. I thought it was happening elsewhere and that it was perfectly safe here,' the bemused entrepreneur confessed.

If conditions were bad in Sarajevo, they were unimaginable in Goražde, Žepa and Srebrenica. The lack of medical supplies was most keenly felt in these areas where many operations and amputations were undertaken without anaesthetic on children as well as adults. Cyrus Vance warned in October 1992 that thousands were likely to die over the winter, and although in the eastern Bosnian enclaves dozens and probably hundreds did fall prey to cold and hunger, in January and February, the fortuitous combination of a relatively mild winter and UNHCR supplies kept the number of victims down to a remarkably low level. If the war were to enter a second winter, the number of deaths through exposure would probably increase exponentially.

By the end of October, the great Bosnian Serb offensive had largely come to an end when Jajce finally fell. The Serbs took the foundation stone of Tito's Yugoslavia for neither strategic nor sentimental reasons. If the Bosnian Serbs are ever persuaded to make territorial concessions, Jajce is the first town they are likely to hand over to the Moslems, while the Croats will almost certainly receive Kupres as a gift. Jajce's chief importance for the Serbs lies in the power station just to the west of the town which is the main source of electricity for Banja Luka. When the town finally fell in November, the Croats blamed the Moslem fighters for retreating like cowards, while the Bosnian government blamed the Croats for handing the territory over to the Serbs as part of a more long-term strategy. When the dust settles over Jajce, it may be possible to find out what the exact story was. The immediate importance of Jajce, however, was that it allowed the Serb forces to concentrate their offensive efforts on the remaining Bosnian government strongholds in the east: Srebrenica, Čerska (which soon fell), Žepa and Goražde. The Bihać-Cazin region in the far north-west, which is dominated politically by Fikret Abdić, had come under sporadic and occasionally intense artillery attack by Serb forces, but the area remains of secondary interest to the Serbs for the moment. In all probability, its survival as a Moslem-dominated region will depend on the overall course of both the war and any negotiations over Bosnia's future.

Wherever they could, the Moslems used the considerable sympathy which they enjoyed in the outside world as a cover to undertake military operations. In December and early January, they launched an intensive offensive from Srebrenica with the aim of regaining control of Bratunac, to the east on the river Drina. The Serbs were caught unawares by the attack and the Moslems moved swiftly through Serbian villages, slaughtering a large number of civilians on the way. Because the atrocities were being perpetrated by the Moslems, they received relatively little attention in the world media. They also provoked a fearsome counter-attack by the Serbs who had soon driven the Moslems back to Srebrenica. Politicians and journalists were quick to condemn the Serbs for this operation but they entirely neglected to point out that it had been provoked by the original Moslem offensive.

By the autumn of 1992, the situation in Bosnia-Hercegovina had begun to attract considerable attention in the United States. George Bush had studiously avoided any major initiative in the former Yugoslavia although his Administration had recognized not only Bosnia, but Slovenia and Croatia as well on 7 April. The shocking pictures of camps in northern Bosnia were sinking in to the consciousness of an American public which until this time had expressed relatively little interest in the Yugoslav conflict. In his presidential campaign, Bill Clinton, the Governor of Arkansas, seized on the subject as an example of Bush's feebleness. This in turn strengthened the nascent sense among American politicians that Europe had failed abysmally in the former Yugoslavia and that only the United States was capable of clearing up messes which the Europeans had created. The State Department was also picking up signals from its allies in the Islamic world, in particular from Turkey and Saudi Arabia, that pressure was building up within the Islamic Conference Organization (ICO) to help the Moslems in Bosnia.

In Europe, the approach towards the crisis in the former Yugoslavia had altered substantially since Germany won the battle of Slovene and Croat recognition. After this policy success, Bonn withdrew from the diplomatic front line. This was partly because since Genscher's resignation, there was nobody in the German cabinet prepared to take up his crusading baton. Indeed, such was the apparent indifference to Bosnia's plight that the veteran Post and Telecommunications Minister, Christian Schwarz-Schilling, handed in his resignation to Kohl in disgust. At the London Conference, Klaus Kinkel, Genscher's successor, had denounced Belgrade with some intemperate rhetoric but Bonn's commitment to an independent Bosnia seemed lukewarm in comparison to the zeal with which it prosecuted the case of Croatia. Unlike Britain, France and Spain, Germany had also contributed no troops to the UNPROFOR peace-keepers for perfectly understandable reasons. But this contribution had strengthened these three countries' influence over Yugoslav policy. The appointment of Lord Owen as co-chair to the Geneva Conference was also decisive.

This shift had substantial implications for European policy. The British and French regarded the war in Bosnia as a civil war, first and foremost, which had been provoked by the breakdown of

Bosnia's constitutional consensus. While recognizing that Belgrade's logistical support for the Bosnian Serb war-machine constituted a form of aggression, the Foreign Office and Lord Owen pointed out that the overwhelming majority of Serbs (and for that matter Croats) fighting in Bosnia-Hercegovina were born and bred on the territory. In the United States, the issue was perceived very differently. The war was a straight case of aggression by one state, Serbia, against another, Bosnia-Hercegovina (the role of the Bosnian Croats or Croatia was simply not considered, a fact which caused complete confusion on the news desks of American newspapers when fighting between Croats and Moslems started to run out of control in spring 1993). The issue, then, was to roll back the Serbs and send them back to their republic, rather as the Americans had pushed the Iraqis out of Kuwait in 1991. This was the beginning of a serious diplomatic conflict between the United States on the one hand and Europe and the UN/EC Conference on Yugoslavia on the other.

From its inception, the Geneva Conference on Yugoslavia took its work extremely seriously. With a core team of highly skilled international civil servants who overshadowed the bundle of dead wood also floating around the conference floor, the co-chairmen, Cyrus Vance, appointed by the UN, and Lord Owen, the EC representative, set about their work with gusto. Within three months, they had produced a draft constitution and the outline of the Vance–Owen peace plan (VOPP) for Bosnia-Hercegovina. It was an incredibly complex diplomatic task which involved negotiating with three delegations headed by Izetbegović, Karadžić and Boban; presidents Milošević (Serbia), Tuđman (Croatia), Ćosić (Yugoslavia) and Bulatović (Montenegro); the Yugoslav Prime Minister, Milan Panić; the three Bosnian army commanders, Sefir Halilović, Ratko Mladić and Milivoje Petković; and the chiefs of the *Vojska Jugoslavije* (the Yugoslav Army) and the *Hrvatska Vojska* (the Croatian Army), generals Života Panić and Janko Bobetko. The whole operation had to be co-ordinated on the ground with the UNPROFOR force commander, General Satish Nambiar, and the head of UN Civilian Affairs for Yugoslavia, Cedric Thornberry. In addition, the work required extremely close co-operation with the UNHCR which was led by Sadako Ogata. Various *ad hoc* bodies and agencies also vied for the conference's attention.[5] The conference was also responsible for examining all political problems associated with the former Yugoslavia, such as Kosovo, as well as the burning issues of Krajina and Macedonia.

Matters were made more complicated by the fact that many of the characters from inside the former Yugoslavia refused to talk to one another. President Izetbegović initially insisted on special treatment over Boban and Karadžić because he was the elected head of a sovereign government. Once the mediators had dismissed this, they had to overcome Izetbegović objections to holding face to face talks with Karadžić. His refusal to meet the Bosnian Serb leader was understandable but until he relented, little progress could be made.

At first, people were concerned that Cyrus Vance and Lord Owen might not make up an effective team. In fact, they complemented each other remarkably well. Vance has no match as a patient diplomat. He was able to cool down the most fervent passions and gently force the delegations to address the substance of the issues. On those occasions when the whip needed cracking, Lord Owen told the various parties bluntly that they had better start reconsidering their position or be named as the guilty party.

The VOPP is an exceptionally good document which has been roundly abused by politicians and the media throughout the world and particularly inside the former Yugoslavia and the United States. In my experience, many who denounced the plan had either not read it or they wilfully misinterpreted its provisions. It was never intended as a definitive solution to the Bosnian crisis. Its function was to provide an interim political solution which would facilitate the scaling down of military operations in the republic. It certainly provided a very clear framework and direction for any future constitutional order but it was not considered immutable by the authors.

5. In one of its least inspired appointments, the United Nations named Tadeusz Mazowiecki, the former Polish Prime Minister, head of the commission investigating human rights abuses in the former Yugoslavia. Whoever came up with the bright idea of selecting a leading lay Catholic intellectual for a job which involved talking to the Serbs should mug up on his or her European history.

The VOPP proposed the division of Bosnia-Hercegovina into ten provinces. Of these, nine would be under the control of a specific national group, three provinces being accorded to each nation. The tenth province, Sarajevo, would be controlled by a body representing all three national groups. The degree to which these provinces would be autonomous from the centre was in part stipulated by the plan and in part would be determined by its implementation.

The VOPP involved both the Bosnian government and the Bosnian Serbs making substantial concessions. The Bosnian Croats, and by extension the government in Zagreb, were perfectly satisfied with the plan.[6] President Izetbegović's first response to the VOPP was to reject it as it involved the collapse of his aim of restoring a unitary Bosnia-Hercegovina with a decisive central government in Sarajevo. The plan also demanded that BiH be demilitarized, which meant that there would be no central army, a concession to the Serbs. So the Bosnian government clearly lost on the constitutional arrangement.

However, although it gave the Serbs wide-ranging powers in the areas designated to them, it contained punitive measures against them as well. Firstly, it insisted that they hand back 60 per cent (25 per cent of Bosnian territory as a whole) of the territory which they had conquered militarily in what they perceived to be a civil war (a unique outcome to a civil war). This included such crucial towns as Zvornik, Bratunac, Višegrad, Foča, Bosanski Novi and Rogatica. They would be denied a northern corridor, while the southern route to eastern Hercegovina was also broken. In addition, the VOPP specifically denied them their central war aim – the formation of an independent state outside Bosnia-Hercegovina with the right to forge constitutional links with third parties (i.e. Serbia and the Krajina). So the VOPP was hard for both Moslems and Serbs to swallow, although the problem for the Bosnian government was

6. If there was one major structural problem, it was that there were two losers and one winner, the Croats. It probably would have been preferable to have three losers which would have involved giving some Croat territory to the Moslems. However, if there had to be one winner, it was most sensible for it to be the Croats as there was a lower risk of revanchist violence in the event of this Croat mini-victory.

ameliorated somewhat inasmuch as their options were strictly limited because of their military weakness.

Enter the United States. After his election defeat at the hands of Bill Clinton in November 1992, President Bush developed a seemingly mischievous policy towards the former Yugoslavia. Back in Belgrade, Slobodan Milošević was hatching a plan to defeat the Prime Minister, Milan Panić, and by implication the federal President, Dobrica Ćosić, by inflicting a deadly blow against them in the forthcoming elections. After some dithering, Panić decided to challenge Milošević for the Serbian presidency and after some more dithering, Ćosić backed Panić's candidacy. By doing so, Ćosić, Milošević's only truly influential opponent within the Serbian body politic, was preparing a showdown with his erstwhile pupil. Ćosić bears considerable moral and intellectual responsibility for the revival of Serbian nationalism and, specifically, for the war in Bosnia. But by the autumn of 1992, he had become genuinely appalled by what was going on in Bosnia-Hercegovina and the fact that politically, economically and morally, his beloved Serbia was being driven into the ground. At the Geneva Conference, the Yugoslav President had made significant progress in forging links with President Tudman. Indeed, Ćosić had signed a provisional agreement with Tudman which would have starved the engine of war in the northern Balkans of its essential fuel: the Serbo-Croat conflict.

Milošević was unable to accept Ćosić as the Balkan peacemaker, as the man who might reconcile Serbs and Croats and thereby facilitate an end to the war in Bosnia. So, in order to defeat the Ćosić–Panić ticket in the elections of December 1992, Milošević resuscitated his hard-line support, not only for the Bosnian Serbs but for the Croatian Serbs as well – the Greater Serbian project was back on the rails. The Serbian media, above all Radio TV Belgrade, portrayed Panić as an unscrupulous opportunist being payrolled by the Americans. The hysterical campaign which portrayed the Serbs as victims of a worldwide, Washington-led conspiracy, played on ordinary Serbs' feelings of insecurity to Milošević's benefit.

A victory for Panić would have disrupted Milošević's power base and given a real boost to the peace efforts in Geneva. Regrettably, the world did nothing. The Bush Administration appeared not to register the election or regarded it as irrelevant; the European Community ignored it; and even the Vance–Owen team bent over backwards not to interfere in the internal affairs of Serbia. Despite this indifference and despite Milošević's total control over the broadcast media and a large part of the print media, Panić's campaign began to pick up. He committed himself to working towards an equitable solution to the war for all three sides in Bosnia; for a normalization of relations between Serbia and Croatia; he even, to Ćosić's dismay, spoke of recognizing Macedonia. Some doubted his ability, but nobody doubted his sincerity. Yet, not a word of support from the international community. Had governments indicated that in the event of Milošević's defeat, they would have advocated that the United Nations reconsider the sanctions regime, then it is certainly possible that the outcome of the elections might have been different. Instead, the United States, in the shape of Lawrence Eagleburger, spoke a week before the elections. He denounced the Serbs and said that the United States would be seeking to prosecute ten men as war criminals. At the top of this list stood Milošević, Karadžić and Mladić. Nothing could have been better designed to ensure Milošević's election victory than this statement and, sure enough, the Belgrade media made a lot of noise about it. Lawrence Eagleburger spoke Serbo-Croat, having served as ambassador to Belgrade. He also knew the Serbian mentality well, having extensive business contacts in Serbia before the fall of Yugoslavia. Either he knew exactly what he was doing or he had been forced into it unwillingly by George Bush or he had lost his grip. Whether it was aware of it or not, the Bush Administration made a substantial contribution to Milošević's victory.

The Serbian President still felt it necessary to engage in a little electoral manipulation (observers estimate that between 5 and 10 per cent of the ballot was rigged). Panić gained 34 per cent of the electorate's trust in a straight fight with Milošević for the presidency. In the face of the hostility of the Milošević Administration, that was an extremely impressive result which reiterated that opposition to the Serbian President is widespread in Serbia, although it is poorly served by its leaders. Had Panić received a little support from the west, his challenge might have been still more impressive.

Following the Eagleburger intervention, the Bush Administration continued to express its concern about Serb aggression in Bosnia, egged on by the incoming, yet inexperienced Clinton team and some blood-curdling leader articles in *The New York Times*. This atmosphere was stoked by the Bosnian Moslem lobby, led by the Foreign Minister, Haris Silajdžić, and Bosnia's ambassador to the United Nations, Mohamed Sacirbey. They advocated the scrapping of the Vance–Owen plan and in its place the lifting of the UN arms embargo. The package was wrapped up with the phrase: 'If you will not defend us, at least give us the arms with which we can defend ourselves.'

The Europeans, in particular Russia and those countries whose troops were serving with UNPROFOR in Bosnia-Hercegovina, expressed considerable disquiet about the idea of supplying weapons to the Moslems. They argued that not only would this place UNPROFOR troops in considerable danger, but that by pouring more weapons into the Bosnian fire, there was an increased danger of the Balkan conflict spreading to other areas. The Croats, still nominal allies of the Bosnian government, were extremely alarmed at the prospect. They considered the VOPP to be in their best interests and they were concerned that a strengthened Bosnian government army might turn its guns on Croat-held territory. Croat opposition to the lifting of the arms embargo was not merely academic. The only supplies reaching the Bosnian government came across Croat territory. Indeed, on 25 April 1993, when relations between the Croats and Moslems in Central Bosnia and Mostar were deteriorating rapidly, Franjo Tuđman held talks with Alija Izetbegović in Zagreb to discuss the worsening relations between the HVO and the Armija BiH in central Bosnia and western Hercegovina. During this meeting, Tuđman turned to the Bosnian President angrily with the rhetorical question, 'And just how do you think you are going to get these weapons, Alija?'

Soon after his inauguration, Clinton identified Bosnia as the most pressing foreign policy issue facing his new Administration. He dismissed the VOPP because in his view 'it appeased Serb aggression and legitimized ethnic cleansing'. This was nonsense. Serb aggression was not appeased because the VOPP emphatically prevented the creation of a Greater Serbia. Neither did it legitimize ethnic cleansing because it forced the Serbs to hand back so much conquered territory and included explicit provisions for the return of property acquired by force. If the VOPP faced a problem, it was a question not of principle, but of implementation.

There followed a month-long period of procrastination on the part of the Clinton Administration accompanied by much negative rhetoric about the Vance–Owen plan. When the Secretary of State, Warren Christopher, finally unveiled the Clinton plan, it was identical to the VOPP with one exception. 'We're not happy with the maps,' Christopher muttered, meaning the Serbs had been given too much territory. If anything, the opposite was true – the Serbs had been given too little territory, in particular, some provision should have been made for the Serbs to establish the northern corridor. The procrastination and the sabre-rattling of the Administration encouraged the Bosnian government to hold out against the VOPP. It also made life easier for Karadžić because as long as the Moslems were against the plan, he was not under much pressure to sign it either.

Throughout March and April 1993, the Clinton Administration seemed determined to go ahead with lifting the arms embargo and using selective air strikes against Bosnian Serb artillery positions. What neither the Americans nor the Bosnian government seemed to appreciate was that Russia, Britain and France, the three European members on the UN Security Council, would not tolerate a lifting of arms embargo under any circumstances. Despite a high-profile tour around the European capitals and despite the support which Clinton had publicly given Yeltsin in the run up to the Russian referendum on 25 April, the Europeans would not budge. Andrej Kozyrev, the Americans' greatest friend in Moscow, spelled it out to the United States in late April. 'Do not do anything unilaterally,' he warned Washington, 'if you want to avoid a Balkan war.'

The Bosnian government was swift to react to the collapse of the Clinton–Christopher initiative. Within a matter of two weeks, it was pressing for the immediate implementation of the VOPP. There were two reasons for this. Firstly, this was now the only option open to it which would stop the Bosnian Serbs from consolidating their control over 70 per cent of Bosnian territory. Secondly, the Croats, tired with the failure of diplomacy, had decided to implement the Vance–Owen plan in their regions. This involved the crushing of Bosnian government influence in HVO controlled areas. The war between the Moslems and Croats, which had been in gestation for twelve months, could begin in earnest. The VOPP had allotted eight districts with an overall Moslem majority to the Croats: Travnik, Donji Vakuf, Bugojno, Gornji Vakuf, Fojnica in province ten in central Bosnia, and Jablanica, Konjic and Mostar in province eight, western Hercegovina. The Moslems in these regions had from the outset of the war resisted the imposition of Croat political structures. In March and April 1993, the HVO and Boban's government of Herceg-Bosna decided to solve this problem by asserting its authority militarily. At the same time, the Moslems were staring defeat in the face and decided to compensate for the massive military defeat that they had suffered at the hands of the Serbs in the east and the north by laying claim to the same areas.

After several weeks of on–off combat around the towns of Gornji Vakuf and Vitez, the Croats embarked on a spree of blood-letting culminating in the massacre of Moslem civilians in the village of Ahmići, a site of considerable religious significance for Bosnia's Moslems. In a cynical action worthy of Ratko Mladić at his most cunning, Croat artillery began shelling the village to force its inhabitants to flee across an open field to the south. Lying in wait at the bottom of the field was a Croat unit which opened fire on the civilians. The village was torched (UN investigators found the body of a three-year-old child which had been doused in petrol before being set alight) and hundreds killed in cold blood.

Some of the fiercest fighting broke out in Mostar. The centre of the town was systematically razed to the ground as the HVO attempted to obliterate the Armija BiH positions on the eastern bank of the Neretva river. Amazingly, the old bridge, one of the most famous symbols of Bosnia-Hercegovina and a masterpiece of Ottoman architecture, still just stands although it has been badly damaged. When I visited Mostar during the fighting, the attitude of Croat fighters, which had been so welcoming to foreigners during the war in Croatia, had degenerated to the level of Serb fighters. The Croats began to cleanse western Hercegovina systematically.

At this stage, the fighting in Bosnia-Hercegovina began to break the bounds of imagination. Around the Konjic area, Serb units guaranteed the Croats safe passage as they were retreating. When Gornji Vakuf was being contested, a fight between Croats and Moslems was being monitored by a nearby Serb unit. After some hours, the Moslem guns fell silent. The Serb commander radioed his Moslem counterpart. 'Why have you stopped firing?' he asked. 'We've run out of ammunition. Give us some ammunition,' the reply came. Instead, the Serb commander requested the Croat co-ordinates which the Moslem commander duly supplied. Over the next four hours, the Serb unit pounded the Croats into surrender. The following morning at dawn, the Moslem commander ordered his men to run up the Yugoslav flag instead of the Bosnian ensign in order to thank the Serbs.

In late May and June, the Moslems struck back at the Croats, launching a vicious offensive around the Travnik and Vitez areas. The atrocities they committed should convince anybody that if the Moslems were permitted a free supply of weapons, then this would not level the 'playing field', as Warren Christopher maintained, it would merely level the 'killing fields', as Lord Owen retorted.

While the Croats and Moslems were slaughtering each other in a grab for territory, pressure was increasing on the Bosnian Serbs to accept the VOPP. If the Bosnian Serb signature could be secured, then the United Nations would have real authority to strengthen its mandate in Bosnia-Hercegovina and enforce the scaling down of military operations in the republic. President Slobodan Milošević had now become the most powerful supporter of the VOPP within the Serb community. Having delivered a crushing blow to Ćosić, who following Panić's election defeat had ceased to wield any influence over Serbian policy, Milošević effected one of his frequent Machiavellian turns and presented himself as the Balkan peacemaker. In April 1993, he and Tuđman reopened their dialogue which resulted in the resumption of talks between the government in Zagreb and the authorities in Knin.

Throughout the war in Bosnia, the conflict between Serbs and Croats over the Krajina had simmered merrily. The Knin Serbs had consciously violated the Vance plan for Croatia which had established the United Nations Protected Areas (UNPA) in the eastern and southern peripheries of Croatia. In particular, they had prevented any progress on the issue of the return of Croatian refugees to their homes in the Krajina. In late January 1993, with Croat patience running extremely thin, President Tuđman ordered an offensive against three crucial strategic points under Serb control in the Krajina: the bridge at Maslenica, Zemunik airport and the Peruća dam. At one point in this offensive, which achieved much less than at first the Croats claimed, the UN feared greatly that it might spark off the large Serbo-Croat war. The situation calmed down. But it highlighted the fact that although the Krajina was no longer a theatre of active war, it still represented a tremendous threat to the stability of the entire region.

In April and May 1993, Milošević both applied tremendous pressure on the Bosnian Serbs to accept the VOPP and offered Tuđman a deal over the Krajina which would have seen Croatian sovereignty restored in the region while granting the Serbs extensive political autonomy. The war in Bosnia-Hercegovina was coming to a slow, if painful end. That is, until the international community stepped in. On 23 May, the foreign ministers of the United States, Russia, France, Britain and Spain (the latter three all having troops stationed in Bosnia-Hercegovina) proclaimed the Washington Declaration or Joint Action Programme. Still licking its wounds after the diplomatic defeat it suffered over the issue of the arms embargo, the Clinton Administration was not prepared to give its full backing to the VOPP. Instead, it agreed to a proposal advanced by the Russian Foreign Minister, Andrej Kozyrev, which envisaged the creation of six safe areas around the besieged Moslem enclaves of Sarajevo, Goražde, Žepa, Srebrenica, Tuzla and Bihać. The VOPP was downgraded, which meant that the international community had discarded the only political programme which it had to deal with the war in Bosnia-Hercegovina.

All three sides in the Bosnian conflict recognized the significance of the Washington Declaration immediately. The international community no longer had the stomach to enforce a political solution on the warring factions. Fierce fighting flared between Croats and Moslems, while the Serbs understood it as a green light to finish off the extraordinary resistance of Goražde's defenders. Worse than this, the Washington Declaration led Milošević to drop his support for a negotiated settlement and within two days of the new policy being announced in Washington, the Knin Serbs cancelled their negotiations with Zagreb. Emboldened by the failure of the international community, the Krajina Serbs announced they would be holding a referendum to decide on whether to unite with the Bosnian Serbs, a move which, if realized, will set the stage for a massive Balkan war.

As I write, the leaders of the Bosnian Serbs, Croats and Moslems, together with presidents Tuđman and Milošević are engaged in cabal-like negotiations at a secret address in Geneva. With them are Lord Owen and Theovald Stoltenberg, the former Norwegian Foreign Minister who replaced Cyrus Vance as co-chair of the Geneva Conference. At the same time, Moslems are now continuing their brutal offensive against Croats in central Bosnia, Bosnian Serb forces are obliterating Goražde, while the Krajina Serbs are preparing for a referendum to decide on whether they will unite with the Bosnian Serbs and destroy the Vance plan for Croatia.

In the south of the Balkans, the Former Yugoslav Republic of Macedonia (FYROM), as it has been designated by the United Nations, is limping along. Its dispute with Greece over its name still looks nowhere near a resolution, while relations between the Albanian minority in FYROM and its Slav Macedonian majority remain tense. At the end of June, demonstrations of nationalists opposed to the bond with Serbia have been held in some Montenegrin towns. Kosovo is battered and bruised. Bulgaria is heaving under another political crisis as the former supporters of the President, Zhelyu Zhelev, are trying to engineer his removal. The international community lurches from one misconceived policy to another. The latest of these, the Washington Declaration, is as catastrophic in its potential as the premature recognition of Croatia and Slovenia by Germany. This time, however, it is the Americans who are muddying the waters.

A large-scale Balkan war remains a distinct possibility. While the international community has been vainly attempting to apply sticking plasters on the bleeding wound of Bosnia-Hercegovina, it has done nothing to address the underlying problems which affect not merely the Balkans but large areas of Eastern Europe and the former Soviet Union.

And the two great nations of the former Yugoslavia? Serbia has become an economic cesspool in which the only relevant political factors are Milošević, his police and state-run television. Tuđman's will has been imposed throughout the media in Croatia, reducing almost all print and broadcast outlets to the role of slavish lap-dogs. The economy is falling down an abyss while Tuđman proclaims his country is on the verge of an 'economic miracle' comparable with that of post-war West Germany. The Serb-controlled Krajina has become a murderous medieval statelet (in which the victims of politically motivated killings are equally likely to be Serbs as Croats). My friends in Sarajevo are alive, but only just. My dear friend, Lenka Raos, a Croat living in Belgrade, was killed by accident in a shooting incident at a Belgrade restaurant in May 1993. I keep writing in the hope of improvement but with a conviction which is ever diminishing. I hate the Balkans. I hate Europe. But we have nowhere else to go.

EPILOGUE 1992:

The Revenger's Tragedy

No East European country has demonstrated quite so clearly as the former Yugoslavia the dangers which were inherent but largely unrecognized in the process of democratization. The central conflict which destabilized Yugoslavia was between, on the one hand, the desire to create or consolidate (in the case of Serbia) a state in which one national group was dominant, and on the other, the perceived or demonstrable vulnerability of minority populations in these projected states. With a largely homogeneous national composition, Slovenia was able to secede early in the crisis after a war which, when compared with what was to come, was peaceful. Almost everywhere else, a plethora of minorities inhabited the disputed territories: in Croatia, in Bosnia, in Serbia, in Macedonia. The issue of minorities was only uncontentious in Montenegro, although the smallest Yugoslav republic was still heavily involved in the crisis.

For a long time (indeed until just before the declarations of independence by Croatia and Slovenia in June 1991), Western Europe and the United States appeared unwilling to recognize that Yugoslavia was disintegrating and that the presidents of its six constituent republics were never remotely capable of regulating this process in a peaceful manner. There were two main reasons for this.

After the collapse of communism in the autumn of 1989, Western policy-makers identified Hungary, Czechoslovakia and Poland as the three former socialist states which could be integrated most rapidly into the market structures of the European Community and the United States. The collapsing Soviet Union also absorbed considerable attention by dint of its size and its possession of a nuclear arsenal and huge stocks of conventional weaponry. In this scheme, the Balkans were regarded as uninteresting both from a political and economic point of view. Only the United States, which developed a busy diplomatic programme in Bulgaria, Greece, Turkey and later Albania, appeared aware of the importance of the Balkans. This was largely determined by strategic interests in the Middle East and the growing importance of Turkey in regional affairs. American policy in the southern Balkans notwithstanding, the peninsula was considered by the West to be of little value, where trouble could be contained should it break out (although few were predicting destabilization).

The second reason for the West's support of federal Yugoslavia was more localized. Ante Marković, the Prime Minister, achieved notable success in 1990 in his attempts to heal Yugoslavia's sick economy. He was viewed as a man with whom the West could do business and who would ensure that there would be no serious default on Yugoslavia's external debt. For a long time, he appeared to have the confidence of the army leadership. Above all, he presented himself as a man with a programme of *rational* transition in both the economic and political arenas. (In fact, as many Western policy-makers later learned to their cost, Marković never evolved any concept beyond the presumption, especially naïve in the Balkan context, that a successful management of the economy alone can amount to a political strategy.) The West looked at Yugoslavia through the filter of the Soviet Union – as Yugoslavia was careering towards an explosive war, caused to a large degree by Serbia's commitment to a unitarist structure, the West supported this political anachronism for fear that an outbreak of secession among the constituent republics might have provoked a similar process in the Soviet Union. The European Community and the United States should ideally have been guiding the inexperienced or opportunist Yugoslav leaders towards an agreed break-up of the country. The excuse diplomats give, which cannot be lightly dismissed, is that during the run-up to the Yugoslav wars, foreign ministries around the world were concentrating on developments in the Gulf and the Soviet Union. Since the collapse of the Soviet Union, the limited resources of most diplomatic services have been stretched beyond capacity. None the less, if we judge foreign policy by concrete results, Yugoslavia must be considered a major failure.

Once the crisis became a war, divisions both within the European Community and between some members of the EC and the United

States soon became apparent. The most striking policy division emerged between Germany on the one hand and the United States and the United Kingdom on the other. As the conflict developed, the 'great power' interests of Russia and Turkey also started to mature. The European Community was quick to negotiate a withdrawal of the Yugoslav army and the *de facto* secession of Slovenia. But there was no agreement concerning Croatia. From an early stage, Germany advocated full recognition of the republic, while the United States and Britain argued for a comprehensive political solution to be agreed on at the Yugoslav conference in the Hague chaired by the former British Foreign Secretary, Lord Carrington. Both arguments contained flaws.

Hans-Dietrich Genscher, the former German Foreign Minister, who was the keenest supporter of recognition, cited the two Helsinki principles of the inviolability of borders and the right to self-determination in favour of granting independence to Zagreb. These were ideas which were inextricably linked to Cold War diplomacy – the West understood self-determination to mean the right of East European countries to leave the Soviet bloc (whereas there was much lobbying in favour of the independence of the GDR, Poland, Czechoslovakia or Hungary, supporters of self-determination for the Ukraine barely got a hearing from Western governments). Following the collapse of communism, it was, of course, not surprising that Croatia wished to apply this criterion in its own bid for independence. This meant leaving Yugoslavia in those internal borders outlined by Tito, thus taking a partly unwilling Serbian minority with it. With reference to those Serbs, does such a policy mean that the right to self-determination is subordinated to the principle of inviolable borders? Croatia's leaders failed to address this problem with any seriousness, while Germany ignored it as irrelevant. Germany wished to see its natural allies in the region being granted the independence it felt they deserved. Germany has been connected with Slovenia and Croatia by dint of culture, economics and religion for many centuries. The self-confidence which it developed after unification brought with it an understandable desire to play a more forceful role in European affairs, particularly in regions of traditional interest like Slovenia and Croatia. But in doing so, not only did the Germans commit a cardinal error of ignoring the neuralgic question of the Serb minority in Croatia, they blithely ignored the implications of recognition for Bosnia-Hercegovina and Macedonia (Bonn's diffidence towards the appalling fate of these two republics can partly be explained by the fact that neither territory was historically an integral part of the German sphere of influence).

The war in Croatia was in part a nationalist war and in part a war of territorial expansion sponsored by Serbia and the JNA. Where Bonn refused to see the nationalist aspect, Washington and London were often prepared to give the JNA and President Milošević more credit than they were due in the initial stages of the war. Both parties, Milošević in particular, exploited the genuine fears of Serbs in Croatia quite cynically by invoking the most blood-thirsty, genocidal images as a way of consolidating his own power. But the essential idea which the British and Americans upheld, that recognition should only be granted once a comprehensive solution to the Yugoslav crisis could be found, was well argued. One notion that withstands no serious scrutiny was that put forward by the German Foreign Ministry and many Croats which claimed that if the European Community had recognized Croatia upon the declaration of independence, then there would have been no war. It supposes that if recognition had been forthcoming, the well-armed Serb minority and the JNA would simply have capitulated in the face of this diplomatic defeat, packed their bags and left the disputed territories for Serbia proper – this is the most wishful of thinking and shows a chronic lack of understanding of the Balkan mentality.

Yugoslavia's disintegration and wars in the north and centre of the former federation have had a profound impact on the uncertain political development in the south of the Balkans. Four issues, which are closely connected, are especially significant. The first concerns the national aspirations of the three Albanian communities in Albania proper, in Kosovo and in western Macedonia. The second is the dreaded Macedonian question. The third concerns the growing rivalry between Greece and the emerging regional giant, Turkey. The final issue focuses on the intense activity of American diplomacy in the southern Balkans. Unless great care is taken, the delicate fabric of regional security could be torn, particularly since Serbia hovers like a wraith in the background, threatening to ignite a Balkan war which it can do overnight if it so decides.

With the demise of Albania's rotten Communist Party as the ruling power, Kosovo has risen rapidly up the political agenda in Albania. President Sali Berisha has publicly warned that Albania will not stand idly by if fighting breaks out in Kosovo. In addition, it is Albania's stated policy to achieve peaceful unification with Kosovo and western Macedonia through the processes of European integration. Greece, Macedonia and Serbia have all made known their implacable opposition to Albanian unification. In addition, the United States (whose influence among the Albanians is decisive) indicated in the first half of 1992 to the leaders of all three Albanian communities that it does not support Albanian unification – the Kosovars and the western Macedonians must be granted the full autonomy stipulated by the Carrington peace conference but the inviolability of borders remains in force for Serbia and Macedonia just as it does for Bosnia and Croatia. While the Americans have succeeded in toning down the rhetoric of Berisha and the western Macedonians, the Kosovars' principled position from which they are not budging is full independence from Serbia under international (presumably UN) protection. Regardless of the moral strength of their position, the secession of Kosovo means war between Serbs and Albanians. Kosovo is the most pressing problem for the region because it is the closest to conflict.

Although not as familiar as the Kosovo problem, the Republic of Macedonia lies at the heart of the conundrum in the southern Balkans. Yugoslavia's southern-most republic is inhabited by one and a half million Macedonians, Slavs who speak a language which is very closely related to Bulgarian. They inhabit a territory known as Vardar Macedonia although historically they have also lived in Pirin Macedonia (now in Bulgaria) and Aegean Macedonia (now in Greece). There is a large Macedonian minority in Bulgaria (which is not recognized by Sofia) and small ones in Greece (not recognized) and Albania (recognized). The Serbs and Albanians recognize the Macedonian nation, but the nationalists among the former sustain claims on northern Macedonian territory while the latter has contemporary aspirations to western Macedonia; the Bulgarians have recognized the state even though they refer to it colloquially as Western Bulgaria, but they have refused to recognize the Macedonian nation (i.e. they are really Bulgarians); the Greeks refuse to recognize either. Indeed the mere mention of the name Macedonia (which the Greeks call the Republic of Skopje, after its capital) induces hysteria in even the most peaceful Greek. The Greeks believe the name Macedonia is exclusively Hellenic property and that the recognition of Macedonia as an independent state would imply the approval of territorial pretensions which Athens claims Skopje has on Greek territory stretching down to Thessaloniki. If fighting were to break out either in the Sandžak (a Moslem enclave in Serbia) or in Kosovo, this would immediately threaten the stability of Macedonia, which during the Balkan wars at the beginning of this century was the host to bloody battles as its four neighbours fought over the same issues which have re-emerged during the past year.

Greece's implacable opposition to Macedonian recognition has caused severe embarrassment to its partners in the European community, particularly since its hostility to Macedonian statehood has led to the revival of its close Christian Orthodox ties with Belgrade. Greece lobbies intensely on Serbia's behalf within the European Community, making a coherent approach by the EC to the Yugoslav crisis very difficult. But by refusing to contemplate Macedonian independence, Greece is shooting itself in the foot as the government in Skopje is being driven into the hands of Turkey, Greece's real regional competitor.

Turkey has offered all Balkan countries membership in its new Black Sea Economic Community which includes all the Turkic republics of the former Soviet Union. The diplomatic activity between Ankara on the one hand, and Tirana, Skopje and Sofia on the other, intensified greatly in 1992. The development of the BSEC is Ankara's response to the EC's repeated refusal to allow Turkey into the European Community. As Turgut Ozal said during a trip to Washington in May 1992, the fluid situation in the Balkans has presented Turkey with 'a once-in-a-lifetime opportunity for Turkey to restore its economic, diplomatic and cultural influence among Moslem vestiges of the Ottoman empire'. Greece fears the creation of an overarching pro-Turkish influence in the region which eventually could translate into a security threat. Turkey, snubbed for so long by the European Community at the behest of the Germans and Greeks, is responding by creating a community of its own which may develop into a significant economic, political and possibly military competitor to the EC.

The significance of the BSEC has clearly not been lost on the State Department. While showing the appropriate diplomatic interest in countries like Poland, Czechoslovakia, Hungary and Romania, Washington has developed its relations with Sofia, Tirana and (tacitly) with Skopje with an unparalleled zeal since the collapse of communism in the three republics. The central focus of US policy is Turkey, which Washington recognizes as the major regional power with considerable potential for expansion. America's policy is explained by its strategic and economic interests in the Mediterranean and the Middle East – from now on, the Turks are the key nation in the region. This is bad news for the Greeks and bad news for the Serbs. Although they may deserve little, if any sympathy, a regional struggle for influence of this kind, while Serbia is still at war, is also bad news for the rest of us as we have all the ingredients required for a Balkan war. This likelihood increases as the economies of Albania, Macedonia and Bulgaria grind to a halt because of wilful or unwitting obstacles to co-operation imposed by the European Community. Europe is not integrating, it is dividing again along the line of the Great Schism, the most persistently unstable border on the continent.

The re-emergence not simply of old Balkan conflicts but of local and more international alliances and strategies implies considerable danger for the stability of southern Europe, central and eastern Europe and the Mediterranean. The Yugoslav collapse provided the international community with an opportunity to grasp the essence of the regional political problem: the question of minorities and nation states. It has also largely ignored related factors such as the low level of economic development in the region. With armed conflict breaking out steadily along the periphery of the former Soviet Union, struggles in the Balkans could overlap and encourage destabilization to the East, particularly as the economic situation of Russia and the Ukraine appears to be deteriorating and not improving. One thing that all these conflicts share (Armenia–Azerbaijan,

Moldova–Transdniestr, Georgia–South Ossetia, etc.) is the presence of a nationalist dispute concerning a minority population. Throughout the Cold War, only poorly funded human rights organizations addressed this problem with any seriousness. If the problems of the Balkans and the former Soviet Union are to be solved, politicians and diplomats must consider it with equal gravity.

Return to Purgatory

On the morning of Saturday, 5 February, I was working in my hotel room in Zagreb feeling unusually relaxed, when I tuned to the BBC World Service: 'A mortar has exploded in the middle of a crowded market-place in the Bosnian capital, Sarajevo . . .' Even at this early stage, when reports were still coming in, it was clear that this was a particularly callous attack on Sarajevo's civilian population. The final death-toll reached sixty-eight, a record number to have been killed by a single mortar at the time in the Bosnian war (another single mortar, which landed in a crowded café area in Tuzla in August 1995, would claim the lives of seventy-one, mainly young men and women). I took the first available plane down to Sarajevo.

It was, of course, no solace for the hundreds of thousands of other victims of this war that this single incident became the focus of so much attention. Yet an act as barbarous as this reflected the quintessential evil, which has characterized much of the prosecution of this war. (Such obscenities are not, of course, a unique feature of the Balkans in the late twentieth century, as many inhabitants of Rwanda, Liberia, Sudan, Somalia, Afghanistan, Chechnya, Georgia, *inter alia*, have experienced at firsthand.)

Much of that attention zoomed in on Lieutenant-General Sir Michael Rose, a former chief of the British Special Air Services, who had been in charge of UNPROFOR's BiH Command in Sarajevo for a month when the missile struck. General Rose had initially been received warmly by the people of the Bosnian capital. He had begun his tour by strolling through the city and greeting passers-by, despite the threat from snipers and shells. He made it clear that his intention as Commander was to open up the city – not merely to provide it with utilities, but to enable its citizens to come and go as they please. His openness was considered a welcome change from the behaviour of his immediate predecessor, the Belgian General François Briquemont, who had spent most of his tour bunkered down inside the UN Headquarters on Đure Đaković St., largely oblivious to what was happening outside.

By the time the mortar struck, however, Rose's relations with the Bosnian government were becoming strained. In order to win the war, the Bosnian leadership had one central strategy (as Vice-President Ejup Ganić has openly admitted) – to entice the Western military, and the Americans in particular, to enter the conflict on its behalf.

Rose was not convinced that the Bosnian Serbs had fired the mortar. The initial UNPROFOR study carried out by a team of French ballistics experts suggested that Bosnian government forces had in fact been responsible for the massacre. It later emerged that a crucial mathematical error in this report rendered it worthless. The document none the less played a role in the curious political intrigues that immediately followed the attack.

The United States called an emergency meeting of NATO ministers which demanded that the Bosnian Serbs withdraw all their heavy artillery surrounding Sarajevo in the space of ten days. Rather confusingly, Rose had also drawn up a plan (formulated largely by Viktor Andreyev, the Russian head of Civilian Affairs in Sarajevo) which also envisaged the pull-back of the Serbian artillery. While NATO was trying to decide on the Western response to the mortar, Bosnian government military commanders failed to turn up at a meeting arranged by Rose at Sarajevo Airport to finalize his plan for the demilitarization of Sarajevo and the pull-back of the Serbian artillery. Furious at this snub, Rose drove from the airport to the presidency building in downtown Sarajevo. He marched into the president's office and threatened Izetbegović with the publication of some unpleasant facts about the mortar attack if Bosnia's representatives did not get to the airport straight away. According to an eye-witness at this meeting, Izetbegović was deeply unnerved and dispatched his commander to the airport where the Rose plan was promptly accepted. This does not prove that the Bosnian government fired on their people. It does suggest, however, that President Izetbegović was unsure as to what the origin of that shell was. There were eight subsequent ballistic reports on the mortar. None of these was able to reach a definite conclusion about who launched it, as the shell had hit part of a market stall on its way down, rendering an accurate assessment impossible. The UN teams did place the firing position between Serbian and Bosnian lines, but this simply meant that either side could have fired it.

As the ultimatum ticked away, journalists streamed into Sarajevo, elbowing each other for the best view of the bombing campaign. The presence of Peter Arnett from CNN led everybody to believe that the NATO threat was really serious. The Bosnian Serbs started handing in artillery in dribs and drabs to the UN collection points. With three days to go before the ultimatum expired at midnight, on Sunday, 20 February, the Serbs had only handed in 10 per cent of their weapons and a large number of these were out of commission. The Serbs were not running away – as many people claimed subsequently – they were bracing themselves for NATO raids, presumably under the impression that the Yugoslav Army would support them in the event. The Russians were implacably opposed to NATO bombing, indeed their Foreign Minister at the time, Andrej Kozyrev, averred that this would spark a much wider war in the Balkans. British, French and UN officials were all concerned about the Bosnian conflict developing into a proxy struggle between the United States and Russia.

On Thursday evening, 17 February, President Yeltsin made a surprise announcement that Russian troops would be deployed in Sarajevo to ensure that the Bosnian government forces do not exploit the absence of Serbian heavy weapons by launching an infantry offensive outside the city. This was probably the boldest and most intelligent decision made by Russia during the entire Yugoslav conflict. Wherever possible, Moscow avoided involvement, and its support for the Serbs was usually grudging, motivated not by pan-Slavism or pan-Orthodoxy, but by its own strategic interests in Europe. President Yeltsin never forgave Milošević for supporting the coup leaders in August 1991, while he, Kozyrev and Vitaly Churkin (for a long time, Yeltsin's envoy to the former Yugoslavia) were positively revolted and regularly angered by Radovan Karadžić and General Mladić. The decision to deploy Russian troops in Sarajevo (an idea which, six weeks prior to the mortar attack, had been categorically ruled out by Moscow) defused the tension around the ultimatum. The Serbian and the Bosnian government forces began handing in weapons to UN collection points. The Serbs never fulfilled their commitment, keeping a large number of weapons back. But for several months, the people of Sarajevo were afforded a breathing space. The shelling of the capital died down and a degree of normality, returned. The trams started running again and the UN and the local authorities were able to restore part of the city's infrastructure. Nobody was safe from the ubiquitous snipers and gradually the Bosnian Serbs chipped away at the agreement as time drew on, preparing for the final showdown, which was to take place in 1995.

To the west and north-west of Sarejevo, the conflict between the Moslems and the Croats had been raging since April 1993 with a ferocity that equalled any other phase of the wars of Yugoslav succession. The pattern of warfare between the Moslems and Croats was similar to that between the Moslems and the Serbs, with the latter enjoying a superiority in artillery and the former in infantry. Predictably, this translated into inordinate suffering for Moslem civilians, although large numbers of Croats were also run out of their homes in central Bosnia. The struggle was symbolized by the fate of Mostar, a city that was both homely and majestic. Over a period of months, eastern Mostar, with a predominantly Moslem population, was bombarded daily with between 100 and 600 shells (according to one UN official I spoke to, it received 1,000 shells over one 24-hour period). On 9 November 1993, a group of Bosnian Croat soldiers pummelled the famous sixteenth-century Ottoman bridge spanning the Neretva river in Mostar. It is difficult to describe to those who do not know the region well just how deep a psychological wound this inflicted on the vast majority of citizens in the former Yugoslavia. This single act seemed to represent the utter senselessness and misery of the entire conflict. Not surprisingly, this example of overweening hubris, like most others but hopefully not all during the war, is unlikely to lead to nemesis.

The opening up of a second front placed tremendous strains on the Armija BiH, although the military leadership was confident that it could make serious inroads into Croat-held territory in the long term. The price of having engaged the Croats was substantial and the grim vision of a total division of Bosnia-Hercegovina between Serbia and Croatia became ever closer, particularly since the signs of a tacit agreement between Tuđman and Milošević proliferated once again.

In response to this development, the Germans and the Americans began working closely on the idea of ending the Moslem–Croat war by creating a federation between the two communities in Bosnia. They began to put out feelers to both Zagreb and Sarajevo, noting a willingness on both sides to explore a negotiated outcome to the war. This was a significant development which represented a desire on the part of Washington to become more closely involved in the nitty-gritty of negotiations. This would mean the Clinton Administration getting its hands really dirty in the Balkans for the first time since the outbreak of the conflict and indeed the Federation Agreement amounted to the first step on the road to the three-way partition of Bosnia, finally enshrined in the Dayton Agreement in November 1995, which the Americans had always proclaimed anathema.

The negotiations leading to the Federation Agreement, which was signed in Washington on 18 March 1994, were tough, and considerable pressure had to be applied on the Moslems and the hard-line Hercegovina Croats to commit themselves to the compromise solution. None the less, the Washington Agreement is without question one of the most impressive examples of both German and American diplomacy in this war, as it brought an immediate halt to the suffering of Croats and Moslems alike. Very few of the solemn commitments made in the agreement were actually respected: the Croats did not dismantle their parastate, the Republic of Herceg-Bosna, while the idea of a joint command of the two armies, the HVO and the Armija BiH, remained a fiction. The Croats claimed that the Moslem side repeatedly tried to gain undue influence in the mixed cantons created by the Federation.

The Federation was a shotgun wedding and amounted to nothing more than a glorified cease-fire. That, however, was a monumental achievement in itself. But it did require that Sarajevo cede part of its sovereignty to Croatia (in particular, Zagreb interpreted the agreement to mean that Bosnian Croats were entitled to vote in Croatian elections, a device that proved very handy for President Tuđman when the Bosnian Croats provided an extra 150,000 votes for him and his party in the Croatian elections of November 1995).

As such, this represented the beginning of the partition of Bosnia-Hercegovina, which was sanctioned by member states of the United Nations, NATO and the European Union. This process would deepen with the presentation of the Contact Group Peace Plan in the late spring of 1994, envisaging the division of Bosnia into two entities, the Bosnian Croat Federation and the Republika Srpska – the former would receive 51 per cent of Bosnia's territory, the latter 49 per cent.

With regard to American policy, the Federation also marked another turning-point. From now on, the rhetorical support, which Washington had always offered the Moslems would transmute slowly but steadily into practical support for Croatia, encouraging the build-up of the Croatian armed forces as the only possible way of combating Serbian military dominance of the region. While this turned out to be an effective policy, it not only ensured military equality between the Serbs and Croats, it also guaranteed Tudman that his forces would be able to dictate policy to the Moslems and to the forces of the Armija BiH.

Throughout the four years of devastation in Bosnia-Hercegovina, the Republic of Macedonia, as it calls itself, lived in an uneasy peace. In early 1993, I moved to Thessaloniki, the great port of the southern Balkans. I had decided to leave Vienna for the capital of northern Greece because of the disturbing parallels I believed existed between Macedonia and Bosnia-Hercegovina. As Greece's hostility towards the new Macedonian state was having a major impact on political developments in the region, I felt it important to understand whence Greek fears sprung. I was also convinced that not enough attention was being paid to the problems facing Macedonia, where there existed a latent potential for extreme violence not too far below the surface. My obsession with Macedonia and the regional stability of the southern Balkans would sometimes provoke amused comments from some of my colleagues, who believed that I was unnecessarily alarmist about the country. At times, I did exaggerate the immediate threat to peace in the southern Balkans, but I did so in order to try to shake the complacency which assumed that Bosnia-Hercegovina was a specific problem which existed outside the wider context of Balkan stability. As I write this, I remain unconvinced that the threat has been lifted from the southern Balkans, although 1995 registered some very encouraging developments which suggest that there may yet be a way out for Macedonia and the region as a whole.

In May 1991, a month before war engulfed the former Yugoslavia, the presidents of two constituent republics. Alija Izetbegović of Bosnia and Kiro Gligorov of Macedonia, spared no effort trying to reconcile the widening gulf between Serbia and Croatia. Both men understood that in the event of an armed conflict their two republics were potentially the most bloody theatres of war. Bosnia was especially threatened since the territory formed a wedge between the Serbs and Croats, both of whom were attempting to establish the borders of their new nation-states by force.

So far Macedonia (or the Former Yugoslav Republic of Macedonia, FYROM, as it is officially called by the United Nations) has escaped the horrors which its twin, Bosnia, has suffered. Yet if the Dayton Agreement were to fail, a gradual destabilization of FYROM is almost certain to accelerate, threatening the state's existence and the wider security of the southern Balkan region. The political problems facing FYROM are remarkably similar to those which destroyed Bosnia-Hercegovina. Both republics were dependent upon the protection of the Yugoslav federation to ward off territorial claims by their more powerful neighbours.

The majority populations of Bosnia and Macedonia are relative newcomers to the Balkan drama. The Moslems and the Slav Macedonians have only properly assumed the characteristics of a modern nation since 1945, partly thanks to a gradual process of historical maturation and partly due to Tito, who encouraged their development in order to dilute the influence of the Serbs and the Croats within the federation. They are no longer satisfied to play the role of spear-carriers allotted to them during the Second World War. This time they have claimed their place centre stage, making the current crisis more complicated than its predecessor between 1941–5.

But the chief similarity lies in the two republics' importance for the region. Dominance in Bosnia-Hercegovina is the key to control of the Adriatic coast. Bosnia can act as a bulwark against Serbian expansionism. Croatia, on the other hand, can only overcome its awkward crescent-like topography if it controls substantial parts of Bosnia. These geo-strategic considerations underpin the rapacious desire of Serbia and Croatia to prevent the establishment of an independent Bosnia-Hercegovina: it gets in their way.

FYROM is the only territory where the Balkan mountains can be traversed from north to south, from Orthodox Belgrade to Orthodox Thessaloniki, and west to east, from Moslem Durrës in Albania to Moslem Istanbul. This is why these two republics have repeatedly suffered as the main theatres of war in the Balkans when dramatic political change in Europe has questioned the constitutional order of the region – their geo-strategic importance is paramount.

To survive in the modern period, Bosnia and Macedonia have always required the protection of an external power – be it the Austro-Hungarians, the Ottomans or federal Yugoslavia. Without that guarantee both republics must rely on the goodwill of their minority populations for security – Serbs and Croats in the case of Bosnia, Albanians in the case of Macedonia. If that goodwill is withdrawn unconditionally (as happened in Bosnia in 1992), the republic is finished. FYROM is now heading down the same path. While it is true that Albanians have nothing approaching the military potential of Serbs and Croats, it is also true that the Macedonian state is even less well equipped to defend itself than Bosnia. Should the delicate consensus between Albanians and Macedonians break down, then the Serbian, Albanian and Bulgarian states will consider how best to fill the resultant power vacuum in this strategic corridor. That may then properly be called the Third Balkan War – the continuation of the dreadful struggles of 1912 and 1913, known as the first and second Balkan wars. For Macedonia to survive, Albanians and Macedonians must learn to live together. Towards the end of 1994, the two communities veered dangerously towards conflict.

Tetovo lies nestled under the noble protection of the Šar mountains which form a natural border between western Macedonia and northern Albania to the west and Kosovo to the north. Aside from the rather uninspiring small square, which is dogged by socialist realist architecture and frequent building work, it is a pretty little market town with meandering streets, saturated in the tempting smell of čevabčići and baklava. The noise and bustle are typical of a lively community in what was once Ottoman Europe, with a variety of faces, dress and headwear, although the egg-shaped Albanian *plis* dominates.

It is only half an hour's drive from the Macedonian capital, Slopje, but as the stronghold of Albanians in the country, Tetovo sometimes seems as though it could be another planet. On 13 December 1994, I was confident that I would not succeed in reaching the town as I set out from Skopje on a bright, cold Saturday morning. Ostensibly, there was nothing abnormal about the drive along the road which arcs gently to the south from the western edge of the Macedonian capital. The steady stream of traffic bearing Skopje, Tetovo or Swiss number-plates (the latter belonging to Albanian *gastarbeiter* back on holiday or business) were monitored vigilantly as always by the Macedonian police.

I broke through the valley, flanked either side by picturesque Macedonian, Albanian and Turkish villages, only to notice how especially threatening the Šar mountains looked that morning. The clear air ensured that I could see every cliff and ravine marking these great peaks. It was as if these magic mountains were waving a finger at me, half in sympathy, half in admonishment: 'You won't get there you know!'

The posse which stopped me as I took the exit for Tetovo town centre did not only comprise the usual couple of cops intent on handing out a $40 speeding ticket. On this occasion, the traffic policemen were surrounded by five mean paramilitaries hidden underneath full-face helmets, waving large semi-automatic weapons and clad in thick flak jackets. No number of identity cards and accreditation letters would allow me through to witness the preposterous, but genuinely popular attempt by local radicals to found an independent Albanian university. It is suitably inappropriate that education has become the main field of struggle between Albanians and Macedonians. The Albanians demand the right to be schooled in their own language right up to university level. The Macedonians insist that this privilege should be restricted so that all citizens may learn the state language, Macedonian, fluently. On this day, the Albanians had promised to inaugurate their university and the Macedonian authorities had promised to stop it. The police were extremely wary about allowing any foreigners in to witness the proceedings. Western diplomats had been warned to keep away and journalists were most definitely unwelcome.

After my car had been rigorously searched, I continued on the road towards Gostivar. Just five miles further on, I found a large, dingy Albanian café. The clientele was entranced by a huge television above the bar. It was showing an atrocious semi-pornographic American movie. However, the film was interrupted every fifteen minutes by the latest events in the centre of Tetovo, which were being filmed on VHS and then rushed to the shoebox studio of the illegal TV station. A mass of some 2,000 Albanians swayed back and forth, alternately confused and excited by the steamy rhetoric of Fadil Suleymani, the designated 'rector' of the university. The crowd sloshed against 200 heavily armed Macedonian policemen, who were guarding the university's proposed headquarters. There was a distinct whiff of colonialism about the juxtaposition of the two nationalities.

Nothing violent happened that day, although it could have done. Two months later, in February 1995, there was another attempt to establish the university. Shooting broke out and one Albanian was killed. Not for the first time since 1991, Macedonia teetered on the edge of conflict. For those who consider the idea preposterous, the Macedonian director, Milan Manchevski, has produced a stunning film *Before the Rain*, which reveals the dynamics of how relations between the Albanian and Macedonian communities in western Macedonia could break down in the future.

On that cold December afternoon, I headed back to the capital, depressed as ever. But I had an important appointment in Skopje which I was looking forward to. Macedonia was due to play a qualifying game in the European soccer championship and I was determined not to miss it. On occasions during the Balkan crisis, the strained or violent relations between nationalities have expressed themselves freakishly in sporting fixtures. This was just such a special occasion served up with the lobotomized sensibility peculiar to the European Union of Football Associations, which was sufficiently asinine to pitch Macedonia in the same group as the Greeks of Cyprus.

For the Cypriots, as for most Greeks, Macedonia and its people are a fiction, a communist plot invented to rip the northern Greek port of Thessaloniki away from the true inheritors of Alexander's greatness. Both Greek and Cypriot television decided against taking a feed of the game from Macedonian television, partly because this would have bestowed legitimacy on a state which they refuse to recognize in any respect. But also because the sight of a stadium drenched in gold Vergina stars, a sacred symbol dating back at least to Alexander's father, Philip of Macedon, would have generated a collective heart-attack among Greek viewers.

And drenched it was. The Cypriots were clearly shocked as they entered the arena. For the invention theory assumes that there is no real commitment among ordinary Slavs to the Macedonian identity – is something which nasty communists, like the President Kiro Gligorov, foisted on an unsuspecting peasantry who had been quite happy as Bulgarians and Serbs. The Cypriot footballers were confronted with something which the Greeks are psychologically incapable of recognizing – these people's great grandparents may have considered themselves either Bulgarians or Serbs, but three generations have now grown up for whom the Bulgarians and Serbs are related but definitely foreign cultures. In the past fifty years a process of ethnogenesis, begun in the second half of the last century, has been completed – a Slav nation which understands itself to be Macedonian has been born. None of this delicate little infant's neighbours or siblings is pleased about the new arrival. Quite the opposite.

Had the Greeks been watching on television, two incidents would have confirmed their worst fears. At half-time a group of Macedonian supporters unfurled a banner in Greek: 'OLI I MAKE-DONII APO TIN FLORINA GIA TIN MAKEDONIA' (All Macedonians from Florina[1] are for Macedonia). This threat was compounded by the chant in English which resounded round the stadium during the second half as Macedonia routed the Cypriots 3–0: 'Macedonia U-NI-TED!'

Naturally, not a single one of Macedonia's 500,000 Albanians (a quarter of the country's population) was at the game, nor were any rooting for the country of which they are citizens. They are only

---

1. Florina is a town in Greek Macedonia with a large Slav-speaking minority.

interested in the results of Albania (one of a group of legendary no-hopers in European soccer). Albanians and Macedonians continue to rub along together quite happily on an everyday level. But 13 December revealed quite starkly that Macedonia remains a country divided into two quite distinct entities.

The first independent Macedonian state was approved by its inhabitants in a referendum held in September 1991. Like his Bosnian counterpart, the Macedonian head of state, President Kiro Gligorov, a longstanding communist official, worked hard to prevent the outbreak of war in the former Yugoslavia. When the European Community began to encourage independence for the Yugoslav republics in 1991, Gligorov reluctantly pursued that course. But he was particularly concerned about the decision of Macedonia's largest minority, the Albanians, who make up about a quarter of the population of some two million, to boycott the referendum, for he well understood the dangers of creating a weak state with a large, vocal and distrustful minority.

None the less, in a masterly stroke, Gligorov succeeded, after the referendum, in negotiating the withdrawal of the JNA from Macedonia without a shot being fired. True, the JNA took all its weapons with it, leaving the new state wholly defenceless. But at least Macedonia did not suffer from the effects of a scorched-earth policy or from an attempt by Serbia to use the small Serb minority in northern Macedonia as an excuse to reabsorb part or all of Macedonia into what was left of Yugoslavia. This negotiated deal brought sharp criticism from the Moslem leadership in Bosnia-Hercegovina, who were hoping that the Macedonians would create a southern front against the Serbs, thus drawing artillery and supplies away from the war in Bosnia. Gligorov can point to the fact that unlike Alija Izetbegović, he has so far succeeded in defending the lives of all his citizens.

However, it soon became very clear that life was going to be very rough for this tiny, land-locked state, which occupies a key strategic position in the southern Balkans – all main trading routes in the southern Balkans pass through Macedonia.

As soon as it became independent, the Macedonian nation was seen as a disturbing presence by each of its much more powerful neighbours. Albania recognized both the Macedonian state and nation; but made it clear that its goodwill would depend on the status of the Albanian minority in Macedonia. Serbia recognized the state *de facto* by setting up a new Yugoslavia without Macedonia, but it still withholds formal recognition. Bulgaria recognized the state, but has absolutely refused to acknowledge that there is a legitimate Macedonian nation for fear of encouraging secessionist tendencies among the inhabitants of Bulgarian Macedonia, many of whom have rejected a Bulgarian identity in favour of a Macedonian one. Moreover, until early October 1994, Greece flatly refused to accept that Macedonia was a state or that its citizens could legitimately be called Macedonians. Greece considers the name to be Hellenic property. Nationalist Greeks claim, without any substantial evidence, that the new state has ambitions to absorb the Greek province of Macedonia, whose capital is Thessaloniki (in April 1993, the United Nations admitted the country under the compromise name, the Former Yugoslav Republic of Macedonia, or FYROM, which nobody likes).

The kingdom of ancient Macedon produced Alexander the Great, who has never been equalled as a military strategist. Before his death in 323 BC at the age of thirty-three, he subdued the Greek city-states of Attica and the Peloponnese, drove his imperial army into Palestine, smashed the might of the Persian Empire, and reached across central Asia into India.

As Greeks developed a modern consciousness in the second half of the eighteenth century, some adopted Alexander as the symbol of Hellenic greatness. Greek historians emphasize that he was tutored by Aristotle and point out that he spoke Greek as his first language, and they are especially sensitive when outsiders suggest that ancient Macedon was anything but an integral part of Greek society in the fifth and fourth centuries BC. But some distinguished historians, while readily conceding Alexander's Hellenic cultural heritage, suggest that most Macedons may have spoken another language, now extinct, that was not related to Greek. They also cite Alexander's pithy contempt for the Greek city-states; as a supreme opportunist, the argument runs, he exploited his Greek culture and connections solely when it suited his purposes to do so. One point everyone agrees on except for the most fantasist nationalists in today's Macedonia however, is that there were no Slavs anywhere near this territory until the middle of the sixth century AD, when the first Slav marauders began launching raids as far south as the Peloponnese.

The second point of agreement concerns the boundaries of ancient Macedon. Aside from a small strip in modern Albania, the ancient territory covered regions that today include, (1) a substantial chunk of northern Greece, whose inhabitants speak Greek, (2) the southern part of the new Republic of Macedonia, where the majority of citizens speaks Macedonian (a Bulgarian language that is now a separate language) and the largest minority speaks Albanian, and (3) a significant wedge of south-western Bulgaria, whose people speak Bulgarian. The authorities in each place now claim to represent the real Macedonia, and they are deeply suspicious of the others.

The modern origins of the 'Macedonian Question', as the notorious southern Balkan dispute of the late nineteenth and early twentieth centuries came to be known, may be traced back to the year 1878. On 3 March of that year, the war between Russia and Ottoman Turkey ended with the signing of the Treaty of San Stefano. Russia, keen to assert its dominance in the Balkans through the new Bulgarian state, was the moving force behind the agreement, which called for the creation of the principality of Bulgaria; this became, after Greece and Serbia, the third major nation-state to be hewn out of the Ottoman Empire's crumbling periphery. The new Bulgarian state was almost four times the size of Serbia and three times the size of Greece. Among other assets handed over by the Russians to Sofia were all the territories of ancient Macedon, notwithstanding its extremely mixed population of Turks, Bulgarians, Greeks, Jews, Albanians, Vlachs and Gypsies. Control of Macedonia immediately made Bulgaria by far the most powerful state in the Balkans.

There were now two large Christian Slav peoples in the central-southern Balkans, the Serbs and the Bulgarians, both speaking languages classified as southern Slav, although Bulgarian has features unique among all Slav tongues. Serbia gained its independence from the Ottoman Empire in the first half of the nineteenth century. The major step towards Bulgarian independence was the creation of the independent hierarchy of the Bulgarian Orthodox Church in 1870.

Although both Serbian and Bulgarian churches were, and are, under the ultimate authority of the Greek Orthodox Church in Constantinople, their autonomy was complete and in both the vernacular was used in all church business.

Russia believed that by helping to found a large Bulgarian state it could further its ambitious strategic aims in the Balkans. It made Bulgaria its vassal state, insisting that it garrison the Bulgarian principality with Russian troops for two years and have a hand in forming the Bulgarian government.

Great Britain regarded this blatant expansionist move by Russia as an intolerable challenge to its interests in the Near East, and Austria-Hungary saw it as an impediment to its own ambitions in the Balkans. The British immediately dispatched its fleet to the Aegean, while Vienna made warlike protests. Horrified by the sudden arrival of a Bulgarian monster state, Serbia, Romania and Greece all demanded a substantial revision of the San Stefano treaty. Just as a huge conflagration appeared likely, Bismarck offered his services as 'an honest broker'. The Congress of Berlin was duly convened later in 1878, and returned most of Macedonia to the stewardship of the ailing Ottoman Empire. Intimidated by German demands, Russia offered large concessions at the Congress, and the Bulgarian principality was squashed to almost a quarter of its size under the San Stefano agreement; the result was a powerful revanchist ideology that was central to Bulgarian politics until 1945.

Henceforth, Macedonia, where all the major transport routes through the southern Balkans coincide, became the apple of discord between the newly forming nation-states that were destined to replace the Ottoman Empire. This rivalry exploded in the most hideous fashion in the first and second Balkan wars of 1912 and 1913. In the first of these, a grand alliance of the Christian Balkan countries – Greece, Serbia and Bulgaria – shoved the remnants of Turkey out of Macedonia and Thrace. No sooner had the three countries succeeded in beating back the Turks than Bulgaria made a disastrous pre-emptive attack on Serbia. Greece and Serbia then joined forces to wreck the Bulgarian Army and carved up Macedonia between them. The extreme barbarism of these wars has been obscured historically by their proximity to the outbreak of the First World War; but the Balkan wars prefigured what has happened in the region in this final decade of the century.

The period between the Congress of Berlin and the Balkan wars gave birth to an image of Balkan politics and society which still persists – mustachioed bomb-throwers, corrupt and devious governments, endemic indolence, conspiratorial great power interference and, not least, shocking brutality. Certainly there was a steady rise in violence and terrorism by all sides. But it was also a time of heady political organization, combined with the beginnings of industrialization and the opening up of markets in the Ottoman hinterlands.

At the heart of Macedonia's identity lay Thessaloniki, one of Europe's largest and most active ports, which linked the Near East with south-eastern and central Europe. Over half its population were Ladino-speaking Jews who had fled Spain in the 1490s and had mixed with the Turkish, Bulgarian and Greek communities. In addition there were, among others, Vlachs, Albanians and Gypsies – the proverbial *salade macédoine*.

Ninety miles north, in the interior, the town of Monastir (now called Bitola and part of the new Macedonian republic), which had lively Albanian, Vlach and Greek communities, became the centre of the Great Powers' budding intelligence services in the Balkans and a haven for shady business deals. In Monastir's surrounding countryside roved groups of armed men who were bandits one day and political terrorists the next. Most of these groups drew their members from disgruntled Slav peasants, but the Albanians, Greeks and Turks all had their own powerful paramilitary organizations.

The Greek and Bulgarian Orthodox churches (and to a much lesser degree the Serbian church) were in intense competition to win over the inhabitants of Macedonia for their congregations. The chief instrument in this game was the classroom. Under the Ottoman *millet* system, which gave religious communities the right to a degree of self-governance, the non-Islamic religions were able to control primary education.

In 1894 a group of Bulgarian intellectuals from Macedonia, mainly teachers, formed VMRO, the Internal Macedonian Revolutionary Organization, to liberate Macedonia from the Turks. The new group did not initially make it clear whether 'the liberated territory' would then form a new state or whether it would attach itself to Bulgaria. Deeply conspiratorial, it attracted considerable, if fluctuating support inside Macedonia and Bulgaria. And while remaining the most faction-ridden body imaginable, it carried out some of the most spectacular acts of terrorism in twentieth-century history, including the murder of two Bulgarian prime ministers. At times in its early history, the murders of perceived traitors within its own ranks far outstripped the deaths of its proclaimed enemies, the Turks.

While VMRO was confident in its aim of liberating Macedonia from Turkish rule, a split soon emerged in its leadership over whether control of the organization should be based in the Bulgarian capital, Sofia, or inside Macedonia. This developed into a struggle between what became known as the IO (Internal Organization), whose primary goal was the liberation from the Turks of all peoples in Macedonia, and the EO (External Organization), the vehicle of Bulgarian expansionism run from Sofia.

There were other differences between the two groups, but what should be clear is that a distinct Macedonian consciousness was emerging before the Balkan wars; it was not, as the Greeks and Bulgarians later claimed, merely created by Tito for opportunistic reasons during the Second World War. A Macedonian identity became important to the Bulgarians of Macedonia, who rejected the dominance of the heavy-handed authoritarian regime in Sofia over their political movements and their daily lives. Although relatively new historically, Macedonian identity is no less real for that.

The activities of VMRO members hastened the end of the Ottoman Empire in the southern Balkans; their acts of terrorism or liberation (depending on whose side you take) put pressure on Bulgaria, Serbia and Greece to go to war with Turkey in 1912. And the decision to attack Turkey had disastrous consequences for the entire region. The subsequent devastation of Macedonia during the Balkans wars and the horrific crimes committed by all sides, set the pattern for modern nationalist warfare in the Balkans. Anyone who wants to understand the origin of the current bestiality in Bosnia should consider what happened to the Greeks, Turks, Serbs, Bulgarians and Albanians of Macedonia in 1912 and 1913, when large-scale 'ethnic cleansing' was practised on every side.

The Treaty of Versailles of 1919 divided Macedonia among Greece, Bulgaria and the new Yugoslav state, which the Serbs immediately dubbed 'southern Serbia', simply ignoring any linguistic or cultural differences between themselves and the rest of the local population. The Bulgarians and Macedonians in the Serbian region gravitated, respectively, towards Bulgaria and Yugoslavia, and away from Aegean Greece. Many of the Greeks from Yugoslavia and Bulgaria moved towards Thessaloniki and its environs.

After the royal dictatorship of Bulgaria's King Boris was persuaded to join the Axis powers in 1940; Hitler permitted the Bulgarian Army to take over most of Macedonia, while part of the western region came under Italian administration and, in recognition of its strategic importance, the Germans occupied Thessaloniki. This of course meant the end of Thessaloniki's Jews; one of the most vital and accomplished European Jewish settlements was soon eliminated and largely forgotten.

Most of the Slavs who came under Sofia's control at first welcomed the Bulgarians; but this sympathy was quickly dissipated when the occupiers brought with them an insensitive, centralizing bureaucracy, which was soon opposed by the nascent Macedonian Partizan movement. As Tito and his forces began to turn the tide in other parts of Yugoslavia, he began to encourage the separate consciousness of the Macedonians, promising that they would be able to develop their own identity within a post-war Yugoslav state. After the war, he went even further, putting pressure on the Slav Macedonians to support the insurgents in the Greek civil war. In retrospect, it seems fairly clear that Tito wanted to incorporate most Macedonian territories (including the grand prize, Thessaloniki) in his vision of a grand Balkan federation.

Tito's expansionist plans explain the passions and fears that have resurfaced in Greece during the four and a half years since the establishment of an independent Macedonia. Had the Greeks pointed out that only fifty years ago there was an attempt to seize a large part of northern Greece in the name of Macedonia, they might have gained more understanding for their case. Instead, the campaign against the new Macedonian state – objecting to its name, its flag and its constitution – has centred on their claims to the Hellenic culture of Alexander the Great. Apart from being irrelevant to the issues of modern nation-building, this campaign left the outside world mystified and bored. It was bad politics, for which Greece paid a considerable price.

Greece's hostility to the new Macedonian state led Prime Minister Andreas Papandreou to impose a complete blockade in February 1994. This, combined with the devastating effect of UN sanctions against Serbia (which accounted for 70 per cent of Macedonia's markets before the collapse of Yugoslavia), continues to pose tremendous economic problems for Macedonia, which exports mainly such crops as tobacco, grains and cotton. Under Tito, Macedonia also developed into an important industrial centre, particularly as a producer of steel and chemicals. This tiny, fertile country, with its breathtaking scenery and fascinating history, also has considerable potential for tourism. Moreover, Macedonia is different from other Balkan countries, since owing to its inherent weakness it cannot possibly pose a military threat to its neighbours. Despite its tense location, it has a weirdly relaxing atmosphere.

The combined efforts since 1992 of Cyrus Vance, David Owen and the Clinton Administration, notably those of Assistant Secretary of State Richard C. Holbrooke, finally achieved a remarkable breakthrough after four years of frustrating diplomacy. On 13 September 1995, Greece and Macedonia signed a treaty calling for mutual recognition, the opening of commercial routes into the country, and the exchange of liaison offices. The Macedonian government agreed to drop from its flag the disputed symbol of the Vergina Sun, to which the Greeks objected most vehemently. The problem of the country's name remains in limbo. But the agreement showed a novel capacity for mature judgement on both sides; it may even have cleared the way for a historical shift in relations between the diverse nations of the southern Balkans.

It has not, however, solved the primary threat to Macedonia's existence – the tensions between the Macedonians and approximately half a million Albanians who live within the new republic. In Tito's Yugoslavia, the Albanians of western Macedonia and Skopje frequently received worse treatment at the hands of the Skopje authorities than the Albanians of Kosovo. It will take a long time for the western Macedonian Albanians to accept their jailers of yesterday as their colleagues and equals today. None the less, the Albanians in Macedonia enjoy the same voting rights and other civil liberties as other Macedonian citizens. Largely Moslem, they can practise their religion without interference either from the state authorities or from the Macedonian Orthodox Church. They now have far more freedom than the Albanians in Kosovo and even in certain respects than those in Albania itself. The Macedonian government leaders fear, however, that granting special ethnic rights to the Albanians will merely encourage secessionism and the break-up of the Macedonian state. Partly as a consequence, the Macedonians have dragged their feet on two key issues: the rights of Albanians to education in their own language and Albanian representation in state organs, notably the police force.

Moderates in both the Macedonian and Albanian communities are constantly goaded by radicals into taking more extreme positions. Although the Bosnian conflict has had a sobering effect on both, their relationship is characterized by a permanent, underlying tension. Macedonia's vulnerability was underlined on 3 October 1995, when a powerful bomb was detonated as President Gligorov's car sped past the façade of Skopje's old railway station. Gligorov's driver was killed instantly while three pieces of shrapnel lodged in the President's head, one penetrating the skull and entering his brain. Gligorov lost one eye and for several weeks, diplomats assumed that he would not survive. Amazingly, Gligorov, who was seventy-eight at the time of the attack, survived to assume office again, defying the interests of those black marketeers who, it was believed, were responsible for the attack.

The Dayton Agreement, combined with the Greek-Macedonian treaty, should help to relieve Macedonia's internal strains. But the political outcome of the Bosnian war also contains problems for the future of the southern Balkans. If Dayton does crystallize into the partition of Bosnia, then it will undermine Macedonia's attempts to create a multi-ethnic state.

The violent disintegration of Yugoslavia gave cause for considerable reflection. It reminded us that European values need not only mean tolerance, culture and affluence – they can also entail brutality, primitivism and misery. It has enriched our political vocabulary, seemingly for ever, with the phrase 'ethnic cleansing'. In constitutional terms, the Yugoslav break-up gave rise to something much more opaque, yet perhaps just as important – the 'parastate', a remarkable phenomenon that has triumphed, probably for ever, in the mountainous territory that until five years ago was the Socialist Republic of Bosnia-Hercegovina.

The parastate emerges as the mutant offspring of an expiring failed state. If Tito's Yugoslavia could be compared to a normal human being, albeit a bit wobbly in the knees, its children are a bunch of youthful George Romero extras, in varying stages of decay – an arm lopped off here, an eye squeezed out of its socket there. Boasting certain essential attributes of a normal state but grotesquely lacking in others, the parastate was destined to find the most fruitful conditions for its development in those regions of Europe that made up the farthest outreaches of the early modern empire.

In terms of size, the dominant parastate of Bosnia-Hercegovina has been the Republika Srpska (RS). Its identity is bolstered by the relative might of its army and its other security forces. Its democratic credentials are highly dubious as the RS's representatives were all either elected to the organs of a dead entity, the Socialist Republic of Bosnia-Hercegovina (SR of BiH) or appointed by decree after the outbreak of war. Hundreds of thousands of Moslems living on the territory of the RS had been expelled or murdered, underlining Pale's identification with just one of three nationalities already implicit in the parastate's name. Although the RS President, Radovan Karadžić, steadily lost popularity during the war, being regarded by the Bosnian Serbs as a failed gangster, the support of the local Serbs for the RS was always considerable. The bloody birth of this parastate goes a long way in explaining why nobody in the outside world, not even Serbia and Montenegro, was prepared to recognize the legitimacy of the RS, meaning it lacked one crucial attribute of a state. The RS scored a muted victory when the United States Assistant Secretary of State for Europe, Richard Holbrooke, announced that it would form one of the two entities in the Bosnian Union, which was eventually agreed upon in Dayton, Ohio.

Although enjoying widespread international recognition, the predominantly Moslem parastate of Bosnia-Hercegovina has always looked exceptionally weak, wedged between two rapacious Serb and Croat parastates, not to mention the two mother ships, Yugoslavia and Croatia. Naturally, it lacked a strong military, but

compensated for this to an impressive degree by the size and motivation of its infantry sources. The territory under Bosnian government
control also promised greater economic potential than either the RS or
the Croatian Republic, of Herceg-Bosna, although this was dependent
on it securing or gaining an access to the sea or the Sava river. Its
representatives were also elected under the aegis of the SR of BiH,
and the plebiscite which confirmed its independence in 1992 was
encouraged largely along national lines, thus giving the Bosnian
Serbs ammunition for their claim that the Moslems and Croats
intended to use the organs of state to dominate the Serb minority.
As the comprehensive solution to the Bosnian and Croat crises
moved ever steadily towards partition in 1994 and 1995, so did the
political base of the Bosnian government veer towards the creation
of a Moslem-dominated state. This provoked a bitter struggle
within the leadership between Alija Izetbegović and his Foreign
Minister, Mohamed Sacirbey, on the one hand, and the Prime
Minister, Haris Silajdžić, on the other. The latter remained committed to a multi-ethnic Bosnia, as the two former began to accept the
logic of the creation of a core Moslem Bosnia.

The Croation Republic of Herceg-Bosna enjoyed substantially
closer links with Croatia than the RS did with Serbia. Whereas
Milošević imposed sanctions on the RS after Pale's refusal to accept
the Contact Group Peace Plan, Croatia was able more or less at will
to maintain regular Croatian Army (HV) troops in the Republic of
Herceg-Bosna, despite occasional pressure from the Germans to
cease the open co-operation between Zagreb and western Mostar.
While nobody offered Herceg-Bosna recognition, Zagreb always
behaved as though its government was the legitimate representative
of the Croats in western Bosnia. After Croatian influence came to
dominate the Bihać enclave following the territory's liberation from
the Serbs in the summer of 1995, Zagreb held sway over more than
20 per cent of Bosnia's territory, including Bihać itself which
inevitably felt the economic pull of relations with Zagreb over
those with Sarajevo, with which it had no territorial link.

After the tension created by President Tuđman's decision to end
UNPROFOR's mandate in Croatia had subsided, I visited Sarajevo and Pale in March and April 1995. On 31 December of the
previous year, the former US President Jimmy Carter had brokered

a cease-fire between the Armija BiH and the Bosnian Serb Army (BSA) which was set to run until 1 May. Little diplomatic progress had been made in the meanwhile and once again all sides to the conflict were preparing for war. In Sarajevo, the gossip concentrated on one topic alone – the forthcoming offensives. The Moslems were about to dig deep into their reservoir of cannon-fodder and attempt some spectacular liberating activity. Press-gangs were out on the city streets, snapping up young men to dig trenches.

In a darkened café, I listened as Emir, with a shaved head and a pronounced limp, fixed me with dull eyes and spoke in a monotone. A former soldier in the 2nd Army Corps, he was pensioned off in 1993, after much of one leg was blown off, but he maintained his connections with the 2nd Army leadership. 'The plan is to attack on five fronts and stretch the Serbs' logistics to such a degree that their line will break, probably in north-central Bosnia,' he told me. At a private briefing I attended in a dank cellar with a representative of the 1st Army Corps, a less likely plan was revealed. 'We are going to punch a hole out of Sarajevo and begin with the liberation of our capital,' an officer said. From a contact in the Interior Ministry came a different rumour, 'Out of Tuzla, but not south-east towards Goražde and the two other enclaves.' The murmurs were no more than a carefully planned campaign of disinformation – an effort to disseminate as many scenarios as possible, so that the real campaign would come as a surprise.

To add to the atmosphere of anticipation, Sarajevo television shifted fear into parastate overdrive in early March, and over the next few weeks lengthy explanations of passages from the Koran were punctuated by sequences romanticizing the preparations of the Bosnian-government Army for the spring offensive. Some chirpy conscripts were seen huddled together in a mountain bunker, cleaning their weapons, discussing tactics and laughing about their slow-thinking opponents. Cut to a young conscript surrounded by a halo of Vaseline on the lens: in slow motion, he fired his handheld rocket-launcher before turning to the camera with an orgasmic smile on his face and punching the air with his fist in a mock victory celebration. (Had it been the Serbs who were openly boasting about offensives under preparation, the massed ranks of the international media would have been crying foul. But the response was muted when the Bosnian government trashes its solemn commitments to the international community.)

On 20 March the Moslems attacked Mt Vlašić and the Majevica range. The latter juts out east of Tuzla, the second-largest city controlled by the Moslems. From Stolice, one of Majevica's peaks and the site of a key television relay station which links Pale with the Bosnian Serbs' largest city, Banja Luka, one can see the Drina River periodically widen into picturesque little lakes as it stretches southward. You can also see the towns of Zvornik, Bratunac and Vlasenica, where so much blood was spilt in 1992.

On the other side of the front line in Pale, the Bosnian Serb capital, there was growing concern at the renewed vigour with which the Moslems were prosecuting the war. Before the war 6,000 to 7,000 people, Serbs and Moslems, lived in the village ski resort. Now, three years later, it had expanded into a town of an estimated 14,000 – all Serbs. There were no longer any guests – just redundant hosts. Pale had become a beautiful but permanently out-of-season tourist centre. Silent teenagers drift listlessly around the few cafés, playing pool until the establishments close in the early evening. Women and old men occupy themselves perfunctorily with the Bosnian Serbs' central economic activity: selling cigarettes by the side of the road. These years of indolence in Pale had been accompanied by some of the fiercest fighting in the war, just five miles away in Sarajevo. Yet Pale was going stir crazy with boredom and isolation. The only excitement was to be found in the House of Culture, a little shoebox on the main drag which is home to Serbian television – a powerful branch of the otherwise sickly tree of Bosnian Serb propaganda. This particular evening, 7 April 1995, panic had seized the overwrought technicians and journalists stuffed tightly in the building. It was barely three weeks since Mt Vlašić and the Majevica range had come under ferocious attack by the armed forces of the Bosnian government. Both were sites of television relay stations. With ten minutes to go before the main evening news, the television and phone lines to Banja Luka, went down. The face of Dragan Božanić, the presenter cum producer cum editor, looked grim. Like CNN, Serbian television uses a split screen – one anchorman in Pale, another in Banja Luka.

'We can't go on air with the split screen,' Božanić said. Serbian viewers would immediately assume that one or both of the relay stations had been taken by the Bosnian government – and the Serbs were not accustomed to the damaging psychological impact of military defeat.

In fact the Bosnian Serb Army had inflicted a serious defeat on the Moslem forces at Majevica, but the relay station on Vlašić had indeed fallen to the Moslems, although the Serbs were not yet prepared to admit this. With two minutes to go, the Serbian television workers were the grateful recipients of a miracle: thanks to the Majevica relay, the lines came back up.

The news that evening led with the first of regular monthly press conferences to be held by Dr Karadžić. Despite the pomposity of his entrance into a room adorned with the crossed flags of the Bosnian Serb parastate, Karadžić's self-assurance was beginning to fade. After Pale's rejection of the Contact Group Peace Plan, the Bosnian Serb leadership were shunned by representatives of the United States, Germany, Britain, France, and Russia. And, of course, Milošević had also cut commerical and political links with Pale.

Gone were the days when Karadžić's entourage would sweep into the parastate's lakeside villa in Geneva. The endless televised negotiations with important people at the Palais des Nations were but a dreamy memory. With resistance to his rule growing in the Bosnian Serb Army and Banja Luka, where Milošević had created powerful connections, Karadžić now spent most of his time contemplating his parochial might in the rarefied atmosphere of the hotel networks built for the tourists and spectators of the 1984 Winter Olympics. So to the delight of those people across the front line in Sarajevo who rarely miss his televised performances, he compensated for his isolation by becoming evermore majestic in his presidential performances – the Emperor was shedding his clothes. The more flags, the more solemnity and the more circumstance, the more intense the ridicule.

Economic life in the the RS was always unpredictable, although its trajectory was forever downwards. After Milošević decided to impose the commercial blockade on his erstwhile allies, only gangsterism remained, promoting some savage internecine struggles among the parastate's élite. There were two overlapping focuses of these battles: one was the town of Bijeljina and the other was

Karadžić's powerful police force. Bijeljina snuggles up to the border with Serbia, in north-east Bosnia, and it soon became the clearing-house through which all goods smuggled in from Serbia were processed. Anything could be bought or sold in Bijeljina and, as a result, the town enjoyed a prosperity absent almost anywhere else in Serb-held territory. In April 1995, every second house in Bijeljina had a sign outside advertising petrol and diesel at two and a half Deutsche marks a litre, which was only fractionally more expensive than the cost in Belgrade. By the time the fuel reached Pale, a mere two and a half hours' drive away, the price had doubled.

Until the blockade was imposed, the bulk of the wages and pensions paid to the Bosnian Serb police was financed directly by the Ministry of Internal Affairs in Serbia. When these funds were frozen by the blockade, Karadžić replaced the major and the police chief of Bijeljina (traditionally dominated by the police and state security from Serbia proper) with his own people, and assumed control of Centreks – a firm, based near Pale, that had a monopoly on the import of cigarettes and oil, the two goods a Balkan parastate must secure in order to survive. The revenues from this trade were used to pay off some Pale politicians and put the police force squarely in Karadžić's pocket, since his trust in the Bosnian Serb Army was less than absolute.

This was a quaint little political struggle, but it was accompanied by betrayals, mysterious deaths and shoot-outs, sometimes quite violent incidents between Karadžić's police force and the Bosnian Serb Army whose leaders were particularly irritated by Karadžić's attempts to sequester all the fuel from Serbia. Greed was a huge factor: in all the parastates, ideology has been dispensed with in favour of money. Small oligarchies masquerading as popular trib-unes were busy stuffing their pockets with lucre, placing their relatives abroad in diplomatic sinecures or creating private armies for a presumed final showdown.

The RS also began haemorrhaging citizens. Of the 1.4 million Serbs registered in the 1991 census of Bosnia, roughly 200,000, many of them in Sarajevo, lived in areas held by the Bosnian government. An estimated 350,000 fled the territory to live as refugees either inside Serbia proper or in other countries. Another 50,000, mainly young people, nervously awaited the outcome of their visa applications in order to emigrate. Most of them hoped to go to Canada and forget their past.

After this tour of the parastates, I travelled to New York and Washington to visit, among others, Richard C. Holbrooke, Assistant Secretary of State for Europe. I had first met Holbrooke the previous November on a similar trip to the United States. I had received warnings from various friends and colleagues that the new man in charge of America's Balkan policy was ambitious, cynical and not one to suffer fools gladly. Over the years Holbrooke has clearly made an inordinate number of enemies. However, I had listened to so much equivocating nonsense from American policy officials on the subject of Croatia, Bosnia and Serbia over the previous five years that I found his unusually direct approach extremely refreshing.

As I walked into his comfortable office in the State Department, he smiled broadly, but he was quick to indicate that this would not be a meeting laced with platitudes. I had not come to interview him but to discuss the situation in Bosnia. 'Right,' he said 'I am meeting with Warren Christopher in half an hour. So that's how much time you've got to tell me what we're going to do in the Balkans. Can we save Bosnia as a state?' I pointed out to him that his Administration had but six months previously, in March 1994, engineered an agreement, the Croat-Moslem Federation, which had effectively put paid to the idea of a unitary Bosnian state. Quick to defend himself, Holbrooke shot back, 'That wasn't me – I wasn't around at the time.' I had the impression that he had not yet fully grasped the implication of the Federation for Bosnia's future, but since he had only recently returned from his posting as Ambassador to Bonn, I would have been surprised had he already mastered the bizarre ins and outs of Yugoslavia. Indeed, at the time the Administration and State Department officials were still very optimistic about the Federation. Disillusionment would set in the following summer.

Immediately after my opening observation, Holbrooke said, 'Wait a minute – I want to bring in Bob for this.' A few seconds later in walked an unassuming man in a smart pin-stripe suit. Soft-spoken and exceptionally polite (the very antithesis of Holbrooke), Robert Frasure had worked as the United States' first Ambassador to Estonia before being brought back to Washington by Holbrooke to work as Holbrooke's amanuensis on Yugoslavia, later replacing Charles Thomas as the American Ambassador to the Contact Group. Over the next nine months before Frasure's terrible death on the Igman road into Sarajevo in August 1995, I got to know him quite well. Not only was this man full of quiet, perceptive wit, but within a matter of months, he had understood all the fundamental dynamics of the Yugoslav wars. With no pomp, he very nearly achieved a miracle in the first seven months of 1995. His adversaries were many and varied: the leadership of the Bosnian Serbs; part of the Croatian leadership; part of the Moslem leadership; and, most disturbingly, members of the Clinton Administration. There is no question, however, that Frasure's greatest contribution was securing the support of Slobodan Milošević for a peaceful settlement sponsored by the United States.

During that first meeting with Holbrooke, it was clear that he and Frasure were already thinking along those lines. Holbrooke wanted to know the details of the political differences between Milošević, Karadžić and Mladić. I suggested that the only way he was going to stop the war is if he cut a deal with Milošević. Holbrooke was not yet convinced. He was not prepared to put his reputation at stake only to be tricked by Milošević, as he put it. Negotiating with Milošević was a bitter pill for anybody in Washington to swallow. He was directly responsible for so much blood and misery in the Balkans that even to talk to him was anathema. But many diplomats and politicians were unable to see that the policy of sanctions was actually working. In order to maintain control of Serbia, Milošević badly needed a lifting of sanctions. For his longer-term strategy, he needed the support of the West to facilitate Serbia's reintegration into Europe. The Europeans, including the Germans, were now well aware of this. But the Americans did not only regard Milošević with the deepest suspicion, they also believed the Europeans to be spineless conspirators of the Serbian president. Holbrooke certainly made no effort to hide his contempt for Lieutenant General Sir Michael Rose and Lord Owen. Ironically, Holbrooke would end up pursuing a strategy which was extremely similar to that of David Owen.

In November 1994, Holbrooke had not fully taken on board the unhappy fact that in order to stop the war, anybody, American or European, would have to make a pact with the devil. None the less, even then it was clear that Holbrooke was prepared to consider any option – he was not content to repeat the errors of his predecessors, who had made a lot of noise about the crimes committed against the Moslems but were utterly incapable of devising a policy to do anything about it.

In the middle of our conversation, one of his hotlines from a bank of telephone lines started buzzing insistently. Madeleine Albright, the US Ambassador to the United Nations, came on the line. So agitated was she that Frasure and I could hear her across the room. She had just come off the phone with President Izetbegović, who had informed her that Serb tanks were penetrating the outskirts of Bihać and that NATO planes must intervene if the city is to be saved. Albright clearly shared the Bosnian president's assessment.

'So, whaddaya think?' Holbrooke stared at me sharply. 'Should we bomb 'em around Bihać?' I asked whether there was any confirmation of Izetbegović's claim and Holbrooke replied that the weather was very bad which meant they could not confirm it. 'Hold it,' I said, 'I thought you have all this intelligence-gathering equipment which can see ants gathering food?' Holbrooke looked at me and laughed hard, 'We can see a tennis ball on a tennis court if we know where that court is and if the satellite happens to be at just the right spot at the right time and if there are no clouds in the sky. Otherwise, forget it!'

By the next time I visited Holbrooke and Frasure in Washington towards the end of April 1995, Frasure had just returned from intense negotiations with Milošević. At one point, Holbrooke was distracted by the telephone. 'So how did you find Milošević?' I asked Frasure. 'I think he's reinventing himself as a statesman,' Frasure replied before elaborating. 'He's rather like a mafia boss whose gotten tired of doing drugs in the Bronx and now wants to move down to Palm Beach to get into junk bonds.'

That summer, Robert Frasure secured the outlines of a deal with Milošević. In the middle of the most intricate negotiations, the whole business was suddenly muddied when on 25 May NATO jets attacked Bosnian Serb munitions dumps and command and control centres around Sarajevo. As UN officials had been predicting for a long time, the Bosnian Serbs responded by taking hundreds of UN peacekeepers hostage. By broadcasting images of pathetic UN soldiers tied to military and communications installations around Pale, the Bosnian Serb military waved a defiant fist not just at the international community but at Milošević as well, whose patience with Karadžić and his colleagues had all but run out. Under intense pressure from the British, French and American governments, Milošević eventually secured the release of all the hostages by dispatching the Head of the Serbian State Security, Jovica Stanišić, to Pale.

Patience with the Bosnian Serbs was now running extremely thin. However, Frasure was working desperately hard to finalize a deal with Milošević which would have seen the implementation of the Contact Group Peace Plan for Bosnia-Hercegovina and the mutual recognition of the Federal Republic of Yugoslavia and Bosnia. The one aspect of the agreement at which the Americans and Milošević remained at odds concerned the issue of UN sanctions on Yugoslavia. Milošević had agreed to a suspension of sanctions (not lifting). But the two sides could not agree on the mechanism required to reimpose sanctions if Serbia and Montenegro failed to live up to their commitments as part of the Milošević–Frasure deal. The United States wanted an independent commission of three UN member states to decide whether Yugoslavia had lived up to those commitments, while Milošević insisted that only Boutros Boutros-Ghali should have the authority to introduce to the Security Council a resolution demanding reimposition. Privately, Frasure believed that Milošević's suggestion should be accepted but he did not have the mandate to authorize the deal. The day before he left Belgrade, I spoke to him face to face for the last time. I asked him what he would be doing. 'I am going to dump this file on the table, and on Thursday I am going down to my ranch in Shenandoah for a rest. I'll be back in the office on Monday or Tuesday and we'll see if they'll go with it. If they don't, it's out of my hands.'

The bulk of the media was still chewing over the aftermath of the bombing/hostage crisis. But the eyes of Milošević, Tuđman and Izetbegović were turned towards Washington. If the Frasure–Milošević deal failed in Washington, all three were preparing to do final battle in Bosnia-Hercegovina.

I spoke to Frasure just over a week after he returned to Washington. He told me that there was not sufficient support for his plan in Washington. Three days later, the Bosnian government ordered an offensive, aiming to break out from Sarajevo. It failed miserably but none the less acted as the starting pistol for one of the most bloody competitions of the whole war.

In early July, General Mladić travelled to Belgrade to consult with the head of the Yugoslav Army, Momčilo Perišić, who gave the Bosnian Serb commander the go-ahead to attack the three eastern enclaves, Srebrenica, Žepa and Goražde. The first to be attacked was Srebrenica where 60,000 people had been living in the most dire stone-age conditions for three years. The Bosnian Army evidently decided not to offer much resistance and many troops attempted to leave for Bosnian government territory some forty miles away.

Bosnian Serb troops entered Srebrenica on the late afternoon of Tuesday, 11 July. According to the women and children who were escorted out like cattle in trucks, the Serb commanders, including Ratko Mladić, assured them that nothing untoward would happen. Not surprisingly, suspicions were aroused when all men were separated from the women and children. The Dutch UN peacekeepers stood by helplessly. Indeed, their commander was humiliated by Mladić who slaughtered a pig in their presence in a gruesome symbolic display. The truth about what happened to the men of Srebrenica has yet to emerge – perhaps the troops of Ifor (the NATO-led implementation force) will be able to secure clearer evidence. But sufficient eye-witness reports have already surfaced to suggest that this will be one of the darkest stains on the blood-spattered shirt of the Bosnian Serbs. While it is true that the Bosnian Army commander, Naser Orić (once the bodyguard of Slobodan Milošević and one of the few Moslems under investigation for possible war crimes), used Srebrenica as a base for raiding Serb villages up towards Bratunac and that countless Serb civilians were slaughtered in these raids, this will never justify the systematic mass murder which invariably accompanied the conquest of besieged towns by the Bosnian Serb Army.

It was only a matter of days, before Mladić turned his guns on Žepa, another of the three safe areas in the Drina valley. Here the Bosnian forces mounted a heroic last stand, obviously aware that they were going to be killed anyhow. But at Goražde, Mladić stopped – under pressure from the imminent threat of NATO raids and under orders from Belgrade (despite Perišić's original assent to the storming of Goražde).

A group of soldiers, civilian police and journalists jostled for position at the makeshift check-in desk of NORMOVCON (Norwegian Movement Control) at UNPROFOR's base in Pleso airport. As is always the case for extraordinary flights to combat zones, there are more passengers than tickets on this Monday, 7 August 1995. A fortunate few from the media have been granted permission to travel with Yasushi Akashi to Knin just four days after the Croatians launched their thunderous assault on the Republic of the Serbian Krajina (RSK), one of the former Yugoslavia's short-lived parastates, which has all but expired.

After an uneventful flight to Split airport, we strap ourselves into British helicopters and head north-east towards Knin. It is not long before I spot Drniš. This once elegant town which drifts down a north-facing hill and on to the edge of a plain had been partially destroyed in late 1991 by JNA forces under the command of Ratko Mladić. I last visited Drniš in late autumn of 1992. Then a mere 1,000 Serbs were living there, many because they had nowhere else to go. This was a full twelve months after Mladić had completed his handiwork. The authorities of the RSK had not yet been able to restore proper water or electricity facilities nor was there the slightest indication that this dejected little parastate would ever do so. The broken glass strewn in and around the gutted buildings reflected the palpable air of doom in Drniš. I could not spot a single building which had been undamaged by the Serbian push against Croatian forces in 1991, except for the Orthodox Church in the centre of town.

In a dingy room in the town hall, the 'mayor' of Drniš, a bearded melancholic, recited a litany of complaints about life under the Croats, life in the RSK, life in Drniš, life in the past and life in the future. Naturally, potable water was hard to come by but there was no shortage of *rakija*. The policeman who had escorted me from Knin joined in the festivities and by the time we returned to Knin in the late afternoon, our minds had been reduced to the state of empty futility that characterized Drniš itself.

Now, three years later and several hundred metres above Drniš, I can still sense the emptiness – there is no movement except for two ant-like Croatian army motor cyclists speeding north in the direction of Knin. Black smoke still spirals from the ruined villages surrounding Knin. The smoke is evidence of systematic pillage – the fires are not an unavoidable consequence of war.

In the town centre, much less is burning but one wisp of smoke tickles the bottom of the huge Croatian flag which now envelops Knin castle, the mighty thirteenth-century fortress that watches the town from atop a steep, craggy cliff. In the middle of the flag stands the *šahovnica*, Croatia's chequered-board heraldic symbol, a red-and-white rag to the Serbian bull. The bull is now being slaughtered or chased out of town, signalling the most dramatic single development since the wars of Yugoslav secession began in June 1991. Croatia has inflicted what one Serb opposition leader described as 'the biggest military defeat on the Serbs since the battle of Kosovo Polje in 1389'. All the wacky tin-pot characters, the Martićes and Babićes of this world, had fled to be replaced only by innumerable posters proclaiming FRANJO TUĐMAN – ČOVJEK KOJI POBEĐUJE (Franjo Tuđman, – The Man who Wins). Nobody may dispute this rare droplet of truth. The day before our arrival, Tuđman had travelled to the fortress at Knin to kiss the Croatian flag. Immediately after this act of state piety, Tuđman raised his hands in the air as though holding a large globe, a gesture reminiscent of Ante Pavelić, the Croatian Ustasha leader. He then bent slightly at the knees cocked his head downwards and clenched his two fists in the fashion of a teenage soccer player who had just scored his first professional hat trick.

This image of victory is probably the most significant in the wars of Yugoslav succession. Franjo Tuđman was on the verge of achieving his three war aims. He had secured the international recognition of independent Croatia in January 1992. By signing the Washington Agreement of March 1994, he had ensured that the vision of a fully sovereign Bosnia-Hercegovina would remain but a dream. And now, with the exception of Baranja and eastern Slavonija, the 5 per cent of the territory still held by the Croatian Serbs, his military was running the Croatian Serbs out of the Krajina.

This outcome belies the popular perception of the two most

significant characters in the former Yugoslavia, Slobodan Milošević and Franjo Tuđman. Hitherto, the Serbian president was seen as the great teacher, forever leading his eager Croatian pupil into political traps. Yet although a supreme puller of strings, the master puppeteer had failed to write a complete script for his bloody drama. Instead, he created mesmerizing scenes in which he himself gradually lost the narrative thread.

Not so Tuđman. In retrospect, the outcome of the armed struggle between the Serbs and the Croats (and by implications the Moslems) was decided as early as 1991. When the two largest nationalities went to war that year, the odds looked overwhelmingly in favour of the Serbs. For every Croat in the former Yugoslavia, there were two Serbs. In addition, the Serbs enjoyed a massive superiority in weaponry, thanks to the stockpiles of the JNA. Confronted with these harsh facts, Tuđman, the military historian, considered his options. If fighting were to break out, it was bound to be very nasty. Combined with Croatia's location in the middle of Europe, the brutality of the struggle would almost certainly result in the internationalization of the war. It would soon cease to be a merely internal Yugoslav matter – more powerful countries would in one respect or another become involved. This is one of the central reasons why Tuđman cultivated the support of Germany and Austria so assiduously prior to the outbreak of war. The only conceivable way to combat the might of the Serbs was to engage a powerful and reliable backer in the outside world who would fight the Croatian corner in the international forums.

In 1991, Milošević was still infatuated with national bolshevism. The Serbian president evinced a careless xenophobia which would have disastrous consequences for the Serbs. At this time, his only foreign ally was the Communist Party of the Soviet Union. Given that both the Party and the Soviet Union were just a few months away from an ignominious demise, this really was a poor choice. Indeed, Milošević's crass decision to offer public support to the motley band who organized the coup against Mikhail Gorbachev additionally earned him the resentment of Boris Yeltsin, the one world leader who might later be in a position to help him.

Germany's commitment to Croatia was of critical importance in blocking the imposition of economic sanctions on Croatia. After the outbreak of open hostilities between the HVO and the Armija BiH in April 1993, the Americans and Europeans fired some diplomatic warning shots across Zagreb's bow. Even though Germany was not a permanent member of the UN Security Council, the only body with the authority to impose binding sanctions, Bonn prevailed upon its partners in the European Union and NATO not to take this step. In addition, the Croatian government proved to be exceptionally adept at circumventing the arms embargo, diverting billions of dollars towards the purchase of quality weapons and equipment. With the aid of private American military consultants, Croatia developed a highly effective, disciplined and motivated fighting force in four short years. Tuđman would make tactical concessions when it was necessary, but he never lost sight of his goals.

In contrast, Milošević never devised a strategy, preferring instead to play opaque tactical games. In the short term, these appeared both pernicious and successful. But in the long term, a pattern of Serbian retreats and concessions began to crystallize. This had its origins in the decision of 1991 to conspire in Slovenia's departure from the Yugoslav federation. The option of Yugoslavia was replaced by the option of a Greater Serbia. When the Serbs failed to advance in Croatia as far as the JNA leadership had intended, Milošević decided to minimize any further losses by signing up to the Vance Plan in the teeth of fierce resistance from Milan Babić and the leadership of the RSK. The Vance Plan explicitly committed the Serbian leader to concede in time Zagreb's sovereignty over the RSK. His ambiguous relationship to the Serbs in Bosnia and Croatia was evidenced by Yugoslavia's refusal ever to accord official recognition either to the RSK or to Karadžić's parastate, the Republika Srpska (RS). In 1993, Milošević backed the Vance–Owen Peace Plan (VOPP), a treaty which, had it been implemented, would have blocked the Bosnian Serbs' main war aim – the establishment of constitutional links with Serbia proper. It took a long time for the outside world to appreciate that Milošević was willing to modify or even drop his policy of expansion.

As United Nations sanctions began to cut deep gashes into Serbia's social and economic structure, Milošević became evermore intolerant of Radovan Karadžić's maximalist demands which hindered the search for a comprehensive negotiatated settlement to the crisis. The Bosnian Serb started to challenge Milošević's authority among Serbs as a whole. He urged opposition parties inside Serbia and institutions like the Serbian Orthodox Church to back his scatty vision of a warrior-dominated Greater Serbia. Milošević, infuriated with Karadžić's tactics, regarded his protégée in the Republika Srpska as an evermore embarrassing and irritating liability. When the parliament in Pale rejected the Contact Group Peace Plan in July 1994, Milošević's patience finally snapped. He imposed an economic blockade on the Bosnian Serbs, cut telephone lines between Serbia and the RS and banned leading members of the Pale government from entering Yugoslavia.

Karadžić's aim had been to persuade the Yugoslav Army (VJ) to enter the war against the Croat-Muslim Federation, a move which, if successful, would have pitted Serbia against Western Europe and the United States. The split between Milošević and Karadžić is frequently portrayed as a revival of the Partizan/Chetnik division which exploded among the Serbs during the Second World War. While there were certainly strong echoes of these two ideological traditions in the conflict, political competition and economics probably played a more decisive role. While the 'mafia' class in both the RS and Yugoslavia made phenomenal profits out of the war and out of the circumvention of the sanctions regime, a majority of Serbian businesses were extremely hostile to the continuation of the war and its distorting impact on the Serbian economy. In 1994, Milošević appointed Dragoslav Avramović as head of the Yugoslav National Bank. Under Avramović's direction, Belgrade pursued a rigorous monetarist policy, with the aim of preparing Serbia's economy for reintegration into European economic structures. Although the profiteer class made some attempts to undermine the Avramović programme, Milošević received considerable support from factory managers, as well as from a substantial number of entrepreneurs who were frustrated by the contracting domestic market. Naturally, they recognized that this contraction was caused directly by the prolongation of sanctions and the war. Once Milošević had made clear his intention of negotiating an end to the war, he received substantial political support from this class, which was sufficient to overcome the nationalist challenge posed by Karadžić.

The biggest price that Milošević had to pay for a peaceful settlement approved of by the international community was the loss of the Krajina, the most dramatic tactical adjustment he had to make in the entire war. There is no question that Milošević sold out the Krajina. Had he not encouraged the extremely inexperienced and volatile Krajina Serbs to form their own state in 1991, then the population of the RSK would not have had to suffer the misery of being ethnically cleansed in 1995. It is here that Tuđman's strategy of seeking international support for his project of an independent Croatia paid the most lucrative dividends. For Milošević had no choice in 1995 but to sell out the Krajina Serbs. With a gutted economy, a deeply demoralized, Yugoslav Army and a Bosnian Serb Army in decline, the Serbian president could not have sustained a military campaign against the Croats on the periphery of the Serbian national community. The only war the VJ could have waged would have involved punitive missile and air attacks on Croatian cities – a strategy which would have resulted in further opprobrium being heaped on Serbia and which, given Croatia's newly acquired defensive capability, could not have succeeded militarily.

One should not, however, underestimate how complicated Tuđman's task was in securing international support. Until the key moment in March 1994, when the American Administration persuaded Alija Izetbegović to sign the Washington Accords (an agreement which met with fierce resistance in the leadership of the SDA), Germany did not carry sufficient diplomatic muscle to facilitate Croatia's victory. As the Clinton Administration explored ways of bringing the Moslem–Croat war to an end, it began to shift subtly its backing for the Muslims in favour of the Croats. As David Owen noted in his recent memoirs, *Balkan Odyssey*, when he met Gojko Šušak in November 1993, the Croatian Defence Minister 'was focusing on building up Croat military strength and links with the US'. Two months later, Owen noted how 'the Germans were now beginning to decouple themselves from the EU Action Plan, attaching more importance to relations with Washington than with Paris over Bosnia and also to concentrate on Croatia'.

The convergence of views between Bonn and Washington, which regarded a resurgent Croatian military as the key to defeating the

Serbs, marks a most important step on the road to peace. Until this point, the great powers were divided into four camps. These overlapped on certain issues but the positions they held were essentially mutually exclusive.

The United States were keen on using punitive air power against the Serbs, although the Clinton Administration was pulling away from the option of lifting the arms embargo on the Bosnian government despite intense Congressional pressure to do so. The Administration was reluctant to become involved in the negotiating process, but was even more wary of fulfilling the promise made by Warren Christopher in early 1993 to back any peace deal with up to 25,000 American troops. Rhetorically, they offered robust support to the Bosnian government and were critical of any moves by the Europeans which to their mind favoured the Serbs. American involvement deepened after the market-place massacre of 5 February 1994, when they began pushing hard for air strikes against the Bosnian Serbs. On the diplomatic level, their promotion of the Bosnian-Croat Federation signalled an end to American reserve.

Germany equivocated on the issue of the arms embargo, sending out different signals. It remained Croatia's firmest ally even though this relationship came under considerable strain during the Moslem–Croat war, notably while eastern Mostar came under ferocious attack from Croatian artillery. However, Bonn remained committed to a comprehensive negotiated settlement in concert with its British and French partners in the European Union. The Germans felt stung by the continuing criticism of its policy of recognition at the turn of 1991 and was reluctant to force issues within the EU. Not being a permanent member of the Security Council and unable to deploy troops, its influence was channelled chiefly through the structures of the European Union.

Britain and France had been actively involved within the United Nations and the EU as well as having made a substantial military contribution to the peacekeeping forces. The presence of British and French troops in Bosnia generated extreme reluctance on the part of Paris and London to agree to an extensive bombing campaign against the Bosnian Serbs. They were deeply worried that in such an event their soldiers would be taken hostage or used as targets by the Bosnian Serb Army. Both Britain and France were convinced that the only solution to the Bosnian and Croatian crises was political. Their strategy was to encourage the split between Miloševié and Karadžić so that the former would be able to sign a deal above the heads of the Pale leadership.

Russia's position was close to that of the British and French, although Moscow's envoys tended to emphasize the importance of lifting economic sanctions against Serbia in order to ease Milošević's task of ditching the Bosnian Serbs. Boris Yeltsin was exceptionally sensitive to suggestions of lifting the arms embargo or to the deployment of NATO air power in Bosnia-Hercegovina. This was partly due to the pressure he was under in Moscow from a broad spectrum, especially in the Duma. But the Russians were also motivated by their own strategic needs – the use of NATO in the middle of Europe before the Russians and Americans had clarified their strategic relationship in the post-communist era was considered a worrying precedent, which explains why Russia insisted so firmly that any decision to bomb should only be taken after close consultations with Moscow.

These differences were deep enough to create a log-jam in the search for a solution to the hot war in Bosnia and the frozen war in Croatia which was always threatening to thaw. However, once the Germans and Americans combined their diplomatic strength and backed a solution which favoured Croatia both above the Serbs and the Moslems, the resistance of the British, Americans and Russians began to weaken. It is important to note, however, that the Federation plan quite clearly demanded of the government in Sarajevo that it cede part of its sovereignty not just to the Bosnian Croats but to Croatia as well. The Federation thus represented the first step on the road to partition, which in one fundamental respect moved the German and American positions closer to the British and French, who had decided after the failure of the Vance–Owen Peace Plan that partition was the only way out of the crisis.

The Krajina Serbs were inevitably marked down as sacrificial lambs. Indeed, to rub salt in the wounds of this largest single exodus made up of 150,000 Serbs from Croatia, the American ambassador to Zagreb, Peter Galbraith, remarked that this did not constitute ethnic cleansing as 'ethnic cleansing was a speciality of the Serbs'. Senior American officials also noted, correctly, that the creation of a strong Croat military altered the strategic balance in the Balkans, thereby facilitating a solution not merely at the expense of the Croatian Serbs but of the Bosnian Serbs as well. What the Americans did not point out was that this would also be at the expense of a unified Bosnia and the Moslems in particular.

Such speculation and theorizing is of no interest to the latest batch of civilians, hundreds of thousands of them from the Krajina, who have been caught in the deadly pincers of terror wielded by local military commanders. Several hundred Serb refugees who succeeded in making their way to the UN headquarters in Knin from outlying villages and the city itself offer bald testimony to contradict the protestations of Croatia's government that it is protecting Serb civilians. Vacillating between tearful hysteria to the numb indifference of deep trauma, a middle-aged woman holds up a tree-stump bandage around her left hand.

'Some shells hit our village which began to burn, so the whole family, seven of us, piled on to our tractor and left without taking anything. We were just outside Knin when some Croatian soldiers hidden by the side of the road opened up with machine guns. Three of our men died immediately. I suppose I was lucky just to lose three fingers.'

'Now that you've come, they've cleaned up the bodies that were lying on the street 'till yesterday,' said an embittered 38-year-old who would only give her first name, Dušanka. 'The civilians were mainly shot as they rushed to the UN compound, but at least two men we know of have had their throats cut.' Croatian army units sweep up and down the roads of Knin with the unmistakable swagger of military conquerors, one hand holding up the V for victory sign, the other clasping a bottle of beer. Knin, which has had a majority Serb population for over three centuries, will soon have but a handful of Serbs left.

Aside from a few confused old ladies picking their way through the broken glass which lies in front of every shop on the town's long main street, there are no civilians visible in Knin.

'About 80 maybe 85 per cent have fled the town, about 30,000 people from the whole district,' said Draženka Koluvija, a nurse who stayed at her post attending the hundreds of wounded who swamped the city's hospital on Friday and Saturday. 'The rest all want to leave,' she stuttered, constantly on the verge of tears.

Yasushi Akashi can do nothing but offer calming platitudes. 'The UN has no influence. The Serbs should not make the decision to leave during this temporary passion,' Mr Akashi averred. Unfortunately, this is no temporary passion. It stretches back over 50 years to the shattering memory of the Second World War. 'All my grandparents were killed by the Croats, and two uncles,' explained Dušanka, 'nobody believes them here and we are not going to stay.'

Although over 1,000 shells have hit Knin last weekend, there is little structural damage to civilian buildings. Every single shop, however, has been looted. A band of merry soldiers were heaving bottles of spirits on to a truck on the road to the hospital. 'There has been no looting in Knin,' General Ivan Cermak, the new Croat military governor for the region, flatly contradicted the evidence before our eyes. A used-car dealer who had got to know President Tuđman through his friendship with the president's daughter, Cermak was beginning to enjoy his new role as governor.

Croatia's 'Operation Storm' is another vicious twist in the spiral of Balkan vengeance. Up to 120,000 Croat fighters had gathered around the borders of the Krajina. They were imbued with tremendous spirit and motivation after suffering years of military humiliation at the hands of the Serbs, they were about to get their own back. Since the Croats were driven out of the Krajina, the government in Zagreb has spent 5.5 billion dollars on the purchase of arms according to Croatia's maverick weekly newspaper, *Globus*. The army has been reorganized with the help of an American firm, Military Professional Resources Inc., which dispatched a number of senior retired US Army officers to Croatia for the job.

On the other side of the border, the equipment of the now defunct army of the Republic of Serbian Krajina has been steadily going to seed. Far away from its powerful parent in Serbia, the RSK was an economic cripple. After the Croats successfully overran the first UN Protected Area, western Slavonija, in May, President Milošević dispatched a new general from Belgrade, Mile Mrkšić, to reorganize the RSK Army. 'The sad truth is,' one angry junior officer of the Yugoslav Army tells me three days later in Belgrade, 'Milošević sent Mrkšić to the Krajina to organize the evacuation of the territory. His job was to extract as much artillery as possible in the event of a Croatian attack and to protect civilian refugees wherever possible.'

As Knin and the southern Krajina collapsed like a pack of cards, the Serbs of the northern Krajina put up a much stronger fight. These were the descendants of the partizans of the Second World War, whose ability to use the undulations of the Petrova Gora hills as a military stronghold is legendary. But the sweep through the Krajina produced an important side-effect in the Bihać pocket in north-western Bosnia. Fikret Abdić had grown dependent on the artillery power of the Krajina Serbs to keep his fellow-Moslem enemies at bay.

As soon as the Krajina Serbs were attacked by the Croats, Abdić's defences collapsed. So too did his Republic of Western Bosnia which had been founded only a week earlier, affording it the rare distinction of being the shortest-lived out of the twelve states which have been proclaimed since Tito's Yugoslavia expired in 1991. Ironically, although the government in Sarajevo want Abdić on charges of treason, its ally, Croatia, decided to extend gracious hospitality to him. Perhaps Zagreb intends to use Abdić as a proxy ruler in the Bihać pocket at a later date. Who knows?

With the road from Bihać open, the Bosnian government's 5th Army Corps charged through Abdić's capital, Velika Kladuša, and broke into northern Krajina. 'Even though they were crossing an international border, the Croats did nothing to stop them,' explained a UN official in Zagreb. 'Once in Croatia, they drove up to the Serb town of Topusko burning and shooting everything in their way.' Indeed, the UN suspect it was the 5th Army Corps and not the Croats who shelled a column of Serb refugees fleeing toward the Bosnian Serb town of Banja Luka, killing five and injuring fifteen.

The fighting had started to provoke another biblical movement of people. At least 150,000 Serbs were on the move, the largest single exodus in Europe since the expulsion of the Sudeten Germans. The entire offensive was undertaken by the authorities in Zagreb with the support of the United States government. President Clinton himself welcomed Operation Storm, suggesting that it may open the way to a solution of the Yugoslav conflict.

The rest of the international community was visibly shocked by America's encouragement of Croatia. 'This marks a new point in the war. Until now at least the international community has been united in its condemnation of ethnic cleansing,' remarked one European Union diplomat, clearly shocked by Washington's position. 'Now it seems one of its members is openly supporting the mass movement of population by the most terrible force.'

Carl Bildt, the former Swedish prime minister, who had been appointed to replace David Owen as the European Union's mediator on the former Yugoslavia was even more explicit. He called for the International Tribunal on War Crimes in The Hague to investigate President Tudman for his decision to shell Knin. 'If we accept that it is all right for Tudman to cleanse Croatia of its Serbs, then how on earth can we object if Yeltsin cleanses Chechnya or if one day Milošević sends his army to clean out the Albanians from Kosovo?'

From the beginning of the offensive, Croatia's leaders have persistently denied that they are cleansing the Serbs. But President Tudman is fully aware that the Krajina Serbs are terrified at the prospect of living in a Croatian state. To this end, the Croatian Army left open several corridors from the main population centres down which the Serbs could flee, either into Bosnian-Serb-held territory or directly into Serbia.

The symbolic importance of Knin's fall to the Croats cannot be overestimated. As the leadership in Zagreb rightly pointed out, the entire balance of power in the Balkans had now shifted in the space of five days. The offensive would also save Croatia's economy from collapse. Several hundred thousand Croatian refugees who have been living in miserable conditions for the past four years would soon start to populate the Krajina. At last, the rail link between Zagreb and Split would be able to run again. The treasured goose may again lay golden eggs. But it also signalled the end of a centuries old community in Croatia. President Tudman knew full well that the Serbs in the Krajina were terrified of the Croat authorities. He knew that almost 150,000 people would now leave the country to join almost 200,000 who had left Croatia's cities in 1991.

With the sustained support of Germany and lately the United

States, whose representatives have given qualified approval to the attack on Krajina, Croatia could now achieve one of its main strategic aims in these dreadful wars. The Serbs of Croatia, who have contributed greatly to the cultural, economic and political life of the country for over 300 years, would be no more. Another dark day for Europe as the Balkans take another step in the creation of bizarre, intolerant and ethnically pure states. Had that been the end of the process, perhaps Europe could have breathed a huge sigh of relief before undertaking the vast task of trying to understand how it may prevent another Yugoslavia. But as the Serb hordes discarded their battered motor cars and tractors when they ran out of fuel and made their tortuous journey to Serbia on foot, they brought with them more chaos to the Balkans.

After one week, about one-tenth of the expected total of refugees had arrived in the overflowing reception centre in the Serb town of Sremska Mitrovica. The hall was once a temporary home for Croats captured by Serbs after the fall of Vukovar in 1991. After their release, these Croats told terrible tales of torture and maltreatment at the hands of the dreaded Serb Chetniks. Now it is the turn of the Serbs to tell how, as they trudged through the Croat town of Sisak towards Serbia, angry Croat civilians turned on them, throwing stones and bricks at the refugee column and beating people senseless at the side of the road. 'The Croatian police and army just stood by and watched this all happen,' blurted out a young mother from the northern Krajina town of Glina. Still shaking with fear on her arrival, she held her baby out to reveal wounds on its face and legs caused by the Croat stones. By the time she arrived, six days after the beginning of the offensive, the hastily organized refugee centres throughout Serbia were all filled up. With ten times as many people still to arrive, Serbia's decaying infrastructure, shattered by three years of United Nations economic sanctions, was about to receive a killer blow.'Quite simply, we have no idea where all these people are going to go,' said a worker at the Yugoslav Commissariat for Refugees. 'There is no space left, we have no idea what to feed them with and if things are not sorted out urgently, we will have the most frightful situation in the winter when the power cuts start coming. This is a disaster with incalculable consequences.'

Some of the refugees were willing to stay in Bosnia where

doubtless some of the retreating Krajina soldiers intended to link up with the men of General Mladić to make the life of the Bosnian Moslems even more intolerable than it already is.

In Belgrade, thousands of young men once again began sleeping in a different bed every night. 'My mother told me last week that my call-up papers had arrived,' Vlado, a nineteen-year-old cigarette-seller said. 'The mobilization is in full swing, so I'm going to have to be very careful indeed.' There is nothing surprising about the huge mobilization. This was officially announced and all Western diplomatic missions were informed of it.

In Zagreb there is no problem with morale. Soldiers returning from the front are greeted as heroes. Croatian television has switched over to a permanent jamboree mixing shots from the deserted and now Croatian Krajina with patriotic songs and symbols. 'We may take a breathing space now, but we'll soon be ready to take back eastern Slavonija,' whooped Hrvoje, fresh from taking part in the conquest of Knin. Gojko Šušak, President Tuđman's hard-line Defence Minister, agrees with Hrvoje. 'If it is not returned through negotations, then we will definitely use military means,' he thundered.

Šušak's bullishness is backed up by the build-up of Croatian troops around eastern Slavonija, mirroring the artillery muscle-flexing of the Serbs inside what is left of the RSK. Since Paddy Ashdown, the leader of Britain's Liberal Party, revealed the map of a divided Bosnia-Hercegovina which he claims Tuđman wrote for him on the back of a menu when they dined together at a banquet in London, the world's media were buzzing with details of the alleged conspiracy theory. Tuđman gets the Krajina, the theory goes, Milošević gets eastern Slavonija and the Moslems get nothing.

For many Moslems, the creation of a new regional military power, Croatia, was a very ominous development indeed. 'Croatia's borders,' President Tuđman informed the world after the Krajina offensive,' 'do not separate two peoples, they separate two worlds.' Which world, Moslems were obliged to ask themselves, do we belong to?

With his tremendous success in the Krajina, President Tuđman's state now circled over western Bosnia-Hercegovina like an impatient vulture. 'The attack on the Serbs of the Krajina,' explained Milorad

Pupovac, the moderate leader of the Serb minority in Zagreb, 'has given a legitimacy to the practice of ethnic cleansing and the creation of ethnically pure states. Krajina as a multi-ethnic community is finished. It's no use crying over spilt milk, the important thing is to make sure that the practice is not repeated elsewhere in the Balkans.'

There was virtually no mixed community left in Bosnia or Croatia which had not been touched by the disease of ethnic cleansing and murder. The Moslems of the Drina valley, northern Bosnia, the Lašva valley, western and eastern Hercegovina had been massacred in an unprecedented example of racist militarism in post-war Europe. The Croats of central Bosnia and large parts of the Posavina had been driven away for ever, as had the Serbs of the Krajina. The former Yugoslavia has become the arena of a vast population exchange, engineered chiefly by Milošević and Tuđman, and has been executed through a series of small, very vicious wars.

But even after this disgraceful, tortured episode in European history, the international community still had to fit the mangled feet into mangled shoes. As the United States had predicted, the success of the Croatian Army in the Krajina had a fundamental impact on the strategic position in Bosnia-Hercegovina. Since late 1993, a civil war between Moslems had broken out in the Bihać pocket between those in the south who supported the 5th Army Corps of the Sarajevo government, and those in the north who backed Fikret Abdić. Often ignored by the outside world, probably because it was such a confusing twist, this was another deeply unpleasant war. Abdić depended on support from the Bosnian and Croatian Serbs. Days after the Croat victory, his forces were routed by the 5th Army Corps under the extremely competent leadership of Atif Dudaković, who no longer had to fight the Croatian Serbs as well as the Bosnian Serbs. This provoked the flight of 20,000 Moslem refugees from Abdić's stronghold, Velika Kladuša, in the face of the advancing Moslem Army. In addition, the Croats now had full control of the strip of land which separated Bihać from western Hercegovina. For the first time since the outbreak of war, the Bosnian Serbs were taking substantial territorial losses. Morale in the Bosnian Serb Army (BSA) had been seriously undermined. The battlefield losses, the flood of refugees from the Krajina into Banja Luka and the evermore acrimonious three-way political struggle between Karadžić, Mladić and Milošević combined to induce a profound sense of fatalism among the Serbs of Bosnia-Hercegovina.

Urged by President Clinton, who was keen to see a Bosnia peace-deal in order to strengthen his political position in the United States, Richard Holbrooke embarked on a remarkable diplomatic tour at the beginning of which Robert Frasure was killed in a dreadful vehicle accident on the Mt Igman road into Sarajevo. Ironically, his most pliable partner in the Balkans was Slobodan Milošević, who was evermore ready to make substantial concessions in order to secure a lifting of UN sanctions. Radovan Karadžić and Ratko Mladić were, however, prepared to fight, while the Bosnian government leadership were becoming ever bolder in what they were demanding from the negotiations. At this fateful juncture, another mortar smashed into Sarajevo's market-place on 28 August. Again the origin of this shell was controversial although the United States and the United Nations were quick to blame the Serbs. This event triggered a ferocious NATO bombing campaign against Bosnian Serb positions on 30 August throughout the territory they held, culminating in a strike of 13 Tomahawk cruise missiles on the command and control centre close to Banja Luka. Ratko Mladić held out for several days before conceding to NATO's demand and withdrawing the Serbian heavy weaponry from around Sarajevo. Many regard the NATO raids as final proof that bombing the Bosnian Serbs was the only way out of the crisis and that it was a tactic which should have been used much earlier. This is an over-simplification which obscures the complicated politics behind the bombing.

First, in order to be guaranteed that the use of massive air strikes would succeed, the United States had to be confident that Slobodan Milošević would acquiesce and prevent the Yugoslav Army from becoming involved in the conflict as a result. As Holbrooke himself has admitted, one of the keys to success lay in Milošević's ability to bludgeon Karadžić into an agreement whereby the Serbian president would negotiate on behalf of the Bosnian Serbs. No matter how much Karadžić and Krajišnik objected in the Geneva, New York and finally Dayton talks, Milošević was able to ride roughshod over their complaints. Indeed, Holbrooke tells how the Bosnian Serbs were excluded by Milošević and the Yugoslav delegation from any meaningful discussions.

Secondly, it was clear that the Americans' intention was not to inflict a massive military defeat on the Bosnian Serbs. They were bombing them to the Contact Group map as evidenced by their warnings to both Sarajevo and Zagreb not to attack Banja Luka, the largest town in the Republika Srpska, even though the BSA was in rapid retreat. Militarily, NATO bombing amounted to a pacification of the Bosnian Serbs. But politically, it also persuaded the Moslems, who were increasingly inclined to continue the fight against a weakened BSA to persist with negotiations and not pull out of the Holbrooke discussions as they threatened to do on the eve of the bombing campaign.

It is hard to imagine that the three sides would have reached Dayton without the mediating personality of Richard Holbrooke. To mediate is hardly the appropriate verb. The Assistant Secretary of State for Europe was brutal and blunt whenever necessary – cajoling, heckling and insisting. He had to threaten all three sides – the Serbs with more bombing and the maintenance of sanctions; the Moslems with the limits of American support ('It is your right to continue the war,' he told Alija Izetbegović at one point, 'but don't expect the United States to provide your airforce.'); and the Croats with a withdrawal of American diplomatic sympathy – one phone call from President Clinton to Franjo Tuđman, just as it seemed that Dayton was collapsing proved sufficient to save the talks.

Holbrooke is adamant that the Dayton Agreement, finally concluded on 21 November 1995, does not amount to the partition of Bosnia-Hercegovina. To judge by most commentators and indeed the behaviour of most political instances in Bosnia-Hercegovina, it does. The documents from Dayton are incredibly complex, leaving room for both partition and some form of a united state. The constitution includes probably the most advance provisions for the protection of human rights anywhere in Europe. But it also omits any mention of the armed forces, a *sine qua non* for any modern constitution, especially one which has been so ravaged by war as Bosnia-Hercegovina. None the less, a full third of the book-size Agreement is devoted to two military annexes, Ia and Ib. These assume that the HVO and the Armija BiH will eventually come under a single command (a rather bold assumption), but concede that at the very least there will be two armies operating in Bosnia, the Federation forces and the Vojska Republike Srpske (VRS). Military Annex, Ib, specifies how much hardware each army will be allowed to stock.

NATO is commanding the 60,000 Ifor (Implementation Force) troops inside Bosnia-Hercegovina, whose mandate will expire around December 1996 (conveniently soon after the Presidential elections in the United States). Nowhere in the Dayton Agreement does it state that Ifor's job goes beyond the establishment and policing of cease-fire zones, corresponding to the territorial divisions worked out during the talks. The response of Ifor commanders within the first month of deployment makes it clear that they do not consider two key aspects of the Agreement, freedom of movement between the two entities (the Bosnian Federation and the RS), and indeed within the Federation between Croat and Moslem areas, or the right of refugees to return to their homes. The ultimate authority in each entity, particularly once the Ifor troops leave, is almost certain to rest with the local military authorities.

Such internal contradictions of the Agreement are no longer the responsibility of the United States which did so much to formulate them. Instead, they are now the joint concern of Ifor, whose role is unlikely to go beyond the policing function, the EU's special envoy to the former Yugoslavia, Carl Bildt, and the Organization of Cooperation and Security in Europe (the OSCE, offspring of the Conference SCE). The latter's job is to organize elections, which will be a mammoth task.

The main problems facing Ifor and Bildt in the initial stage of the Dayton Implementation were the cities of Sarajevo and Mostar. In the Bosnian capital, tens of thousands of Serbs who lived in RS areas until the Agreement were faced with a choice of remaining in their homes under control of the government they had opposed in the war, or joining the millions of other, displaced peoples in the former Yugoslavia. Given but the vaguest assurances of their safety by the Bosnian government in Sarajevo, and frightened by stories from their own leadership in Pale, tens of thousands of Serbs from Sarajevo embarked on a voyage of uncertainty, literally digging up the relics and bones of their fathers and mothers to drag them into Serb-held territory.

The departure of these Serbs from Sarajevo provided the most dramatic evidence that the Bosnian government and the Bosnian Serbs are content to interpret the Dayton Agreement as a blueprint for partition. Although the international sponsors of the Agreement continued to insist that this was not the case, they, too, permitted the logic of partition to assume a firmer grip during an emergency meeting held in Rome on the weekend of 17 February 1996. The most important issue in Rome was the status of Mostar, which had been under EU administration for eighteen months. The Moslems of Mostar wanted to see closer integration of the two halves of the city separated by the river Neretva.

The EU mayor of Mostar, the German Social Democrat Hans Koschnick, had drawn up a plan which would divide the city into two zones of influence, one Moslem, one Croat, but which also created a large joint zone in the middle of the city. The day after the Rome meeting, the Moslem mayor of east Mostar, Safet Oručević, resigned in protest at the deal, claiming that the international community had capitulated to the demands of separatist Croats. Even more revealing was an interview given in early April to the Austrian newspaper *Die Presse*, in which Hans Koschnick revealed that he felt 'abandoned' by the German government delegation at the Rome meeting. Koschnick continued that the delegation's intention had been to 'support Tuđman at all costs'. He further speculated that there had to be 'military interests' involved. 'It is easy to abandon the man in Mostar,' Koschnick said, 'when the final details of an accord leading to co-operation between German and Croatian armies are being discussed.' Apart from suggesting that Germany was prepared to watch the federation between Moslems and Croats continue to decay, this was the first time that a German official involved in the former Yugoslavia had been prepared to accuse his government of favouring the Croats – not just over the Serbs, but over the Moslems as well.

The further implementation of Dayton will be immensely difficult. Tensions between the Moslems and Croats are likely to be especially difficult to solve. It is quite possible that however peaceful Bosnia-Hercegovina is during Ifor's stay there, that the country will slide back into war after the departure of the NATO-led force. That is one possibility. If peace is maintained, however, Bosnia will almost certainly be divided into three. The Croat and Serb entity will be under the more or less direct control of Zagreb and Belgrade respectively. The cause of democracy will have been advanced in neither Bosnia nor in Herceg-Bosna, nor in the Republika Srpska, nor in Croatia, nor in Serbia. Indeed, as peace approached in Bosnia, it was noticeable how Presidents Milošević, Tuđman and Izetbegović tightened their grip on what in certain respects are one-party states.

The misery of Yugoslavia has been borne by civilians, the bulk of them Moslems, but many Croats and Serbs as well. The regional leaders, still wallowing in the mire of political power, appear impervious to the concept of personal responsibility and morality. They are unlikely to learn many fundamental lessons from their experiences of the past five years. But Western Europe, Russia and the United States must learn the lessons of their first great crisis in post-communist Europe. It may, of course, not yet be over. But we must hope that it is. For if the past five years are anything to go by, the future of Europe is anything but safe.

Glossary of Terms and Political Movements

APC: Armoured personnel carrier

Arkanovci: Fighters loyal to the Serb nationalist militia leader, Željko Ražnjatović – Arkan

Armija BiH: The largely Moslem army of Bosnia-Hercegovina

AVNOJ: *Anti-fašističko Vijeće Narodnog Oslobođenja Jugoslavije.* Anti-fascist Council of National Liberation of Yugoslavia

Beli orlovi: The White Eagles. Chetnik militia loyal to Dragoslav Bokan

Chetniks: Serb nationalist movement founded in the nineteenth century. Involved in fratricidal war with the Serb-dominated Partizans during the Second World War. Associated with extreme Serb nationalism during the wars in Croatia and Bosnia. Used as a generic term for Serb nationalists by Croats, Moslems and liberal Serbs

Cominform: Communist Information Bureau. The umbrella organizations of post-war Communist parties controlled by Stalin. Expelled the Yugoslav party for Tito's resistance to Stalinist hegemony in June 1948

Crna legija: The Black Legion. Croat Fascist militia which re-emerged during the war in Croatia

DS (Srbija): *Demokratska Stranka.* The Democratic Party in Serbia

Dušan Silni: Notorious Chetnik unit

HDZ: *Hrvatska Demokratska Zajednica.* The Croatian Democratic Union

HDZ – BiH: *Hrvatska Demokratska Zajednica – Bosna i Hercegovina.* The Croatian Democratic Union – Bosnia-Hercegovina

HNS (Hrvatska): *Hrvatska Narodna Stranka.* The Croatian National Party

HOS: *Hrvatske Odbrambene Snage.* The Croatian Defence Force (military wing of the HSP)

HSP (Hrvatska): *Hrvatska Stranka Prava.* Croatian Party of Rights

HTV: *Hrvatska Televizija.* Croatian Television

HV: *Hrvatska Vojska.* The Croatian Army

HVO: *Hrvatsko Vijeće Odbrane.* The Croatian Defence Council (the army of the Bosnian Croats)

HZHB: *Hrvatska Zajednica Herceg-Bosne.* Community of Herceg-Bosnia (Bosnian Croats)

HZP: *Hrvatska Zajedica Posavine.* Community of Croatian Posavina (Bosnian Croats)

ICO: Islamic Conference Organization

ICRC: International Committee of the Red Cross

JNA: *Jugoslovenska Narodna Armija.* The Yugoslav People's Army

Martićevci: The colloquial name for the police of the Serb-held Krajina in Croatia. Named after the force's founder, Milan Martić

MBO: *Muslimanska Bošnjačka Organizacija.* The Moslem Bosniak Organization

NDH: *Nezavisna Država Hrvatska.* The Independent State of Croatia. The wartime Fascist state run by the Nazi-installed Ante Pavelić

OS BiH: *Odbrambene Snage Bosne i Hercegovine.* The Defence Force of Bosnia-Hercegovina (the forerunner of the *Armija BiH*)

Partizans: Tito's victorious communist guerilla army, dominated by Serbs and Montenegrins but with strong Croatian, Macedonian, Slovene, Albanian and Moslem participation in various regions

Pokret za Jugoslaviju – SKJ: The Movement for Yugoslavia – League of Communists of Yugoslavia, also known colloquially as the Generals' Party. Formed from the ruins of the SKJ

RSK: *Republika Srpske Krajine.* The Republic of Serbian Krajina

RTV Beograd: *Radio Televizija Beograd.* Radio Television Belgrade

Sabor: Croatia's Parliament

SAO: *Srpska Autonomna Oblast.* Serbian Autonomous Region. Self-declared Serb-held areas of Croatia and Bosnia-Hercegovina

Glossary of Terms and Political Movements

SČP: *Srpski Četnički Pokret.* The Serbian Chetnik Movement

SDA (BiH): *Stranka Demokratske Akcije.* The Party of Democratic Action (Moslem) in Bosnia-Hercegovina

SDA (Sandžak): *Stranka Demokratske Akcije.* The Party of Democratic Action (Moslem) in the Serbian region of Sandžak

SDP (Hrvatska): *Stranka Demokratskih Promena.* The Party of Democratic Changes (Croatia). The reformed Communist Party

SDS (BiH): *Srpska Demokratska Stranka.* The Serbian Democratic Party in Bosnia-Hercegovina

SDS (Hrvatska): *Srpska Demokratska Stranka.* The Serbian Democratic Party in Croatia

Šešeljovci: Fighters loyal to the leader of the Serbian Radical Party, Vojislav Šešelj

SFRJ: *Socialistička Federativna Republika Jugoslavija.* The Socialist Federal Republic of Yugoslavia

SKJ: (and associated republican organizations) *Savez Komunista Jugoslavije.* The League of Communists of Yugoslavia

SNO (Srbija): *Srpska Narodna Obnova.* Serbian National Renewal [Party]

Specijalci/MUP-ovci: The Specials. Name given to Croatian special police units formed after the elections of 1990. The MUP refers to the police force in all republics

SPO (Srbija): *Srpski Pokret Obnove.* The Serbian Renewal Movement

SPS: *Socialistička Partija Srbije.* The Socialist Party of Serbia

SRS: *Srpska Radikalna Stranka.* The Serbian Radical Party

TO: *Teritorijalna Odbrana.* Territorial Defence. Created under the communist period. Local defence force organized on the level of republics

UDBA: *Uprava Državne Bezbednosti.* State Security Administration (Communist)

UNHCR: United Nations High Commission for Refugees

UNPA: United Nations Protected Areas (in Croatia)

UNPROFOR: United Nations Protection Force (in Croatia and Bosnia-Hercegovina)

Ustashas: The movement of the Croat wartime Fascist leader, Ante Pavelić

Vitezovi: Militiamen loyal to Serb nationalist leader, Mirko Jović

VJ: *Vojska Jugoslavije.* The Army of Yugoslavia (successor to the JNA)

VMRO – DPMNE (Macedonia): *Vnatrashna Makedonska Revolutsionerna Organizatsija – Demokratska Partija za Makedonsko Natsionalno Edinstvo.* The Internal Macedonian Revolutionary Organization – Democratic Party for National Unity

VOPP: The Vance–Owen Peace Plan

ZNG: *Zbor Narodne Garde.* The National Guard Corps (predecessor to the Croatian Army)

Index

Abdić, Fikaret, 152, 153, 185, 186, 221, 284, 288
Adžić, Blagoje, 61, 122
Agrokomerc, 152
Ahmići, 230
Ajduković, Gordana, 106, 138
Akashi, Yasushi, 274, 283
Albania, economy, 241, and Kosovo, 15, 238; and Macedonia, 71, 238; Ottoman influence, 6; revolution, 69; Tirana, 239, 240; unification, 239; United States and 235–6, 239, 250; and Macedonia, 254–5
Albanians, clan system, 132; Drašković, 39; intelligentsia, 141; in Kosovo, 32, 34, 35, 66, 67, 68, 183, 261, 262, 285; Macedonian, 70–71, 250–55, 261–2; nationalism, 69, 70
Albright, Madeleine, 271
Alexander the Great, 253, 255, 260
Amett, Peter, 245
Andreyev, Viktor, 244
Andrić, Ivo, 22
Arkan, *mafia-style criminal*, 39, 168, 185, 186
Arkanovci, 168, 171
Armed Forces of BiH COS BiH, later *Armija BiH*), 199, 218, 228, 230, 246, 247, 248, 265, 277, 291
Arsenije III, patriarch of Peć, 4, 5
Arsić, Tihomir, 58–9
Ashdown, Paddy, 287
Austria, 112, 189, 212, 276

Austro-Hungary, 250, 257
autoput, 78–9
Avramović, Dragoslav, 278

Babić, Mate, 62–4
Babić, Milan, 277; appearance and behaviour, 16; and Glina Serbs, 93; history, 16–19; and Koljević, 155; message to Ušće, 56; Milošević and, 16, 37, 56; prestige among Serbs, 119; Radio Knin, 21; rejects UN plan, 7; totalitarian methods, 20
Badinter, Robert, 163
Balkan Odyssey (Owen), 279
Balkan wars, first and second, 250, 257, 259
Balkans, political leprosy, 129; problems for peace in, 100; Slovenia, 97; southern, 236, 248–9, 254, 256, 259, 261, 262; threat to stability in, 143; the West and, 236
banditry, 5
Banija, 6, 80, 90, 91, 101, 217
Banja Luka, 151, 155, 184, 185, 200, 206, 207, 208, 217, 266, 267, 284, 289, 290
Baranja, 275
Batele, *Serb from Old Tenja*, 107, 108, 110
Before the Rain (film), 252
Belgrade, 250; Babić in, 17; Brioni Accord, 98; culture, 42; fighting in streets, 46–9; financing of *autoput*, 75; liberal tradition, 41;

He just wanted a decent book to read ...

Not too much to ask, is it? It was in 1935 when Allen Lane, Managing Director of Bodley Head Publishers, stood on a platform at Exeter railway station looking for something good to read on his journey back to London. His choice was limited to popular magazines and poor-quality paperbacks – the same choice faced every day by the vast majority of readers, few of whom could afford hardbacks. Lane's disappointment and subsequent anger at the range of books generally available led him to found a company – and change the world.

'We believed in the existence in this country of a vast reading public for intelligent books at a low price, and staked everything on it'
Sir Allen Lane, 1902–1970, founder of Penguin Books

The quality paperback had arrived – and not just in bookshops. Lane was adamant that his Penguins should appear in chain stores and tobacconists, and should cost no more than a packet of cigarettes.

Reading habits (and cigarette prices) have changed since 1935, but Penguin still believes in publishing the best books for everybody to enjoy. We still believe that good design costs no more than bad design, and we still believe that quality books published passionately and responsibly make the world a better place.

So wherever you see the little bird – whether it's on a piece of prize-winning literary fiction or a celebrity autobiography, political tour de force or historical masterpiece, a serial-killer thriller, reference book, world classic or a piece of pure escapism – you can bet that it represents the very best that the genre has to offer.

Whatever you like to read – trust Penguin.